Children's Glass Dishes, China, and Furniture

By Doris Anderson Lechler

COLLECTOR BOOKS
P.O. Box 3009
Paducah, KY 42001

The current values in this book should be used only as a guide. They are not intended to set prices, which vary from one section of the country to another. Auction prices as well as dealer prices vary greatly and are affected by condition as well as demand. Neither the Author nor the Publisher assumes responsibility for any losses that might be incurred as a result of consulting this guide.

Dedicated to the dealers of antiques who make the world glance and glimmer by providing the old and magical . . . and to my husband, for the same reason

Additional copies of this book may be ordered from:

COLLECTOR BOOKS
P.O. Box 3009
Paducah, Kentucky 42001

@$17.95 Add $1.00 for postage and handling.

Copyright: Doris Lechler, 1983
ISBN: 0-89145-225-7

Printed by IMAGE GRAPHICS, Paducah, Kentucky

ACKNOWLEDGMENTS

This work embodies the personal recollections, knowledge and collections of many friends and correspondents. It gives me great pleasure to thank them.

Pat and Walt Oswald were among the first to offer parts of their collection for the book. They also generously hosted our first collectors' get together in June of 1982.

OSWALD CONTRIBUTIONS:
   Milkglass LAMB spooner and creamer; DUTCH BOUDOIR potty, tray and tray items in blue; blue French candlesticks; pink and blue bath set; amber MENAGERIE turtle (old gold bear and owl); clear with frosted LION heads cup and saucer; clear MONK stein set; red trimmed HAPPIFATS china; glass bakeware sets; RED WING; china PET GOAT sugar. (They also loaned some items which had to be cut from the text due to book size.)

GREEN CONTRIBUTION:
   MISS AMERICA set; RAISED DAISY; HOUZE; STICK SPATTER tea pots; BULLSEYE AND FAN main berry; unknown creamer; NORTHWOOD table set; row 10 in the candlestick section; two decanter sets; three tumble ups in one group shot; SANDWICH caster sets; CIRCLE IN SQUARE caster set; PETITE SQUARE pieces; TWINS bath set; kitchen ware rolling pin set; stoneware sample pottery; pottery bowls; aluminum cannister set; baking table; HOOSIER cupboard; ice box; dining suite; horsehair sofa; pastry set; unknown spooner and butter; ORPHAN ANNIE pieces; china: SEASIDE, SPATTER tea pots, FISH; EASTER

Jerry and Sandy Schmoker have been collecting friends for years. They worked long and hard getting their collection of mugs to the photographer. They also kindly measured each item, writing a brief description as well. Joyce Johnston put the finishing touches to the mug text.

SCHMOKER CONTRIBUTIONS:
   all of the mugs in this publication except for Joyce Johnston's WESTWARD HO and CAT IN A TANGLE; Largent's STIPPLED FORGET-ME-NOT; Welker's LIBERTY BELL, frosted ACORN creamer; ROYAL DOULTON cups, saucers, plates and tumblers; child's oak dresser; SANDWICH compote

Mr. Lynn Welker and his parents have been generous with their collections and knowledge.

WELKER CONTRIBUTIONS:
   Cambridge catalog reprint; clear LIBERTY BELL mug; grape colored luster; three cut glass nappies; split hickory basket; EMPIRE chest; roll top desk; turtle top table; walnut CIRCASIAN table; dining table; MURPHY bed; dry sink; LITTLE TOT coffee grinder; QUEEN ANNE mirror; SNOWBABIES cup and saucer; Revere ware set; TWO BAND pieces; CAT AND DOG cup and saucer; SHERIDAN chest; clear epergne; two tea kettles; bone handled knife and fork; sausage crocks and meat grinder; stein; TIGER MAPLE chest

Dauphine and Howard Lundquest invited me into their lovely home for five days. We assisted Orin Gronau in getting the china collection pictured. The Lundquests made several additional trips to the photographer with late arrivals and with the lovely MAXEL (new) toy furniture. The Lundquests have nearly 140 china sets represented in this publication. I regret, due to space, they cannot be named. Please credit them with the majority of china shown in this book.

When the publisher told me to cut 125 pages, I turned to Joyce Johnston. She and Seth invited me to their lovely, quiet home for a week and we tore the book to pieces. I can never thank her enough for her time, patience and help. She also contributed several valuable pieces to the book as well as her knowledge about antiques. Her quick eye picked up some valuable catalogue proof that I had missed.

JOHNSTON CONTRIBUTIONS:
   KITE FLYER china set; WESTWARD HO mug; CAT IN A TANGLE mug; c-44 candlestick; ORNAMENTAL HOBNAIL cup and saucer; BABY PLAIN PANELS butter; toy plates: LITTLE PIG, CLOCK, JUMBO; ROOSTER, OLD INDEPENDENCE HALL, FROSTED BOUQUET, CHRISTMAS EVE; china set

LUBBERGER CONTRIBUTIONS:
   BUTTONS AND ARCHES butter; LITTLE BO-PEEP and HEY DIDDLE DIDDLE plates; VINE goblet

Ruth E. Smith is a dear friend. Andy and I enjoy her home and having her travel with us.

SMITH CONTRIBUTIONS:
   CLAMBROTH SCENERY table set

Donna Mourning read every word of this text. She allowed an occasional monkey shine, but kept me pretty well within literary boundaries. (She's not a collector, so she made me explain EVERYTHING in print.) Joy Auer typed pages and pages and was very patient.

Helen Feltner has always been generous with her time and knowledge. She provided the PETITE HOBNAIL water set, measurements for the cake and fruit stands and the information about the NORTHWOOD table set and BABY THUMBPRINT pieces.

Blanche Largent from Texas is a kind and generous friend. She and Glenda Lechler researched with me at the grand and flourishing Corning Museum Library. Blanche also found BUTTERFLY TIMES for my collection.

LARGENT CONTRIBUTIONS:
   CHIMO pieces; small KING Co. candlestick; STIPPLED FORGET-ME-NOT mug; SAWTOOTH sugar; blue tumble up with under plate; HEISEY cone holder (not a toy); HOOK creamer and mug

Dora Rosenberger kindly allowed David Grim to photograph some of her lovely items for this publication. Mr. Grim, in turn, contributed these lovely pictures.

ROSENBERGER CONTRIBUTIONS:
   two environmental settings shown in the furniture section; MONK fruit dish; MAJOLICA tea set (color plate); etched decanter set

Sharon Boren has one of the largest adult Depression Glass collections in the nation. She kindly delivered all of her toy Depression and Akro sets to my home so that the photographers could photograph them. She shared her knowledge of this ware with me. In addition, she brought some furniture and dolls. I appreciated her help.

BOREN CONTRIBUTIONS:
CHERRY BLOSSOM, CHERRY DELPHITE, DORIC and PANSY; HOMESPUN; MODERNTONE; LAUREL; SHIRLEY TEMPLE items; STACKED DISC and PANEL; Heinrich Handwerck's socket head doll; German and Japanese dolls; SCARLET by Madam Alexander; LEMONADE and OXBLOOD; CONCENTRIC RING; STACKED DISC water set; CHIQUITA; OCTAGONAL; MARBELIZED; two rockers; kitchen cupboard (roll curtain style); black Jappanned kitchen cupboard; cherry cupboard; pot metal candlesticks; three china sets

Art Edwards, my mentor from the wonderful Fenton Art Glass Company, contributed the glass making information and much more. He is a man who knows that beautiful things are dependable, consistent, predictable and satisfying. That must be why he married Jean.

Mr. Charles Funaro is a new friend from California. He was generous with his Sowerby catalogues and knowledge.

Mr. and Mrs. Ray Early are friends and dealers of lovely antiques. They loaned me a beautiful yard-long print by Maude Humphrey and a dragon tea set as well as a charming ''cat'' cup and saucer.

The subscribers to the newsletter *The Miniature News* loaned their support and encouragement.

Dr. Jim Measell contributed an "in the box" picture of the AUSTRIAN #200 table set and shared his Greentown knowledge with me.

Fred Bickenheuser allowed pictures of some rare examples of Federal glass from his old 1914 trade catalogues.

Susan Stewart sent Kate Greenaway's own pewter toy dinner set to be pictured in this publication.

Fred Horn gave permission to have his photograph of the AMAZON compote copied in black and white for the book.

The dealers who searched for unknown treasures for this book are: Tom Neale and Glen Schlotfeldt from Bridgewater, Va.; Jean Dorney; Mr. and Mrs. Ray Early; Clifford Hanson; Norman Alford; Helen Simmons; Bob Jones; Shevell and Zinman; and Trudie and Pegge whom I adore. Jim of the Rare Book Exchange on Market Street in Corning, N.Y., helped to find research publications for this text. He's a master ''thing finder''.

Two great photographers spent months on this book: Mr. Tom Maloy and Mr. Paul Wilcox. They photographed my collection and parts of the Oswald, Welker, Johnston, Lubberger, Boren and Largent contributions. The Ohio State University Department of Photography and Cinema have two fine gentlemen working for them. Thanks, too, to Linda Wall for developing their work and to Katie Miller for her patience.

Two more great photographers spent one whole Saturday perfecting the cover for this book; Chuck Smetana and Rosario Tripepi from the Richardson Printing Corp.

Orin Gronau photographed the Lundquest china collection and their MAXEL furniture.

Al Achterberg of Holdrege, Nebraska pictured parts of the Schmoker mug collection, their Royal Doulton and furniture pieces.

Chip Decker of Stroudsburg, Pennsylvania pictured the Anna Green contributions.

The staff of the Corning Glass Museum Library gave their time, resources and permission unselfishly. Norma Jenkins arranged for fifteen trade catalogue photographs to be taken at the museum for this publication.

Cathryn J. Mc Elroy of the William Penn Memorial Museum arranged for two trade catalogue photographs to be taken. Permission was granted by the Pennsylvania Historical and Museum Commission to print them.

INTRODUCTION

The fancies of childhood in which we are so interested were created by magical masters at the potters' wheels, around the glory holes, and in the wood shops. Inglorious themselves, and willing to be so, they believed in the glory of children. The toys of china, glass, and furniture which they created whisper us into a time when England held the world in a fasionable philanthropic embrace. Americans were insatiable importers of the niceties of life, receiving nearly one third of all that was exported. Therefore, the trinkets of time bind us yet to the Mother Country, allowing us to participate in the enjoyment of distant scenes of the past.

Primarily, this text will stress items which were made expressly for the entertainment and educational enrichment of children who lived in the nineteenth and early twentieth centures. These toys were procured from American and European shops, nurseries, playhouses, attics, and collections of today.

The concentration of material in this publication will serve the collector, the dealer, the fact enthusiast, and the nostalgic excapists who delight in child-size baubles in china, glass and wood. Collectors and dealers who are interested in a frill free approach to the facts will find research data grouped on each page in a clear concise form with lucid photographs to further serve their needs. The words and pictures will carry those who wish to be voyagers through time to an era brilliantly lighted by great wealth, yet shadowed by devastating poverty. Rosy-cheeked children enjoyed the sparkle and glitter of objects fit for fairy housekeepers while at the same time pinched-faced infants worked in the countless side street potteries of Staffordshire, England. The industrial bound New World rendered its share of insufferable working conditions as well. The domestic and foreign markets were demanding--and they were served.

Now as the twentieth century grows old, the fruits of those vast harvests are enjoyed by collectors whose memories have been gathered on the feet of gold-fuzzed bees that hover over youth. These recollections create a special magic capable of turning wrinkles into smiles.

So . . .

> If you are a dreamer, come in.
> If you are a looker, a wisher, a sigher,
> A dealer, a collector, a magic bean buyer . . .
> If you're a pretender, come sit by my fire,
> For there are memories to tap-to-spin.
> Come in . . .
> Come in.

Doris Anderson Lechler

TABLE OF CONTENTS

Section I: Glass Dishes 9
Glass Companies and Their Pattern Contributions 10
Acorn 33
Alabama 34
Amazon (Variant) 34
Austrian No. 200 35
Baby Flute 36
Baby Thumbprint 36
Bead and Scroll 36
Beaded Swirl Variation 37
Block and Rosette 37
Braided Belt 38
Bucket 38
Bullseye and Fan No. 15090 38
Button Arches 39
Button Panel 39
Buzz Star 40
Cake and Fruit Stands 40
Cambridge Glass Company Contributions 42
Candlesticks 43
Caster Sets 46
Chateau No. 714 48
Chimo 48
Clambroth Scenery 48
Clear and Diamond Panels 49
Cloud Band 49
Colonial 50
Cups and Saucers 50
D & M No. 42 51
Decanter Sets 52
Deep Stars and Octagons 54
Depression Glass and Akro Agate Toy Ware 54
Dewdrop 58
Doyle's No. 500 59
Drum 59
Dutch Boudoir 60
Enameled Lemonade Sets 60
Epergnes and Lusters 61
Euclid 62
Fenton's Kittens 63
Fine Cut and X's No. 379 63
Fine Cut Star and Fan 64
Fish Set 64
Flute 64
Galloway No. 15071 65
Grape Vine With Ovals 65
Grape Stein Set 66
Hawaiian Lei 66
Heisey's Sawtooth Band No. 1225 66
Hobbs Water Sets 67
Hobnail With Thumbprint Base No. 150 67
Horizontal Threads 68
Ice Cream Cone Holder 68
Ice Cream Set 69
Lacy Daisy 69
Lamb 70
Large Block 70
Liberty Bell 70
Lion 71
Little Jo 72
Menagerie 72
Michigan No. 15077 73
Monk Stein Set 74
Mugs 75
Northwood Hobnail 94
Nursery Rhyme 94
Oval Star 96
Pattee Cross 97

Pennsylvania No. 15048 97
Pert 98
Petite Hobnail 98
Petite Square 99
Plain Pattern No. 13 99
Plates 99
Pointed Jewel 103
Portland 103
Reproductions and Reissues 103
Rex 105
Rooster 106
Sandwich 107
Sawtooth 108
Singles, Pairs and Possibilities 109
Sowerby Glass Works 115
Standing Lamb 117
Steigel-type Lemonade Set 118
Stippled Dewdrop and Raindrop 118
Stippled Diamond and Stippled Forget-Me-Not 118
Stippled Vine and Beads 119
Style 120
Sultan 120
Sunbeam No. 15139 121
Tappan 121
Thumbelina 122
Tulips and Honeycomb 123
Tumble Ups 123
Twist 127
Two Band 127
Wabash Toy Series 127
Wee Branches 128
Wild Rose 129
New Toy Glassware 130
Brief Description of Today's Glassmaking Process 131

Section II: China ....
China To A Tea 132

ANIMAL SERIES:
American Kittens and Chariot 135
Cat Teaching the Rabbits 136
Dog and Cat In The Cream Pitchers 136
Dressed Animals and Verses 137
Fish 138
Group of Five 138
Hunter and Dog 139
Japan's Mickey Mouse 140
Kittens In A Boat 140
Kittens, Puppies, Musicians 141
Peter Rabbit 142
Rabbit Pulling A Cart 142
Roosevelt Bears 142
Sinful Pigs 143
Sports Minded Bears 144
Swan On The Lake 144

FLOWERS AND FANCY TRIMS SERIES:
Apple Blossoms From Japan 145
Bird and Foliage 145
Blue Bands 146
Brown-Maroon Flowers 146
Castle Staffordshire 146
Chowder 146
Christmas Holly 147
Crusade 147
Dauphine's Wedding Ring 147
Davenport Maltese Cross 148
De Jeuner 148

Delhi 148
Egg Shell 148
Enamelware 149
English Cottage 149
Feathery Ferns 149
Flower Pots 150
Flowers and Caramel Luster 150
Flowers and Vines 150
Flowing Blue and Berries 151
Gaudy Staffordshire Dahlia 151
Gold and Orange Buds 152
Gold Corn Decoration On White 152
Gold Flowers On White 152
Gold Tea Leaf 152
Gray With Blue Leaves 153
Lavender and Red 153
Lea Flower 153
Lilac and Begonia 154
Little Pinks 154
Majolica 154
Meissen Style 154
Nieman-Marcus 155
Old Moss Rose 155
Old Paris 155
Orange Poppies 156
Oyster Stew 156
Paula 156
Peach and Pink Roses 156
Periwinkle Enamelware 157
Petite White With Gold Trim 157
Pink Chintz 157
Pink, Gold And Black Banded 158
Pink Spring 158
R.S. Prussia (eight sets) 158
Red Roses Petite 160
Shaggy Asters 160
Spatter Tea Pots 160
Staffordshire Chowder 160
Tete-A-Tete 161
Thee Service 162
Thimble Tea 162
Tiny Blue And White 162
Tree In A Meadow 163
Two Tones Red And Yellow Roses 163
Victorian Roses 163
Victorian Majolica Fruit And Dessert 163
Willow 164

PEOPLE SERIES:
Afternoon Tea 166
American Kate Greenaway 166
Beyreuth Children 166
Black And White Staffordshire 167
Blossom Children 167
Boy And Dog 168
Boy And Swans 169
Boy On A Bench And Friends 169
Buster Brown 170
Busy Day 171
Busy Girl 171
Children And Toys 172
Children And War Games 172
Children At The Table 173
Children On Sled 174
Children Pulling Sled 175
Circus And Clown 175
Dutch Boy And Girl 175
Dutch Children On White 176

Flower Boat Children 176
German Kittens And Chariot 177
Girl With A Whip 177
Goat Cart 178
Haviland 178
Having A Ride 179
Humphrey's Clock 179
Kate Greenaway-style 180
Kite Flyers 180
Little May 180
Little School Teacher 181
Little Women 181
Lustered Merry Christmas 182
Merry Christmas 182
Old Fashioned Girl And Dog 183
Princess Driving A Bird 183
Robinson Crusoe 184
Rose O'Neill Kewpies 184
Royal Bayreuth Nursery Jingles 185
Santa With Pack 185
Seaside 186
Skating Children 186
Sled And Kite 187
Three Girls And A Dog 187
To Grandmother's House 187
Toys And Children 188
Two Girls With Doll 188
Two Toned Green Dutch Children 189

RHYMES JINGLES AND TALES SERIES:
Alice In Wonderland 189
Cat And The Fiddle 190
Cat And Fiddle And Other Tales 190
Cinderella 191
Fairy Tales 191
Four On A Blank 192
Golliwags 192
Hey Diddle Diddle 193
House That Jack Built 193
Japan's Disney Characters 194
Little Miss Muffet 194
Noritake Nursery Rhymes 195
Palmer Cox Brownies 195
Punch And Judy 196
Puss In Boots On Shore 196
Red Riding Hood 196
See-Saw Margery Daw 197
The Wolf And Red Riding Hood 197

China Singles, Pairs and Possibilities 198
General Accessories 206
Section III: Furniture 208
Bibliography 216

SECTION I: GLASS DISHES

Samples of miniature glass from the late 1800's to the late 1900's are shown in this section. They consist of mostly American pressed or blown glass with an in depth look at some Sowerby products from England. Besides the "proven" toy glass there will be some miniature adult glass counterparts which have yet to be research-proven as falling into the toy glass classification. These items are included in this text because they are glass miniatures found in many toy glass collections across the nation.

OLD TOY GLASS - This classification of glass has been termed as toy in trade publications from the late 1800's through the first quarter of the 1900's. This glass was played with in nurseries, playhouses and bedrooms and is child-sized. It is too large for dolls' houses.

GLASS MINIATURE ACCESSORIES — This text includes old glass which is termed "miniature" but research so far has not been proven to be "toy". These miniatures are counterparts of adult pressed or blown glass and are: epergnes, lusters, six to eight inch cake plates and fruit baskets.

SINGLES, PAIRS AND POSSIBILITIES — Proof has been found in trade publications that partial sets and single pieces were made and labeled "toy". An example of a single item is the toy loving cup produced by United States Glass; a pair example is the Jewel pattern open sugar and creamer; the possibility examples are sets in the Alabama pattern or the Block and Rosette pattern which have yet to have "toy" as part of their ad descriptions.

DEPRESSION TOY GLASS — In this section will be some colored glass made primarily during the late 1920's through the 1930's in amber, green, pink, blue, red, yellow, white, and crystal. These were all made for children.

REPRODUCTIONS OR REISSUES - Part of toy glass history or miniature history is the limited number of PATTERNS of toy glass which have been reproduced from old moulds. This glass section includes these items as well as glass produced from new moulds which have been directly copied from old glass sets. Both classifications are very limited pattern-wise but are rendered in a multitude of colors and combinations.

NEW TOY GLASS - Another part of toy glass history deals with the new collectibles for children and adult investors. These are limited editions created with new designs, new moulds and marketed as new.

The glass pieces and sets will be found in the following combinations.

PUNCH SETS - Complete when consisting of a punch bowl and either four or six matching cups.

TABLE SETS - Complete when there is a covered sugar, a covered butter, a creamer, and a spoon holder. (A "spooner" is a small stubby vase used in the second half of the 19th century for spoons.)

LEMONADE OR WATER SET - Complete when the set includes a pitcher and either four or six tumblers.

CASTER SETS - Complete when a metal holder having from two to five holes contains matching bottles replete with stoppers and caps.

BERRY OR DESSERT SETS - Complete when a main bowl has either four or six matching counterparts.

CANDLESTICKS - Complete by the pair or collected singly in glass, china, or metal. (This publication contains single examples due to space limitation.)

MUGS - Mugs in this publication range from toy through the usable size, being designed and produced for children.

CAKE PLATES - Toy cake plates measure from approximately two to four inches in diameter while the salvers measuring six to eight inches are usually considered to be miniature accessories.

GLASS COMPANIES
AND THEIR PATTERN CONTRIBUTIONS

AKRO AGATE

"Chiquita"
"Concentric Rings"
"Marbelized Interior Panel"
"Octagonal Opaque"
"Stacked Disc"
"Stacked Disc and Panel"
"Lemonade and Oxblood"
"Raised Daisy"
"Miss America"

The Akro Agate Company began in Akron, Ohio in 1911. The company made marbles and games, staying ahead of the foreign marble importing companies. The company moved to Clarksburg, West Virginia where gas and materials were more cheaply available. The Akro Agate Company ruled the marble world for forty years and florished in the doll dish market during World War II. In 1951 the company was sold to the Clarksburg Glass Company.

ALEXANDER J. BEATTY & SONS
THE BEATTY-BRADY GLASS COMPANY

"Rea" toy mug after 1891
"Vandyke" toy mug, 1885, made in amber, blue, canary, crystal
No. 100, "Hobnail with Ornamental Band" cup (also made by Columbia Glass Company)
No. 86 and No. 87 toy mugs, 1888, known as "Opalescent Rib"
No. 1220 "Block" toy mug and cream pitcher

ATTERBURY & COMPANY

"Ceres" (Medallion) toy mug

This company was established in 1858, producing pressed tableware, lamps and bottles. One of Atterbury's most popular novelties was the covered animal dish series.

BRYCE, McKEE & COMPANY
BRYCE, RICHARDS & COMPANY
BRYCE, WALKER & COMPANY
BRYCE BROTHERS (Factory B of U. S. Glass Co.)

"Amazon" table set, 1890, reissued by U. S. Glass Co. after 1891
"Pert" mug which collectors call "Ribbed Forget-Me-Not", 1880
"Ribbon Candy" cake plate in clear, green, 1885
"Bucket" table set, also known as "Wooden Pail", made in clear, 1885
"Stippled Forget-Me-Not", 1880, later produced by Model Flint Co. after 1891
"Sultan" table set, 1880 (see McKee Glass company)
Mugs: beaded handle series with pleated bases -- dog racing through the woods, dog beginning to point, bird on a twig, "Heron and Peacock", cardinal; short loops; chick mug #1200; deer eating from branch #1201; berry cluster #1202; bird peeking at the ground #1203; basket weave called "Happy Thoughts"; tall stemmed flower in middle with a scalloped panel trim; scalloped wheel

"Buzz Star" table set, punch set
"Pattee Cross" berry set, water set

Fred M. McKee, James Bryce and Robert D. Bryce formed a glass company known as Bryce, McKee & Company in 1850. In 1854 the firm became Bryce, Richards & Company, producing pressed and cut table ware. In 1865 the company name was changed to Bryce, Walker & Co. Later the Bryce family operated the company as Bryce Brothers until it was united with the United States Glass Company where it was known as Factory B.

BRYCE, HIGBEE & COMPANY
THE J. B. HIGBEE GLASS COMPANY

"Drum" table set and mugs, 1880
"Menagerie" table set
plates: "Emma", "Rover", (A B C)
"Hawaiian Lei" table set
"Euclid" (Rexford) table set and cake stand
"Style" (Arrowhead-in Ovals) table set and cake stand
"Fine Cut Star and Fan" table set
"Clambroth Scenery" (no proof) table set

In 1879 the Homestead Glass Works, also known as the Bryce, Higbee & Company, was formed by John Bryce, John Higbee, and Joseph A. Doyle. After the turn of the century the company reorganized and was known as the J. B. Higbee Glass Company, adopting a trademark which consisted of a bee with the letters "H" and "G" appearing on the insect's wings and the letter "I" on its body. The firm was still operating in 1915. This company issued many pressed glass novelties and was responsible for some very collectable toy glass.

THE CAMBRIDGE GLASS COMPANY

"No. 1 Toy" water set
"Colonial" No. 2630 table set
#2697 "Buzz Saw" table set
#2635 "Fernland" table set
"Wheat Sheaf" punch set, berry set, wine set
"Inverted Strawberry" punch set, berry set
"Sweetheart" table set
toy candlesticks in clear and peachblo; toy candelabra (3 branch)

This company was built by the National Glass Company at Cambridge, Ohio in 1901. This was the only new factory the company ever built, choosing the site because of the natural gas deposits. The company had two trademarks. The first was a "C" within a triangle, the second consisted of the words "Near-Cut". In 1960 Imperial acquired the Cambridge moulds.

CENTRAL GLASS COMPANY

"Pennsylvania" table set (possibly)
mugs: "Rabbit" mug (with a tree in the background) #702
#3831 Old No. 100, "Rose Mug"
"Oak Wreath" mug
"Elephant" mug #728
Old No. 0 leaf motif with a smooth handle

Although this company made a great deal of famous glass patterns, they did not make many pieces of toy glass . . . other than mugs. This company began in Wheeling, West Virginia in 1863 with only $2,000 in capital. By 1939 the plant was closed due to foreign imports.

This company is represented in this publication (in addition to the mugs) because in 1939 the Imperial Glass Company acquired Central's moulds and machinery. Imperial has been known to reissue from old moulds; perhaps collectors need to be aware of the moulds obtained through the years.

CHALLINOR, TAYLOR & COMPANY, LIMITED

mugs: #351 cat
#352 bird in a nest
#353 rabbit eating
#355 shell foot

small owl creamers with glass eyes (not to be used in the "Menagerie" series) Ca. 1885

"Ear of Corn" pitcher (dark green glass) not a part of a toy series

This company started in 1866 with the name Challinor, Hogan Glass Company. It became a member of the United States Glass Company in 1891. Challinor specialized in colored glass and hand painted glassware.

COLUMBIA GLASS COMPANY (Factory J, Findlay, Ohio)

"Dewdrop" (Dot) table set, 1891
"Pointed Jewel" table set, 1891
Old No. J "Tycoon" toy mug with all over giant's teardrops, #3822 3¾ oz.
Old No. 3 toy mug, Tycoon #3823
#3824, 6½ oz., Tycoon J
#3825, Old J
Old No. J "Dewdrop" cup

The Columbia Glass Company started in Findlay, Ohio about 1886. This was one of the plants which never reopened after the big strike of 1893.

It was a member of the United States Glass Company.

THE BEAVER FALLS CO-OPERATIVE GLASS COMPANY
THE CO-OPERATIVE FLINT GLASS COMPANY, LIMITED

Rex Pattern

"Rex" (Fancy Cut) table set, punch set, water set, 1907
#379 "Fine Cut and X's" (author name) berry set
Viking-style stein--sold 300 dozen per barrel

mugs: #214 vertical panel of ferms
#235 vertical strips of protruding bull's eyes
dewdrop style mug (hobnails)
#374 panels
#233 arrowhead style

The Beaver Falls Co-Operative Glass Company, located in Beaver Falls, Pennsylvania was organized in 1879. In 1889 it

Sundries

379—Toy Berry Set
5 piece Bulk, 12 doz. in bbl. Wt. 165 lbs.
5 piece boxed, 9 doz. in bbl., wt. 120 lbs.

was succeeded by the Co-Operative Flint Glass Company. The company was dissolved in 1937.

DOYLE & COMPANY

"Hobnail Thumbprint Base", 1885, No. 150 (also produced by the Phoenix Glass Company in 1884 and the Pioneer Glass Company in 1885). It was reissued by the United States Glass Company after 1891.
"Red Block" mug
"Doyle #500" table set and mugs in two sizes (reissued by U. S. Glass)

Doyle and Company was established as early as 1866 on the south side of Pittsburgh, Pennsylvania. This company was absorbed into the United States Glass Company in 1891.

GEORGE DUNCAN & SONS
GEORGE A. DUNCAN & SONS
GEORGE A. DUNCAN'S SONS COMPANY
DUNCAN & HEISEY COMPANY
DUNCAN & MILLER GLASS COMPANY

"Button Arches" toy butter dish, 1885
"Diamond Crystal" #44, 1900, Button Panel
#42 "Mardi Gras" table set, 1898
#48 "Diamond Ridge"
"Block and Rosette"
chamberstick

Between 1886 and 1889 the name of the firm became Duncan & Heisey Company. In 1891 the company joined the United States Glass Company with Mr. Heisey becoming the firm's first sales manager. In 1894 the company was no longer a link in the U. S. Glass Company chain.

In 1895 Mr. Heisey formed the A. H. Heisey Glass Company. The close association of the Duncan Company and the Heisey Company no doubt caused some mould exchanges which confuse the glass collecting picture.

FEDERAL GLASS COMPANY, COLUMBUS, OHIO

Wabash series (1914): Ice cream set
Fish set
Grape stein set
"Tulip and Honeycomb" table set, punch set and serving pieces
Candy dips in light colors
A "Hickman" individual salt, which is found in little condiment sets, was shown in a 1914 Federal Glass catalogue.

This company was founded in 1900 and recently closed its doors. It contributed one of the most unusual series of children's toy glass of any company. The quality of the glass leaves much to be desired but the ideas and designs were interesting. The company's trademark was a shield with an "F" in the middle.

FENTON ART GLASS COMPANY, WILLIAMSTOWN, WEST VIRGINIA

"Kitten" pattern in clear and carnival colors
"Lechler's Heirlooms of Tomorrow" (1981 and 1982)
Encore's (red) "God and Home" water set, 1981

In 1906 the company was started with just over $200 in Martins Ferry, Ohio. It is now located in Williamstown, West Virginia.

During the first few years the company specialized in crystal and expanded to chocolate glass. Chocolate glass was originated by Jacob Rosenthal who was the first glassmaker to work at Fenton.

Fenton's luster ware became one of the largest selling lines of glass ever produced in America. The company has developed the many possibilities of opalescent glass, producing lovely overlays and cased glass techniques.

This company is a fine family-run organization with quality products.

FINDLAY FLINT GLASS COMPANY

"Stippled Diamond"
"Stippled Forget-Me-Not"

This company was started in 1888. The factory, located in northeast Findlay, was destroyed by fire in 1891 and never reopened.

GAS CITY

"Sunbeam"
"Nursery Rhyme" punch set
"Jewel" toy creamer and sugar
"Galloway" water set

This factory was built by the United States Glass Company in Gas City, Indiana because of the seemingly endless supply of natural resources.

THE FRANKLIN FLINT COMPANY
GILLINDER & BENNETT
GILLINDER & SONS
GILLINDER BROTHERS, INCORPORATED

"Liberty Bell" table set and mug
"Lion" table set, cup, saucer
"Cloud Band" table set
"Sawtooth" table set
plates: boys in cart
          boys falling over log
          "Sancho Panza & Dapple"
A B C deer in center
          flower bouquet (center)
Frolic boy and dog on steps
mugs: Old No. G flower rosette swirled, scroll base
       #427 "Rustic"
"Pennsylvania" table set (possibly)

William T. Gillinder, a glass worker in England, published a book called *The Art of Glass Making*. After its publication he came to America and worked at the New England Glass Company before starting a factory in Philadelphia. In 1876 an exhibition factory was built at the Centennial Exhibition grounds in Philadelphia. There was a great amount of pressed glass produced and sold on the spot, with toy glass claiming a share of the collectible fame.

One of the most important patents ever issued in the glass world was given to William T. Gillinder in 1865. It made mass production in the glass industry possible.

HAZEL ATLAS

"Moderntone" toy glass sets

This company was founed in 1885 at Wellsburgh, West Virginia. They produced opal glass liners for Mason zinc caps. In 1887 the company moved to Washington, Pennsylvania where the operation was expanded. From 1930 to 1940 the company produced three main patterns, one of which was the toy set in "Moderntone". It was made in crystal, green, pink, blue and burgundy.

A. H. HEISEY GLASS COMPANY

"Sawtooth Band" table set
elephant head mug
candlesticks-chambersticks
    #31 (c-25 in this book), #33 (c-21), #5 (c-17) and #30
    (unavailable for pictures)

Augustus H. Heisey created the glass company that bears his name in 1895. Heisey's production was based on quality crystal, both pressed and blown. The ware was all hand finished. There was a limited amount of color in the line.

In 1958, the Imperial Glass Company of Bellaire acquired the name and moulds of the A. H. Heisey Glass Company of Newark, Ohio. They are at present reproducing two miniature candlesticks which do not bear the Heisey trademark. Unfortunately they are not marked as new and collectors are becoming confused (see candlestick section).

HOBBS, BROCKUNIER & COMPANY

Frances Ware water sets, 1886, #323 with No. 7 decoration Hobnail water sets in blue, white opalescent, rubina (frosted and clear)

George Carothers built the company in 1820. It changed hands several times, growing larger with each exchange, until in 1879 the factory was the largest in the United States. The company produced colored glassware in quality batches.

A few years after the death of John Hobbs, Sr. the company was absorbed into the United States Glass Company. Workers strikes closed the factory but it was eventually taken over and operated by Harry Northwood who was a Hobbs employee as well as a United States Glass Company representative in England.

HOUZE COMPANY OF POINT MARION, PENNSYLVANIA

"Houze" blue, yellow, green "Depression" glass toy sets

The "Houze" toy sets are very rare, having been made for only a short time at the Point Marion site. The sets were cast in yellow, blue and green moonstone or opaline type glass. The sets consist of a covered tea pot, covered sugar, creamer, four cups and saucers, and four plates. The company's label was black and gold in a shield form. The label was usually placed in the bottom right corner of the container.

IMPERIAL GLASS COMPANY

"Lamb" reproduction in blue, 1981; in sunburst, 1982 candlesticks reproduced from Heisey moulds; Heisey's #33 (c-25) in this publication

In the 1920's Imperial moulds were used to produce premiums for promotional purposes. The so-called Imperial German Cross (type) trademark was used between 1905-1920. The Nucut trademark was registered in 1914 and removed from all moulds about 1932. The "I" superimposed over the "G" determines reissues. In the late 1930's and early 1940's Imperial bought moulds from Central Glass Company. Another outstanding buy from the Heisey company was made in 1958. In 1960 they moved the facilities of the Cambridge Glass Company to the Bellaire location.

INDIANA GLASS COMPANY

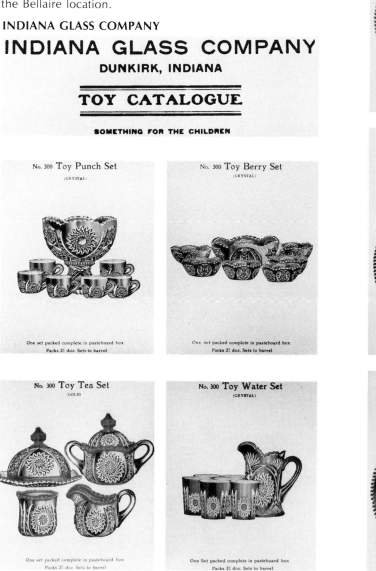

13

No. 300 Toy Birthday Candlestick

Two Candlesticks and three Candles packed complete in pasteboard box constitutes set.

Packs ¾ dozen Sets to barrel

"Oval Star" toy series--see catalogue reprint
plate series--see catalogue reprint (plate series now being reproduced)

This company was operating in 1897. It is possible that this company took over some of the production from The Indiana Tumbler & Goblet Company after their disastrous fire in 1903.

INDIANA TUMBLER & GOBLET COMPANY

"Austrian #200" table set complete in clear and chocolate

This firm was founded in 1894. During the short time it was in operation it produced a great amount of pressed ware. They were famous for chocolate glass, which was developed by Jacob Rosenthal.

IOWA CITY GLASS COMPANY
Animal motto plates:
"Be Affectionate", "Be True", "Be Gentle", "Be Playfull" (sic); "Elaine" series of plates

JEANNETTE GLASS COMPANY
(see Depression Glass text)

"Cherry Blossom"   "Homespun"
"Doric and Pansy"   baking (dish) sets

KING, SON & COMPANY (Cascade Glass Works)
THE KING GLASS COMPANY 1800

"Plain Pattern No. 13"
"Frosted Ribbon Double Bars" #13
Old No. K small, medium, and large "Vine" mugs (not to be confused with #198)
plain footed goblet
4" toy 1 2 3 plate (seated dog)
6" toy A B C plate (chicken center) two styles
"Vine" footed goblet
"Pillar" tumbler, mug
"Prism"
"Rooster" table set and 3" nappy
mugs: #3827 Old K 195 small, #3898 Old K 196 medium, #3829 Old K 196 large; #198 "Vine" mug
"Bead and Scroll" table set has been attributed to this company by researchers (without ad proof)

Using the facilities of the King Glass works, the United States Glass Company broke the strikes which plagued the industry. Unskilled people were brought into the King factory where they lived until the strike was over. Many of these people turned out to be excellent recruits to the "glass" world.

The King Glass Company supplied the toy glass collector with some of the most interesting ware in the miniature realm.

McKEE & BROTHERS

mugs: "Harp and Wreath"--large, medium, small
         "Our Boy"; "Our Girl"
         "Dot"
         "Pillar"
         "Beaded Swirl" with notched handles and beaded bases (three sizes)
"Tappan" table set (1915-1925); Kemple reissued with pieces in color.
"Sultan" table set (1915-1925)
Depression toy ware: "Laurel" toy sets; glass baking sets (McKee produced the "Sunbeam" and "Tex" patterns--it is not known if these patterns were extended to the toy series by this company.)
"Champion" (cake salver)
"Grape Vine and Ovals" table set

The McKee Glass Company began operation as McKee and Brothers in 1853. McKee started large and grew. Originally the factory was in Pittsburgh. Later following the gas supply to Westmoreland County, the company settled in what has been called "the glass city" . . . Jeannette, Pennsylvania.

In 1916, the United States Glass Company and the Duncan & Miller Glass Company granted the McKee Glass Company and the Cambridge Glass Company licenses to manufacture certain pressed, figured, and cut glass under their patents.

"Pres-cut" impressed on the products' bases is said to have been the McKee Brothers first trademark. By 1905 this symbol was within a circle. In 1908 McK and McKee were both enclosed in circles.

The company was sold to Jeannette Glass in 1961. (The Jeannette Glass Company produced toy sets in: "Doric and Pansy"; "Cherry Blossom"; "Homespun" and toy (glass) baking sets.)

MODEL FLINT GLASS COMPANY, FINDLAY, OHIO

"Stippled Forget-Me-Not" table set, mug
"Twist" (common to the Findlay and Albany factories) table set

This company was started in 1888, moving from Findlay to New Albany, Indiana between 1891 and 1894. It operated with the National Glass Company from 1898 to 1902.

MOSSER GLASS COMPANY, CAMBRIDGE, OHIO

reproduced: "Inverted Strawberry" punch sets; Depression glass miniatures;
"Hawaiian Lei" three piece table set based on old design--excluding the H I G on the wings and body.

NEW ENGLAND GLASS CO.

candlesticks and chambersticks

In 1817 the works was bought from the Boston Porcelain & Glass Manufacturing Company. Deming Jarves was a purchaser but left the company in 1825 for the Boston & Sandwich Glass company.

NEW MARTINSVILLE GLASS MANUFACTURING CO. 1900-1907 (art and opaque glass) Period I
NEW MARTINSVILLE GLASS MFG. CO. 1907-1937 (pattern glass) Period II
NEW MARTINSVILLE GLASS CO. 1937-1944 Period III
VIKING GLASS CO. 1944-1972 (new type of glass with a Swedish look)

"Chateau" punch set
"Viking" type stein with or without a metal top
ice cream cone holder
toy plates:
    #531 "Boy A-B-C" plate (H) also called "Emma"
    #532 dog center, "Dog A-B-C"
    #10 "Souvenir"
    #530 "Star A-B-C"

RICHARDS & HARTLEY FLINT GLASS COMPANY (Factory E of the United States Glass Company)
THE TARENTUM GLASS COMPANY

Pattee Cross products
mugs: #3815 Old #12 "Hanover" (looks like embedded stars) small
      #3816, 7½ oz. "Hanover", Old E
      #347, 5½ oz., Old No. E, (looks like buttons and double clear panels) called "Three Panel"

This firm was established in 1866 in Pittsburgh, Pennsylvania. They produced tableware, novelties and lamps at the Centennial in 1876. Richards & Hartley became the Tarentum Glass Company. The plant was destroyed by fire in 1918.

SOWERBY & CO., GATESHEAD-ON-TYNE, ENGLAND

vases, spills, baskets, match holders
1219 "Birds Nest" posy holder
1220 "Mary, Mary Quite Contrary" posy holder
1224 "Witch and Caldron" posy holder (sometimes called "Old Woman Spinning"); sometimes used to hold matches
1226 "Girl on the Bench" posy holder
1227 "Mary Had a Little Lamb" vase
1232 "Old King Cole" posy or nursery match holder
1234 "Shepherd" vase
1235 "Lamplighter" vase
1260 "Lavender Blue" posy holder
1263 "Little Bo-Peep" spill or match holder
1268 "Jack and Jill" vase
1285 "Jack Horner" (bellows shape) posy holder
1293 A "Lemons and Oranges" semi-circles for centerpiece
1293 B "Lemons and Oranges" rectangular pieces; plus the 2 semi-circular pieces

1293 ½ "Lemons and Oranges"
1293 C "Lemons and Oranges" 2 semi-circular pieces and 4 rectangular pieces
1294 "Ma Mammy Dance A Baby" vase or spill

Sowerby & Co. produced about 13 pattern books, two of which have been located to date. The information about these nursery patterns has been procured from the two rare catalogues.

UNITED STATES GLASS COMPANY (a few examples)

"Amazon" table set and compote
"Bucket" table set
"Dewdrop" factory J table set
"Michigan" table set, stein set (1915)
"Nursery Rhyme" table set, punch set, water set, berry set (1900)
"Pattee Cross" berry set, water set, punch set factory B
"Bullseye and Fan" dessert set factory B
"Whirligig" (Buzz Star) (1907) table set, punch set
"Ribbon Candy" cake plate
"Alabama" table set (1892)
"Monk" stein set, "Wild Rose" table set, punch set
"Pennsylvania" table set
"Mirror and Fan" decanter set (1910)
"Sunbeam" (Twin Snowshoes) table set factory U, Gas City
"Portland" water set
Toy beer mug with short-loop-base-panels
A B C mug "Boy At Desk" Adams Co.
Smooth handle, rayed base mug, Adams Co.

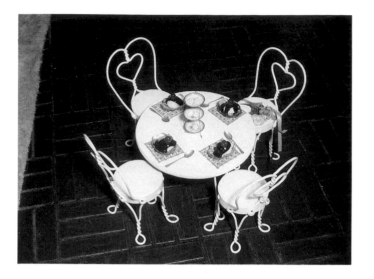

ICE CREAM SET, table 10½'' tall, 15'' across; chair 16'' tall, 6'' across seat.

HEPPLEWHITE MAHOGANY CHEST 7½'' deep, 11'' wide, 12½'' tall; PINE ONE DOOR DRY SINK with dark stain, 8'' wide, 7½'' tall; WALNUT DROP LEAF TABLE with a drawer in the end, 6'' x 12'' with drop leaf and 12'' x 12'' with the leaves up, 8'' tall.

SILVER SERVICES: Right - silver plate child's tea set; Left - sterling silver tea set; Right - "Sunbeam" glass butter dish; Center - sterling silver toast rack; Back - miniature (cherry) butcher paper rack.

CHERRY AND BIRDSEYE MAPLE POST OF-FICE 48″ tall, 21″ wide, 12½″ deep. Post of-fice built by a postmaster and part-time cabinet maker for his children between 1790-1820 in South Carver, MA. Complete with letter slots (that now house a miniature mug collection) and fold down sorting table.

SPINET STYLE DESK; HANGING BRASS (CANDLE) CHANDELIER; MINIATURE BOOKCASE with inlaid wood; STERLING SILVER MINIATURE TEA SET on a plateau mirror; TOY (FUNCTIONAL) LAMP with pot metal base; HANDMADE QUILT by Elizabeth Anderson.

CHILD'S STEAMER TRUNK 12″ high, 20″ wide, 13″ deep with fold out storage and compartments--sturdy and functional.

WALNUT DRESSER WITH BURL INLAY, has small marble slab and candle racks; Stafford-shire perfume (Dutch boy and girl) bottles are on the candle racks; forget-me-not chamber set.

Top - MINIATURE HANGING LAMP; Left to Right - CHILD'S SPICE AND PLAY CUPBOARD with tin Blue Willow ware on top; Center - OAK CHILD'S SPICE CUPBOARD with flip down flour bin; Wall - Maud Humphrey (yard long) Butterfly Time picture. (Maud Humphrey was Humphrey Bogart's mother); Right - CHERRY CUPBOARD with canister set, tea set, Sherwood caster set.

LYRE BACK SETTEE and matching walnut chair; CYLINDER STYLE DESK with swing-out secret bookshelves and swing-out drawer; pink rose buds with gold tete-a-tete tea set; CHILD'S ANTIQUE PICNIC BASKET.

DINING SUITE: table with removable cupboard top; matching buffet with silverware drawer; egg shell tea set; grape luster on buffet surface.

WALNUT DRESSER 55'' tall, 27'' wide, 14'' deep, has marble top; MINIATURE SHAVING MIRROR; HAND MIRROR COLLECTION; CHINA CHAMBERSTICK; CHAMBER SET with caramel luster trim.

FRENCH KATE GREENAWAY-STYLE DIVIDED WASH BOWL and matching equipage.

TEA POTS from complete sets found in the china text.

DEPRESSION GLASS: Top row - ''Moderntone''; Row two - teal ''Doric And Pansy''; Row three - pink ''Cherry Blossom''; pink ''Doric And Pansy''; ''Cherry Delphite'': Row four - ''Laurel''; (new) ''Cherry Blossom'' butter dish.

21

ENGLISH TALL CASE CLOCK, 56″ tall, 7½″ deep; HALL'S LIFE TIME TOYS (canopy bed) 28″ tall, 21″ wide, 32″ deep; toy quilt rack; Heinrich Handwerck's 18″ bisque socket head doll; dry sink, 14″ tall, 14″ wide, 9½″ deep with forget-me-nots on a chamber set.

DUTCH BOUDOIR assemblage: Right to Left - covered potty; blue slop jar without lid and white jar with lid; blue potty without lid; blue water pitcher; blue tray holding two pomade jars and a candlestick.

ROCKER with impressed kitten picture on head rest, has a child's sewing kit resting against it on the floor; CURTAIN-ROLL CABINET with canister sets on top and a Marumon strawberry tea set on the work surface; BRASS MINIATURE SKATING LANTERN; JAPANNED CUPBOARD with white milkglass Nursery Rhyme punch set; PUNCHED-WOOD ROCKER with a Japanese bisque character baby (11″ tall); SPLIT HICKORY EGG BASKET.

MENAGERIE table sets showing the variation of colors.

MINIATURE LUSTERS AND TUMBLE UP (see regular text for information). Top Row: Lusters--L-2; L-3; L-1. Row Two: Tu-4; Tu-19; Tu-3; Tu-14; Tu-2. Bottom Row: Tu-13; Tu-12; Tu-11; Tu-10; Tu-8; Tu-9; Tu-7; Tu-6; Tu-5.

Kate Greenaway-Style DINNER SET.

Palmer Cox Brownies DINNER SET; Amazon TOY BUTTER; ETCHED GOBLETS; Sherwood CASTER SET.

Spatter TEA POTS

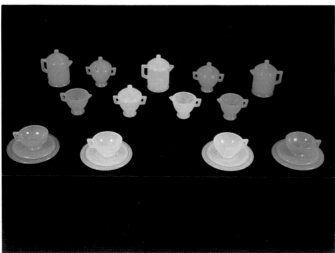

HOUZE COMPANY (Point Marion, Pa.) TOY GLASS SETS in blue, yellow and green.

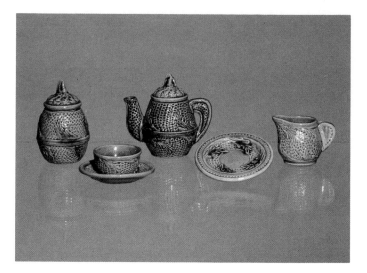

Majolica TEA SET (picture by David Grim; Rosenberger collection).

Delhi by Wileman.

Pink, Gold and Black Banded DINNER SET.

R.S. Prussia Petite TEA SET.

Gaudy Staffordshire (Dahlia pattern).

R.S. Prussia Four Seasons TEA SET; PRESSED STRAW BASKET.

Ram's Head RED VELVET FAINTING COUCH 17'' tall at the highest point, 13'' high at the lowest point, 48'' long, 19'' wide; one from a pair of MARBLE-TOPPED WASH STANDS, 33'' high, 15½'' wide, 12'' deep; ENGLISH SHAVING MIRROR, 7¾'' high, 6½'' at widest point; blue and white CHAMBER BOWL AND PITCHER.

TUREEN examples taken from toy china dinner sets.

TUREEN examples taken from toy china dinner sets.

MILKGLASS: Top row - Dutch Boudoir chamber items; Lavender Blue (vase, spill or match holder); Monk stein pieces; Row two - Lamb table set; Row three - Braided Belt table pieces; Cloud Band table set; chamberstick; Row four - Wild Rose table and punch sets; Nursery Rhyme punch set.

Cobalt Thistle LEMONADE SET and 6½'' ENAMELED EPERGNE.

Christmas Holly TEA SET.

Davenport Maltese Cross TEA SET.

AMBER AND BLUE WARE: Top row - Menagerie table set; Row two - Frances Ware frosted lemonade set; Row three - clear Frances Ware lemonade set; amber Stippled Vine And Beads table set; Hobb's Blue water set; Row four - amber Hobnail With Thumbprint Base table set on a tray; Doyle #500 blue and amber sets on trays.

TEA POTS.

American Kittens And Chariot.

WATCH CASE CLOCK with inlaid wood; CAT CUP AND SAUCER from a child's set; a lavender (etched) LUSTER which is 6½'' tall; a MINIATURE WALNUT BOOK CASE with original books; a sterling silver CHAMBERSTICK.

Twist TABLE SET pieces and a Twist (style) VASE.

AKRO AGATE: Top row, Left to Right - Stacked Disc: J. Pressman;
Octagonal; Stippled Band; Semi-circle - Stacked Disc And Panel;
Lemonade And Oxblood; Marbelized; Akro Luster; Chiquita;
Marbelized: Front, Left to Right - Concentric Rings; Trans Optic.

McKee'e Sultan TABLE SET in various colors.

Cat Teaching The Rabbits TEA SET; Sweetmeat SERVER; Twin CAKE PLATE.

LECHLER HEIRLOOMS OF TOMORROW a new line of toy collectibles by Fenton Art Glass Company (1981). Top row, Left to right - custard lemonade set and tumble up; Row two - custard lemonade set with violets and a set with Christmas holly; Row three - custard tumble up with violets; ruby overlay tumble up; amethyst lemonade set; Burmese lemonade set. All from the ELIZABETH series.

Miss America (marbelized); Miss America (decaled); Raised Daisy.

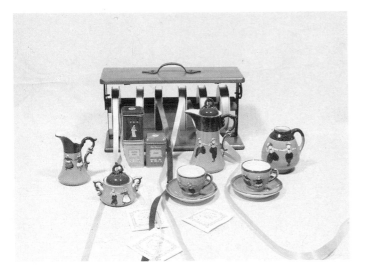

Two Toned Green Dutch Children TEA SET.

Gold Corn decoration on WHITE COFFEE SET; TOY COFFEE GRINDER.

Orange Poppies Tea Set; three metal TEA POT and TRIVET.

ACORN

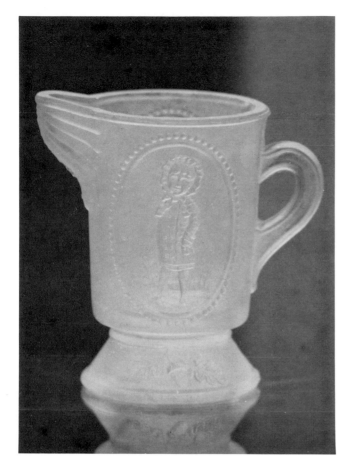

The quality of the "Acorn" glass enhanced by the dignity of the design set the trend for the blueprint which guided the child of the past to great expectations. A child grew to adulthood expecting and receiving superior workmanship. The aesthetically pleasing toys could be used and passed through the generations as a link coupling the qualities of today with the security and peace of the past.

PERTINENT DATA:

Additional pattern names: "Kate Greenaway"
Pattern pieces: Four piece table set

Pattern colors: Clear, frosted
Factory: Unknown
Date: 1890-1900
Classification: Rare
Reproduced: No
Pieces difficult to locate: Whole butter, both lids, all frosted
Features attributable to pattern: All have two handles except creamer; all have collared bases with acorns; all have Kate Greenaway-style children in beaded ovals except the butter

MEASUREMENTS:

Spooner	Boy and pipe; girl and palette; 2-1/8'' across, 3-1/8'' tall
Sugar	Bell shaped lid; base has girl with ribbons and an apron with flowers; boy in short jacket and knickers; 4-¾'' complete, 2¼'' across base top
Creamer	Boy in knickers; girl in coat; 2-1/8'' across, 3-3/8'' spout to base
Butter	Lid matches sugar; base contains all of above except motif found on spooner; 4'' complete, 1-7/8'' base ht.

ALABAMA

This set is in the ''possibilities'' category since there has been no written proof that this pattern was intended for the toy classification. This table set is a United States Glass Company product, #15062, made at Glassport, Pennsylvania.

PERTINENT DATA:

Additional pattern names: #15062
Pattern pieces: Four piece table set
Pattern colors: Clear
Factory: United States Glass Company
Date: After 1891
Classification: Rare
Reproduced: No
Pieces difficult to locate: Butter
Features attributable to pattern: Fringed draping secures the smooth beaded circles encircling the pieces

MEASUREMENTS:

Spooner	Six beaded circles around scalloped rim; six textured cones at bottom; 2-3/8'' ht., 1-7/8'' across.
Sugar	Ribbed finial; draping with diamond drop under circled beads on lid; six circled beads on base with diamond droplets under beaded circle; 4'' ht. complete, 2-5/8'' lid across, 2¾'' base ht.
Creamer	Repeated motif; 3¾'' lip to base, 3¾'' lip to handle, 2½'' across base
Butter	Unavailable for photograph or measurement

AMAZON (VARIANT)
SAWTOOTH MITERED

This sparkling four piece table set has heavy raised diamonds which catch the light, drawing attention to its fine lines. The set is interesting even though it is a variant of the much copied adult design.

A collector of children's glass has a special attraction in his Amazon table set, a fifth piece. It is simply the butter dish raised on a slender stem, creating a beautiful miniature compote in the Amazon pattern. Bryce Brothers could have been trying out different treatments and his compote may be a single result, for that is the only one accounted for to date.

PERTINENT DATA:

Additional pattern names: "Sawtooth Mitered"
Pattern pieces: Four piece table set, miniature compote example
Pattern colors: Clear
Factory: Bryce Brothers
Date: 1890
Classification: Not too difficult to assemble
Reproduced: No
Pieces difficult to locate: Compote, butter and sugar in mint condition
Features attributable to pattern: Jagged edged sawtooth design on sugar, butter, spooner

MEASUREMENTS:

Spooner	Jagged rim; 3'' ht., 2'' wide
Sugar	Mitered sawtooth rim; 5'' complete, 3'' base ht.
Creamer	Sawtooth design stops halfway, clear top; 2-7/8'' ht., 1-7/8'' across
Butter	Mitered sawtooth rim; 4'' across top of lid, 4¼'' complete

AUSTRIAN NO. 200

A find of two complete and mint chocolate Austrian sets in their original boxes caused a ripple across the country matched only by the horror story of the unfortunate husband who accidently placed a brown paper bag containing rare miniature lamps (on their way to the photographers) into his wife's trash compactor. Collectors were "hard pressed" to know which story to discuss first.

It seems the Austrian sets were purchased for 25¢ each, according to the box, at the Pan-American Exposition in Buffalo, New York in 1901. Today's clear or chocolate glass discoveries sell for an exorbitant price while collectors search in vain for complete sets in canary and blue. (It has been deduced that the complete four piece table sets were done only in clear and chocolate.)

PERTINENT DATA:

Additional pattern names: "No. 200"; "Fine Cut Medallion"
Pattern pieces: Toy four piece table set
Pattern colors: Complete in clear and chocolate only
Factory: Indiana Tumbler & Goblet, Greentown, Indiana
Date: Circa 1900
Classification: Rare
Reproduced: No
Pieces difficult to locate: All chocolate, clear butter, sugar
Features attributable to pattern: Four bevelled medallions with tiny squares

MEASUREMENTS:

Spooner	Has beaded rim; rising and falling pattern; short stemmed base; 2-7/8'' ht., 2'' wide
Sugar	Covered plain rimmed bowl; repeated pattern; short stemmed base; 2¾'' base ht., 3½'' over all
Creamer	Has beaded rim and smooth lip pattern rising and falling around the piece; smooth handle; 3'' spout to handle, 3¼'' spout to base
Butter	Has flatish appearance, smooth finial; 3½'' across base top, 2¼'' complete ht.

35

BABY FLUTE

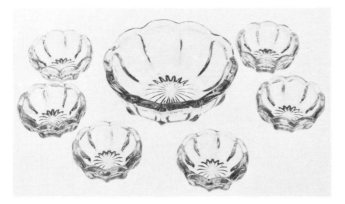

The quality of glass found in the "Baby Flute" berry set is superior to that which is seen in the "regular" toy Flute set. The design of the fluting is delicate and the pieces are attractive.

PERTINENT DATA:

  Additional pattern names: None
  Pattern pieces: 7 piece berry set
  Pattern colors: Clear
  Company: Unknown
  Date: Early 1900's
  Classification: Rare
  Pieces difficult to locate: All
  Features attributable to pattern: Fluting, rayed bases

MEASUREMENTS:

Main berry	20 point ray in base; 10 fluted panels; 1" tall, 3½" wide
Small berry	16 point rayed design in base; 10 fluted panels; ¾" tall, 1¾" across

BABY THUMBPRINT

If we were to forget for an instant the firey baptism of heat maintained in the glass making process, we could imagine a tiny person at the scene of glassmaking, placing uneven finger stamps around these dainty pieces which were made in the early 1900's. A child had to be "running the show" when the Baby Thumbprint cake plates were made, for they are in various stages of crooked charm. Today the cake plates, a compote, and a butter dish comprise the unit attributed to this toy pattern classification.

PERTINENT DATA:

  Additional pattern names: None
  Pattern pieces: Butter, compote, two sizes of cake plates
  Pattern colors: Clear
  Factory: United States Glass Company
  Date: 1900-1920
  Classification: Rare
  Reproduced: No
  Pieces difficult to locate: Butter, cake plates
  Features attributable to pattern: Rows of thumbprints, clear glass

MEASUREMENTS:

Compote	Around the base is a row of sixteen impressions, while the lid has fourteen; 3-7/8" ht., 2-7/8" base ht.
Larger cake	One row of impressions; paneled stem; 3" ht., 4-1/8" dia.
Smaller cake	Two rows of bean shaped impressions; smooth stem; 2" ht., 2-5/8" dia.

The Baby Thumbprint cake stand, 2" tall, 2-5/8" in diamter, was made by Edwin Reeves who produced glass in Alexandria, Virginia, Williamstown, New Jersey, and Royersford, Pennsylvania at various times. This piece was made sometime between 1900 and 1920.

BEAD AND SCROLL

The designer of the moulds for the "Bead and Scroll" set certainly had "glass class". A child who played with the miniature set in this pattern must have been frustrated as an adult in the search for tableware elegant enough to compare in both quality and design. (The adult sets in this pattern are as rare as the miniature.)

PERTINENT DATA:

  Additional pattern names: None
  Pattern pieces: Four piece table set
  Pattern colors: Clear, amber, blue and olive green, red flashed, gold trim, souvenired
  Factory: United States Glass Company
  Date: Early 1900's
  Classification: Rare in color, difficult to locate in clear

Pieces difficult to locate: Butter, sugar in clear, all colored pieces

Features attributable to pattern: Good glass quality, beads, scrolling; irregular bases on all but butter

MEASUREMENTS:

Spooner	Curving scalloped base, rivets of twelve vertical beads and scalloped rim; 2¼″ wide, 2½″ ht.
Sugar	Lid has smooth ball finial, pattern repeated as in other pieces; 4″ complete, 2¼″ base ht.
Creamer	Semi-scalloped rim, smooth lip and handle, twelve rows uneven beads, scalloped base matching other pieces; 3″ spout to base, 2″ side to side
Butter	Lid has smooth ball finial, pattern repeated on lid and butter rim; 4″ complete, 4-7/8″ base width

BEADED SWIRL VARIATION

Judging by the amount of clear, blue and amber glass found in miniature collections, it is evident that the glass houses felt these were the hues of their expertise. However, in this pattern the color innovation is what finally fired the collectors to seek this four piece table set. When a set is found in color, momentum increases and is rewarded in a few rare cases. (It has been discovered, too, that finding a clear, perfect spooner is not easily accomplished.) The four piece table set is the only unit in this toy pattern.

PERTINENT DATA:

Additional pattern names: "Puritan"
Pattern pieces: Four piece table set
Pattern colors: Clear, amber, cobalt
Factory: Westmoreland
Date: Late 1800's, early 1900's
Classification: Frequently found in clear, rare in color
Pieces difficult to locate: Clear spooner, all color
Features attributable to pattern: Teardrop ribs outlined by row of tiny beads; small collared bases

MEASUREMENTS:

Spooner	Scalloped rim; 2-1/8″ wide, 2-3/8″ ht.
Sugar	Finial-plain cylindrical knobs; 3¾″ complete ht., 2¾″ across opening
Creamer	Smooth rim and handle; 3½″ spout to back of handle, 2-5/8″ spout to base
Butter	Finial matches sugar; 2½″ complete ht., 3-5/8″ width of base, 2¾″ width of lid

BLOCK AND ROSETTE

Striving to define once and for all the correct classification for the Block and Rosette pattern has met with defeat. This set is placed in this publication based on the expertise of dealers in the field of miniatures.

At the Corning Glass Library, the 1870 Duncan and Miller catalogue was scrutinized with only the sugar claiming the name . . . the word "toy" was noticeably absent.

PERTINENT DATA:

Additional pattern names: None
Pattern pieces: Supposedly a four piece table set
Pattern colors: Clear, clear with gold

Factory: Duncan and Miller
Date: 1870's
Classification: Rare
Reproduced: No
Pieces difficult to locate: Butter
Features attributable to pattern: Small spooner and creamer, large adult type sugar

MEASUREMENTS:

Spooner	2-3/8'' ht., 1¼'' width
Sugar	4-7/8'' overall ht., 2¾'' ht. of base, 2-5/8'' across base opening
Creamer	2½'' spout to base, 1¼'' side to side

BRAIDED BELT

The mystique of the Braided Belt's origin and date is surpassed only by the questionable ability of the decorator assigned to embellish this four piece table set. A single half daisy hangs on this otherwise well-proportioned unit.

PERTINENT DATA:

Additional pattern names: None
Pattern pieces: Four piece table set
Pattern colors: Clear, amber, transparent light green, whitish-turquoise milkglass
Factory: Unknown
Date: Circa 1900
Classification: Rare
Reproduced: No
Pieces difficult to locate: All
Features attributable to pattern: Half a flower, band design of c's inside c's

MEASUREMENTS:

Spooner	Unavailable for measurement
Sugar	3½'' overall ht., 2-5/8'' across lid
Creamer	2-5/8'' spout to base, 3½'' handle to finial
Butter	2½'' tall, 3-3/8'' across lid, 1-1/8'' across base

BUCKET

Not many complete clear-glass Bucket sets survived unscathed from the turn of the century. All attempts to put colored sets together are thwarted from the start. Collectors are utterly in sync in their desire to attain this wooden slatted design in its entirety. They usually have only the creamer and an occasional spooner to call their own, however.

PERTINENT DATA:

Additional pattern names: "Wooden Pail", "Oaken Bucket"
Pattern pieces: Four piece table set
Pattern colors: Toy set in clear
Factory: Bryce Brothers, Factory B
Date: 1891
Classification: Rare
Reproduced: Creamer may have been made by other companies as well as by Bryce
Pieces difficult to locate: Butter, sugar, spooner
Features attributable to pattern: Textured wooden slats, clear bands, molded glass bails, textured board effect on bottom of each piece

MEASUREMENTS:

Spooner	Wood slats bound by smooth clear bands with a molded glass bail; 2½'' ht., 2'' across rim
Sugar	Smooth finial, molded glass bail, repeated pattern, collared base as on spooner and creamer; 3¾'' complete, 2½'' base ht.
Creamer	Easy to find, smooth rim and handle, repeated design from rest of set; 2-5/8'' ht., 3-1/8'' spout to handle, 1¾'' across bottom
Butter	Smooth finial matching sugar, no collard base, smooth banded rim on base; 2-3/8'' complete, 1'' base ht., 3'' width of base

BULLSEYE AND FAN
No. 15090

Even though salt and sauce "put togethers" are as common as measles, this pattern is the exception. In Revi's *American Pressed Glass and Figure Bottles* the catalogue proof of this toy dessert set is shown. Otherwise, one would assume that these small pieces served a different purpose. This is, in fact, one of the most difficult sets to complete in the toy glass category.

Because the dessert set could not be located for photography, a small cake salver in the Bullseye and Fan pattern is shown here for pattern identification along with the main berry bowl.

PERTINENT DATA:

Additional pattern names: #15090
Pattern pieces: Seven piece dessert set, small cake salver
Pattern colors: Clear
Factory: United States Glass Co. (B)
Date: 1905
Classification: Rare
Reproduced: No
Pieces difficult to locate: All
Features attributable to pattern: Circle looking somewhat like an eye with feathered fan effect above it

MEASUREMENTS:

Cake salver	6½" across, 2" ht.
Main berry	4¼" across top

BUTTON ARCHES

One of the companies to produce this familiar pattern around 1885 was the Duncan and Miller Company. The but-

ter dish in this pattern has just come to light--a complete and welcome surprise.

The pattern of buttons and arches gracing the upper half of the butter lid is carried through to the finial's top. The butter dish shown in this text is a part of the Nancy Lubberger collection.

PERTINENT DATA:

Additional pattern names: None
Pattern pieces: Four piece table set
Pattern colors: Clear, clear with gold or ruby stain
Factory: Duncan and Miller
Date: Circa 1885
Classification: Rare
Pieces difficult to locate: All
Features attributable to pattern: Good glass, buttons and arches design

MEASUREMENTS:

Butter	3¾" tall, 5" across base
Sugar	2-5/8" base only, 4-1/8" (about) overall ht.

BUTTON PANEL
D & M #44

If this set were personified, it would have a sparkling personality. The quality of the dazzling, unobscured glass used in it makes owners happy when they see it cushioned cozily in their display cabinets. Even though it is Duncan and Miller large, one knows that it was made to please a child and certainly to thrill future collectors.

PERTINENT DATA:

Additional pattern names: "D & M" #44, "Diamond Crystal"
Pattern pieces: Four piece table set
Pattern colors: Clear; clear with gold
Factory: George Duncan's Sons
Date: 1900
Classification: Obtainable
Reproduced: No
Pieces difficult to locate: Butter, sugar
Features attributable to pattern: Sparkling glass, patterned finials, vertical columns of cane alternating with a plain path, star designed bases

MEASUREMENTS:

Spooner	Small size, cylinder shaped, scalloped rim; 2-5/8" ht., 1-7/8" across
Sugar	Dome lid, patterned finial; 3" ht., 3" across base
Creamer	Smaller in proportion compared to the butter and sugar, cylinder shaped, pointed zipper pattern cascading around top; 2-5/8" spout to base, 3" spout to handle, 1¾" side to side
Butter	Dome lid, finial matches sugar finial; 3-7/8" ht., 5-3/8" across base

BUZZ STAR
WHIRLIGIG
#15101

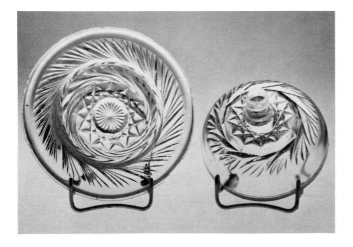

Set No. 15101 is a United States Glass Company product with the company name of "Buzz Star", commonly known as "Whirligig" to collectors.

The main design in this cut-glass style pattern is a pear shaped oval. The interior of the butter lid carries a buzz star design which is often confused with a similar motif found on the set called "Buzz Saw". When the two butters are compared one of the main differences is glass quality. The "Buzz Star" set is clear and light. The "Buzz Saw", with its exterior design of deeply whirling slashes, is thick and klunky.

The covered sugar of the "Buzz Star" set has a petaled rim which flares out encasing the lid. An old punch set is available in this pattern also. A giant mould grabbing boo-boo is connected with the reproduced punch bowl unit. The cups are from the same mould, but the bowl is a different high-stemmed mistake. (The new punch bowl is shown in an old Imperial Glass Company catalogue, No. 100 C, as a jelly compote.)

PERTINENT DATA:

Additional pattern names: "Whirligig", "#15101"
Pattern pieces: Four piece table set, seven piece punch set
Pattern colors: Clear (old)
Factory: United States Glass Company, Factory B
Date: After 1907
Classification: Not difficult to locate
Reproduced: Punch set only, in clear and cobalt
Pieces difficult to locate: Sugar lid
Features attributable to pattern: Cut glass style, pear shaped oval design, lids have an inside buzz star effect

MEASUREMENTS:

Spooner	2¼" wide, 2¼" ht.
Sugar	3-3/8" overall, 3" wide, 2-3/8" width of base
Creamer	3-3/8" spout to handle, 2¼" ht. from spout to base
Butter	2-5/8" overall ht., 3¾" across base
Punch bowl (old)	4¼" ht., 4-5/8" width
Cups (old)	1¼" ht., 1-3/8" wide
Punch bowl (new)	5-7/8" ht.

See the punch set and table set in *Glass Companies and Their Pattern Contributions* section for catalogue proof.

CAKE AND FRUIT STANDS
Miniature Accessories

Pictured in this section are examples of cake or fruit stands with a list and measurements of others that can be found in the six to eight inch classification. These are cake salvers which are not listed, to date, in any trade catalogues as having been made as toys. Collectors, however, display these miniature counterparts of adult glassware, at times, with their toy glass assemblages.

"AMERICAN BEAUTY ROSE"

(Figure 26 in *Children's Glass Dishes*); 6-5/8" wide and 3¼" in height

"STYLE" ("ARROWHEAD-IN-OVALS") (Figure 30 in *Children's Glass Dishes*); 6¼'' wide and 3¼'' tall

"PALM LEAF AND FAN" Stemmed banana stand 4¾'' tall, 5¾'' long; cake stand 3¼'' tall, 5¼'' diam. (turned up edge); cake stand 4'' tall, 6-3/8'' diam., clear or green

"CHAMPION" (Figure 29 in *Children's Glass Dishes*); 7¼'' wide and 3'' tall

"RIBBON CANDY" 3-3/8'' tall 6½'' diam green or clear

"FLOWER WINDOW" (Figure 27 in *Children's Glass Dishes*); 5'' wide and 2½'' tall

"KIDNEY BEAN BAND" Plain or silver rimmed, 2-7/8'' tall, 5'' across

"PEAKS AND BUTTONS"   Cake stand, 4½'' across, 3½'' tall

"TWIN CAKE"   4¾'' wide, 3-3/8'' tall
"TWIN MUFFIN"   4-1/8'' wide, 3¾'' tall
  (or candy)

Available patterns and measurements of cake or fruit stands which are not pictured in this publication:*

"BEAUTIFUL LADY"	Banana stand 5¼'' tall and 6-5/8'' long; flat banana dish 2-1/8'' tall and 5-5/8'' long; cake stand with turned up edge 4-1/8'' tall and 6¼'' diam.; cake stand, straight edge, 3-7/8'' tall, 6¾'' diam.
"CHIMO"	Low footed cake plate, 2½'' tall, 6½'' diam.
"CHAIN & STAR"	Turned-up edge, border of interlocked circles, star and fan medallion in center, 3-3/8'' tall, 6½'' diam.
"FINE CUT STAR & FAN"	Banana stand 5-3/8'' tall, 6-1/8'' long
"LACY DEWDROP"	Banana stand 6¼'' tall, 6-5/8'' in length
"LOUISIANA"	Cake stand 3'' tall, 6½'' diam.
"OCTAGONAL"	Petite eight sided cake plate, plain, 2¼'' tall, 5'' diam.
"EUCLID" ("REXFORD")	Banana stand 4-7/8'' tall, 6-5/8'' long, cake stand 3¾'' tall, 5¾'' diam.
"TINY THOUSAND EYE"	Cake stand 3½'' tall, 5-3/8'' diam.

"WISCONSIN"("BEADED DEWDROP")   Banana stand 4-1/8'' tall, 7½'' in length

*figure 25 in the cake plate section of *Children's Glass Dishes* is not a cake plate. It is an adult cheese compote from the 1930's and fits on a large cracker plate with a ring which holds the compote.

CAMBRIDGE GLASS COMPANY CONTRIBUTIONS

The actual 1909 catalogue ad for the Cambridge toy sets is so clear that it will suffice for photographs. The promoter of this popular glass was quick to inject that only the best tank glass was used in this ware.

THE "NO. 1" TOY WATER SET which is shown first in this ad has only five pieces; the tumblers are the most difficult to locate. The pitcher is 3-1/8" tall and the tumbler is 1-7/8" in height.

THE "COLONIAL" TABLE SET, No. 2630, can be found in cobalt blue; in clear; and in wandering shades of green, ranging from deep lush emerald to a fractious yellowish green. The spooner to this set is 2-1/8" in height; the complete sugar is 3" tall; and the butter is 2-1/8" in overall height. The creamer is 2-3/8" tall.

THE "FERNLAND" TABLE SET carries the factory name as shown in the catalogue proof. The set, #2635, sold for $1.75--for a dozen sets! They were made in the same colors as the Colonial set. The spooner is 2-3/8" tall; the creamer is 2-3/8" high; the butter is 2¾" in overall height and the complete sugar is 3" tall.

THE "BUZZ SAW" TABLE SET, No. 2697, has a butter with deeply swirling slashes on its exterior. The glass in this set is thick and chunky with no resonance. It was made only in clear. The creamer is 2½" from spout to base; the spooner is 2-1/8" in height; the complete sugar is 2¼" in height; and the butter has an overeall height of 2½".

THE "WHEAT SHEAF" PUNCH SET, No. 2660, sold for $2.90 per dozen. It was made only in clear although a pinkish bowl will turn up on occasion sans the cups. The punch bowl is 4¼" wide and 3½" in height. The matching cup is 1-3/8" wide and 1¼" in height. The Wheat Sheaf main berry bowl is 4" wide and 2¼" in height, the small berry is 2-1/8" wide and 1-1/8" tall.

Speculation surrounds the "WHEAT SHEAF" tumbler (1¾" tall) shown here with a matching miniature wine jug. No documentation exists that the set was made as a toy; however, an identical adult set confirms this is indeed a miniature version. Each collector must judge whether to buy this little set as a toy or not. The wine jug is 5" tall. It has a pattern-matching stopper and a wooden bail held by conveniently designed glass loops.

THE "INVERTED STRAWBERRY" pattern was used in adult and toy ware. The toy punch set has been reissued in many colors by Tom Mosser of Cambridge, Ohio. (Originally it was made only in clear.) Mr. Mosser is serving the collector by marking each piece with his M (see reproduction section.) The punch bowl is 4-3/8" wide and 3½" high. The cup is 1-3/8" wide and 1-1/8" tall.

The so-called toy berry set has not been reproduced to date. Collectors seek the 2" high, 4-1/8" wide main bowl and six little counterparts with determination. The small berry dish is 2-1/8" wide and 1" high.

CAMBRIDGE CANDLESTICKS are popular with toy glass collectors. The 2-7/8" candlestick was made in crystal and peachblo in 1924-25. The Cambridge 4½" candelabra was made originally in a clear three-branch style (see Candlestick section.)

THE "SWEETHEART" TABLE SET has been attributed to the Cambridge Glass Company with many sets being marked "Near-Cut". The spooner is 2" tall; the creamer is 2-3/8" from spout to base; the sugar is 3" high and the covered butter is 2" tall.

CANDLESTICKS

The Heisey Glass Company made one complete child's table set, one (heavily reproduced) mug with an elephant trunk handle, and four (single socket styled) toy candlesticks.

The #31 toy chamberstick has a handle that does not touch the candle cup. (Those chambersticks having handles touching the socket are considered to be Duncan and Miller products rather than Heisey.) The #31 chamberstick is the only Heisey candlestick to receive the special color treatments of moonbeam, flamingo, and sahara. This style is being reissued by the Westmoreland company without a mark in crystal glass. (Heisey's #31 is c-25 in the candlestick section of this publication.)

Heisey's #33 (c-21) was made in adult sizes (5", 7", 9" and 11"). The Heisey mark is found on one of the side panels below the neck. It was originally made only in clear glass. This piece of ware is now reproduced by Imperial in crystal and green.

Heisey's #30 (c-20) candlestick, made only in crystal, is marked on the underside of the base. It has not been reproduced to date.

The five inch #5 candlestick is a toy which is marked on the underside of the hollow base. Both the top and base have six sides. This is c-17 in this publication. This candlestick has not been reproduced.

The "c-numbers" are from the book *Children's Glass Dishes* with newly assigned c-numbers for the current additions or corrections to the candlestick list. All candlesticks are in clear glass unless noted.

CANDLESTICKS

c-5*	3-5/8" ht., white, blue, green milkglass
c-8	4" ht.
c-10	3½" ht.
c-11	3-5/8" ht.
c-12	3-5/8" ht.

c-14   4¼'' ht.
c-15   4'' ht.
c-16*   4-5/8'' ht.
c-17   4-3/8'' ht. (Heisey's #5)
c-18   4¼'' ht.
c-20   3-5/8'' ht. (Heisey's #30)

c-21*   3'' ht. (Heisey's #33)
c-22   2-7/8'' ht. (Cambridge) 1924-25 in clear and peachblo
c-34   2-7/8'' ht. marbelized peach, pink, tan
c-23   3'' (Indiana Glass Co.)
c-24   2'' (New England Glass Co.), green, canary, clear, blue, like the chamberstick c-32
c-32   1'' (New England Glass Co.), cased bottom in blue, orange, yellow and all clear chamberstick

c-34   1-5/8'' ht. (Sandwich) clear or color; *M'Kee Victorian Glass* catalogue reprints from 1859/60 to 1871 shows a similar candlestick
c-35   4¼'' ht. Wild Rose
c-36   3-5/8'' ht.
c-37   3-5/8'' ht.

CHAMBERSTICKS

c-25*   2'' ht. (Heisey's #31)
c-26*   1-7/8'' ht. (Duncan and Miller #72)
c-28   2¼'' ht. (KRYS-TOL)
c-29   2'' ht. lacy white milkglass

c-41   1¾'' ht. (King Co. #143) cross hatching and beaded handle
c-6   1-7/8'' ht., some are new French imports in blue and white milkglass
c-42   2¼'' ht. chamberstick
c-43   2'' ht., sapphire blue lacy chamberstick

c-44   3 1/4'' ht. clear chambersticks; also in blue and amber

CANDELABRAS

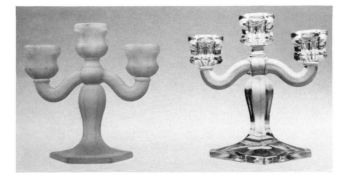

c-1   (Two different bases)
        Cambridge Glass Company made these in clear. Some three socket candlesticks have red paint in the candle cups. These were found in their original box which read:"Cape Cod Candle Co., Hyannis, Mass.'' (The word ''patent'' is missing from the socket rims.) Westmoreland made the three branch candelabra around 1920.
c-2   The four branch candelabra was not available for photo

c-45   7½'' complete, 4'' to the top of the candlesticks. These clear, French hurricane peg lamps are embossed with dots and have shades with frosted etchings of birds. This set is very rare.

c-24   Two photographs were taken to show the difference
c-34   between the Sandwich and the New England Glass Company candlesticks in height and socket openings.

c-1   This group shot shows the branched candlestick
c-12   with its original box (left rear). There is a rhyme
c-47   on the front of the lid which can be read from
c-48   the clear photograph. Inside the lid it says:
c-24   "Handipt Candles/Colonial Candle Company/ of Cape Cod, Hyannis/Massachusetts''.

The right rear of the photograph shows c-12 with the addition of a silver resist-type decoration. The front left of the photo shows a saucer shaped candlestick with the original label in green and gold which says "Swedish Glass". It is 2'' wide; c-47.

The front center of the picture has a 2'' square candlestick shaped in an ashtray form, excluding the indentation; c-48.

c-24 is shown in canary (frosted) glass at the front right of the photo.

c-46   This is an unusual combination of a candy container and a candlestick in ruby glass which has been souvenired. It is 3¾'' tall.

*c-5   Candlestick is the same as the chamberstick c-6

*c-16   c-16 and c-18 are the same in the book *Children's Glass Dishes*. In this text c-8 remains the same, but c-16 is a different candlestick.

*c-21   Is now being reproduced by Imperial; this is Heisey's old #33

*c-25   Heisey's #31 was originally made in clear, moonbeam, flamingo and sahara

*c-26   Comes in clear; this photo, however, shows one of a pair having a solid base of gold paint

CASTER SETS

"Drape"

"Diamond"

"Square"

"American Shield"

"Quilted"

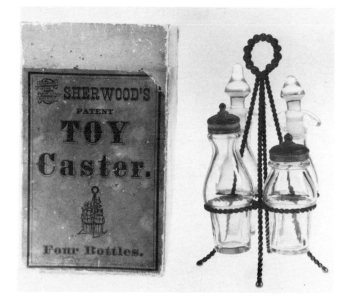

The miniature caster sets are a clever toy counterpart which demonstrates the charm and grace of the Victorian period. These replicas of the larger, more ornate caster sets used by mothers and grandmothers add a special touch to a table display of children's glassware or china.

Adults are delighted and amazed when they encounter these gems in shows, flea markets, or in the homes of avid collectors. The patterns are as numerous and varied as the holders which capture the bottles, stoppers and caps. A set found in the original Sherwood Company box confirms the intended purpose of these dainty objects.

Tiny caster sets which are much smaller than those shown in the book *Children's Glass Dishes* were made. A group shot of three sizes of caster sets is presented in this text which includes: a small "Sandwich" unit with blown bottles, all the same size, 1-5/8" tall without the stoppers . . . the pewter holder is 3¼" tall; the medium size caster set has free hand blown bottles which are also all the same size . . . 2" in height; the largest caster set in the group picture is the elusive "Circle In Square" found in its eagle topped frame. The bottles in the largest set include a cruet with a stopper, a mustard with a glass top and a shaker with a pewter lid. The holder is 5¾" tall.

Other patterns and styles illustrated in this text are the "Diamond", "Large Ribbon", "American Shield", "Quilted", "Drape", "Small Ribbon", "Square" and "Sherwood". The "Sherwood" and the "Circle in Square" as well as one "Sandwich" set have original lids and stoppers which may not be the case for the other patterns shown.

A recent acquisition, not shown in this book, was an American Shield caster set with the pewter holder bearing the words "Centennial 1876".

"Large Ribbon"

CHATEAU NO. 714

714 Toy Punch Set
Chateau

It is unfortunate that more of these punch sets were not made at the New Martinsville factory. Perhaps these sets were made for export; their absence in most collections is glaring. Even though children were rough in the handling of their play items, these sets are sturdy enough to have withstood more abuse than most.

PERTINENT DATA:

Additional pattern names: "#714"
Pattern pieces: Seven piece punch set
Pattern colors: Clear
Factory: New Martinsville
Date: Early 1900's
Classification: Rare
Reproduced: No
Pieces difficult to locate: All
Features attributable to pattern: Bowl is deeply scalloped ending in indented paneled flutes, cups are pouched and paneled

MEASUREMENTS:

Bowl	Curving paneled arches, graceful standard; 3-3/8'' ht, 4½'' wide
Cups	Paneled, sixteen point star on base, panels are pouched; 1¼'' ht., 1'' across base, 1-5/8'' across rim

CHIMO

The old Chimo pieces caused quite a stir when they were first discovered. Today, the disturbance persists because of the quality of glass used to reproduce the spooners and creamers which are found in fractious colors with careless trims.

In the book *Children's Glass Dishes*, a punch cup in this pattern was shown. No bowl has turned up to date, causing many collectors to believe that the so-called punch cup was probably used as a whiskey taster in the past. It is so difficult to find that most collectors buy it when they have the chance in case the bowl does make an appearance.

The L. E. Smith Glass Company in Mount Pleasant, Pennsylvania is producing a Chimo patterned spooner and creamer as #3580 in their line of assorted miniatures.

PERTINENT DATA:

Additional pattern names: None
Pattern pieces: Known four piece table set, a small punch-style cup
Pattern colors: Clear, amber, blue
Factory: Unknown
Date: Turn of the century
Classification: Rare in the old
Reproduced: Spooners and creamers only; clear with various trims, amber, blue and green
Pieces difficult to locate: All of the old pieces
Features attributable to pattern: Star design with dots interspersed among the points

MEASUREMENTS:

Spooner	2-1/8'' tall
Sugar	3'' complete, 2-1/8'' base tall, 2½'' diam., 1-7/8'' lid in diam.
Creamer	2'' tall, 2'' wide
Butter	2¼'' complete, 3¾'' base diam., 3'' lid across
Cup	1½'' tall, 1-3/8'' wide

CLAMBROTH SCENERY

Clambroth is the treatment given the rare souvenired table set pieces which have decals of Gettysburg scenery. Some of the sets were done in a custard style glass with the words "Cincinnati Zoo" and the embellishment of hand painted roses. The thought remains that children visiting tourist attractions across the country could pick and choose the inscriptive design to complete their sets.

PERTINENT DATA:

Additional pattern names: None
Pattern pieces: Four piece table set
Pattern colors: Clambroth glass with Gettysburg decals, custard glass with Cincinnati Zoo hand painted
Factory: Unknown
Date: Circa 1900
Classification: Rare
Reproduced: No
Pieces difficult to locate: Spooner, creamer
Features attributable to pattern: Historical information; souvenired motif

MEASUREMENTS:

Spooner	Pennsylvania Memorial clambroth; 2-3/8'' ht, 2-1/8'' width
Sugar	Jennie Wade House clambroth; 3¼'' ht., 2¼'' ht. of base
Creamer	Jennie Wade House and Monument in clambroth; 2-5/8'' spout to base, 2-7/8'' spout to handle
Butter	1863, Gettysburg, Pennsylvania; gold finial; gold border on butter base; 3-5/8'' across base, 2½'' overall ht.

CLEAR AND DIAMOND PANELS

When the book *Children's Glass Dishes* was written it was not imagined how hard it would be to find the larger of the two butters in this table set. Relying on the standard colors seemingly used for children's glass, the company cast the pieces in medium green, blue and clear. The larger butter has been seen only in clear to date, while the rest of the pieces are frequently found.

PERTINENT DATA:

Additional pattern names: None
Pattern pieces: Two butters, sugar, creamer, spooner
Pattern colors: Clear, blue, green
Factory: Unknown
Date: 1880's
Classification: Small butter and table set frequently found in clear
Reproduced: No
Pieces difficult to locate: Large butter, green pieces, blue sugar lid
Features attributable to pattern: All have modified scallops around edges and panels of cross hatching

MEASUREMENTS:

Spooner	2-3/8'' ht., 2¼'' width
Sugar	2-3/8'' ht. of base, 2-7/8'' side to side
Creamer	2¾'' spout to base, 3¼'' spout to handle, 2¼'' side to side
Large butter	4'' overall ht., 4½'' across base, 3-3/8'' across lid opening
Small butter	3-5/8'' across base, 1¼'' ht. of base, 2-3/8'' ht. of lid, 2-5/8'' across lid bottom

CLOUD BAND

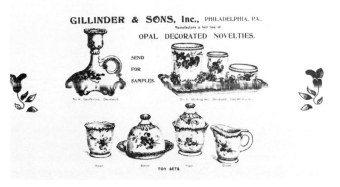

"Cloud Band" was made in a four-piece table set by Gillinder and Sons, Inc., Philadelphia, Pennsylvania. In their trade catalogue proof, an adult chamberstick and smoking set were shown with the toy set. This rare toy set was done in decorated opal glass; the original sets had purple violets and green leaves on each shell-rimmed piece.

In Warman's *Milk Glass Addenda* the spooner to this set is shown as a toothpick and called "Beaded Top." In Kamm's book seven, page 47, the name "Cloud Band" is given.

Gillinder ware became popular because of the exhibition factory at the 1876 Centennial Exhibition where many pressed novelties were turned out for the watching crowds.

PERTINENT DATA:

Additional pattern names: "Beaded Top"
Pattern pieces: Four piece table set
Pattern colors: Milkglass with purple violets
Factory: Gillinder
Date: 1900 ad proof in *Crockery and Glass Journal*; July 26, 1900
Classification: Rare
Reproduced: No
Pieces difficult to locate: Butter base, whole butter, sugar
Features attributable to pattern: Draped design around the top of each piece, ornate finials (crown effect)

MEASUREMENTS:

Spooner	Beaded, scalloped ruffled rim; 2-3/8'' ht., 2-3/8'' wide
Sugar	Crown type finial; 3-7/8'' complete, 2-3/8'' base ht.
Creamer	Smooth rim and handle; 2½'' ht. from lip to base, 2¾'' across spout handle
Butter	Ruffled base rim, beaded crown finial, done type lid; 3¼'' complete, 4-5/8'' base diam.

COLONIAL

This seven-piece punch set has one advantage promoting its popularity. It is the only old toy glass punch set made with stemmed glasses. (Contrary to some opinions, these are not eye-winker glasses.) This set comes in clear crystal and has a slightly murky appearance. At times there is an amethyst tinge which is carried to the water set of the same plain pattern. The purplish tone is not due to sun tinting but is instead a factor in the glassmaking process.

PERTINENT DATA:

Additional pattern names: None
Pattern pieces: Seven piece punch set, water set
Pattern colors: Clear (with a smudged appearance)
Factory: Unknown
Date: Circa 1900
Classification: Difficult to complete
Reproduced: No
Pieces difficult to locate: Punch bowl, correct glasses
Features attributable to pattern: Plain fluting type style, murky glass

MEASUREMENTS:

Bowl	3-3/8'' ht., 4-1/8'' wide
Cup	1-7/8'' ht., 1¾'' wide
Pitcher	3-3/8'' spout to base, 1-7/8'' wide
Tumbler	About 2'', 1-7/8'' across flared top

CUPS AND SAUCERS

"Dog Medallion"

Deep saucer, 3½'' across; cup with long eared dog's head 1¾'' tall

"Lion"

Deep saucer with reclining lion in the base, 3¼'' across; cup has two shaggy headed lions, footed, 1¾'' tall; 2-1/8'' side to side, frosted, clear with frosted lions

"Ornamental Hobnail"

Made by several companies; 2'' cup height, 4'' saucer width; (also issued as mug #3847 by the Beatty & Sons Glass Co.)

"Sandwich" (style) Excess glass; ornate handles; footed; 1¾" in height

"French" (style) Heavy, thick glass, panels; cup 1-7/8" tall, 2½" across (group picture)

"Cat and Dog" Cup, 2" tall, has two pictures in beaded frame, a dog in a garden and a fat cat in quiet repose; saucer 3½" across (group picture)

"Loops and Ropes" Smooth handle, obscured glass which is yellowish, 2" tall; needs a saucer (group picture)

"Stippled Leaf and Grape" Large leaf with grape clusters on each side, 1¾" tall; the leaf and grape appear four times on the saucer (group picture)

"Pillar" Smooth handled mug 1½" tall (group picture)

"Blue Milkglass Diamonds" Cup 1-7/8" x 2¾"; saucer 3¾" across

"Basket Weave" Cup, 2½" x 2-5/8"; saucer unavailable; in clear and amber

"Daisy Band" Cup, 2½' x 2½"; saucer unavailable; clear

"Two Children" Cup, 2½" x 2½"; saucer unavailable, clear

D & M 42
MARDI GRAS

The Duncan and Miller Company produced this five piece table set in the 1890's. It is but one of the sparkling toy renditions made by this quality-minded glass works. Of the table set, the butter and plump creamer are the hardest pieces to locate. The so-called honey jug and the covered sugar are next in procurement difficulty. The spooner, even though residing in several toothpick collections, seems to be easily found.

The set is lovely without the ornate gold trim treatment, but elegant when the gold is found in good condition.

A crystal decanter set with an enameled Art Deco style decoration consisting of large white dots centered within a band of black outlined squares is shown in this publication. The tray is 4'' in diameter and each tumbler is a mere 1¼'' high and ¾'' across the rim. The decanter is only 3¼'' tall.

This example shows a transparent sapphire blue set consisting of a 4¼'' tray, tumblers which are 1-5/8'' tall and 1-1/8'' across (each rim) and a decanter which is only 4'' in height. The design is an enameled motif consisting of white geometric outlines with yellow dots and orange flowers.

DEEP STARS AND OCTAGONS

The glassmakers of the past would certainly be confounded to realize how much debate has been caused due to lack of written verification of their specialty. The debate has not run its course when it comes to the pattern of "Deep Stars and Octagons."

Some collectors declare that this is not a child's set, rather wines used with a creamer. Ladies of age, however, insist that they are lemonade sets with which they played. Collectors scrutinize the bottom of each pitcher discussing the merits of the leaf and grape motif versus the ray design which is also found in the bases of the tumblers.

No catalogue proof has been found to verify any of these deductions. One would have the tendency to assume that the ladies remember their toys with clarity; there could not have been many sets of toys per family. The ones they had were usually guarded and frequently used. In comparison, how many of today's children remember the Christmas bounty from the previous season?

An additional "use" possibility exists. Perhaps these items served the adults as well as the children. Nevertheless, collectors determined to have an example of each glass pattern associated with the word "miniature" count with zeal the eight octagonal deeply set designs which encircle the center of the pitchers and tumblers. Deeply grooved stars complete the set's pattern.

PERTINENT DATA:

Additional pattern names: None
Pattern pieces: Seven piece water set
Pattern colors: Clear
Factory: Unknown
Date: Turn of the century
Classification: Obtainable
Reproduced: No
Pieces difficult to locate: Tumblers
Features attributable to pattern: Eight octagon deep set designs encircle the center of the pitcher with deep stars finishing the design

MEASUREMENTS:

Pitcher   3¼'' spout to base, 2-7/8'' side to side
Tumbler   2'' ht., 1-5/8'' wide

DEPRESSION GLASS
and
AKRO AGATE TOY WARE

Depression Glass has been defined as colored glass made primarily during the late 1920's through the 1930's in amber, pink, green, blue, yellow, red, white and crystal. Most of this inexpensively made, highly collectible glass was produced to induce people to buy other products during that pennyless age . . .the Depression days.

The Akro Agate Company has been "classed" in the Depression era even though it began its days in 1911 in Akron, Ohio. Established to make marbles and games, they were able to best the foreign marble importing companies by moving to Clarksburg, West Virginia where gas and materials were available cheaply.

For forty years they ruled three-fourths of all the marble business in America. The company florished during World War II, controlling the doll-dish market because the metal needed for some of those toy sets was also needed in the war effort . . . and they could, of course, forget the competition from Japan during that time.

Akro Agate did not concentrate on transparent colors, turning instead to mixed batches of glass, producing sets in lovely and unusual combinations of color. These sets sold cheaply while the company's sales record reached a zenith in the years of 1942 and 1943.

In speaking with several glass masters of today, they have indicated that few, if any, companies would attempt to produce such unusual combinations as the "Lemonade and Oxblood'' glass which was made by Akro Agate. It seems the ''recipe'' for keeping the red from bleeding into the lemon color is lost.

With the end of the war and the return of metal and imports, the ''kiss of death'' was bestowed on the Akro Agate Company and it was sold in 1951 to Clarksburg Glass Company.

Collectors who have neglected this classification of glassware will be sad to know that the boat has left the dock . . . the craze for this glass has long begun. The publishers of this book indicated to me that when the last Depression Glass book was published by his company, 38,000 copies were sent out to buyers in four days.

Due to the urgency of mass production during the war, quality often gave way to quantity, so some of this glassware is not especially well made. But, nevertheless, collectors want examples of everything made and if it is in the original box the price escalates. The black and white pictures shown in this text were taken in the original boxes because of the importance of the containers. A clear pattern idea may be obtained from the color plates shown in this publication.

The four groups of the Akro children's line are: the transparents (made in the 1930's); the marbleized two-color opaques; the crystal baked on; and the most common, the opaque solid colors. Several pieces have a crow flying through an A on the underside--this was the Akro trademark.

The Akro Agate shown in this publication is but a small sample of the variety of ware turned out by this company which enjoyed prosperity for 40 years.

The toy Depression glass in this section is part of the Sharon Boren collection. Mrs. Boren owns one of the largest Depression glass collections in the United States with over 25 complete adult sets and several pieces which have not appeared in any publication to date.

Mrs. A. Green provided the unusual Houze toy sets which are a part of Depression toy-glass Americana. These sets were made in transparent blue, yellow, and green for only a short time. The glass is similar to moonstone of Aladdin lamps. It is also a bit like Fenton's opaline. The sets were made by the Houze Company of Point Marion, Pennsylvania.

DEPRESSION GLASS:

''Moderntone'' - The ''Little Hostess Party Set'' was made by the Hazel-Atlas Glass Company, founded in 1885 at Wellsburgh, West Virginia. (The name ''Hazel'' was chosen at random to name a new furnace - a practice of naming the furnaces with feminine names was carried on in the steel and iron industry.) The sets come in many colors; an unusual pink and black combination, burgundy, dark green, blue, and yellowish green.

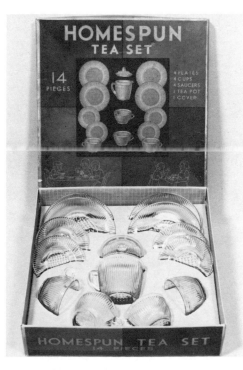

''Homespun'' - This set was made in light pink and clear by the Jeannette Glass Company from 1939-1940. The set consists of cups, saucers, plates, and a tea pot. (Tea pot found in pink only, so far.)

"Doric and Pansy" - These "Pretty Polly" dishes were made at the Jeannette Glass Company from 1937-1938. They were made in teal and pink and consisted of cups, saucers, plates, creamer, and a sugar. These dishes have not been reproduced.

"Cherry Blossom" - These sets were made at the Jeannette Glass Company from 1930 to 1939 in pink and in (blue) delphite. The sets consist of four plates, four cups and saucers, a creamer, and a sugar. A butter dish was never made in toy form by this company in this pattern.

Reproductions - ("Cherry Blossom" set) - A new butter was made in 1973 in shades of blue, green and carnival colors. The cup was reproduced with an imperfect handle and a cherry design inversion mistake which was later corrected. After the correction the color quality slipped a bit. The saucer was reproduced with the design a little off center.

"Laurel" - This set was made by McKee Glass Company and has some unusual combinations. (1930) The colors are plain, Scotty Dog decaled, and plain with colored rims. The set shown in this publication is cream with a red rim . . . four plates, four cups, four saucers, a creamer, and a sugar complete this set.

"Houze" - These sets were made for a short period of time by the Houze Company in Point Marion, Pennsylvania. They were made in lovely "moonstone or opaline" shades of yellow, blue and green. The label from the company was gold and black and it appears in shield form in the bottom right hand corner of the tea set box. The original box contains: a covered tea pot which is 3¼" complete and 2¼" without the lid; a covered sugar which is 2" complete and 1¾" tall without the lid; the creamer is 1¼" tall and 2¼" across the rim; there are four cups which are 1¼" high and four saucers which are 3¼" across; the four plates are 4" across. The man credited with developing this beautiful treatment of toy glass was Henry T. Hellmers. Mr. Hellmers traveled to different companies treating them to his formulas and expertise. He worked at the Akro Agate Company from 1922 to 1930 developing colors for toy dishes and marbles. (Mr. Hellmers also worked for Cambridge Glass Company from 1930 to 1932, developing their important Crown Tuscan.) He worked at the Houze Company from 1935 to 1942 and is responsible for the lovely sets shown from the Green collection in the color section of this publication.

AKRO AGATE:

(See the color section for the group shot and this section for the black and white "in the box" photographs.)

"Shirley Temple" - The cereal bowl was given away with two large boxes of Wheaties. (circa 1935) The mug was given with a large box of Bisquick. The picture on the creamer was from the movie "Captain January." The cobalt plate is very difficult to locate. This photo includes: cobalt pitcher, mug and bowl; plastic and the metal tea set; a 12" doll (1957) and a 14" doll (1961).

Sharon Boren Collection

"Chiquita" - The Chiquita sets were made in solid opaques, transparent glass, and baked-on enamel expressly for J. Pressman of New York; they are marked "J.P." The set in this publication is transparent cobalt with wing-tipped handles: saucer 3½", tea pot with lid 3½", creamer 1-5/8", sugar 1-5/8", cup 1-5/8" (All in the original box.)

"Concentric Ring" - These sets were made in solid opaques or transparent glass. There are six rings banding the pieces with the cups having closely set rings surrounding the cups' centers. The handles are wing-tipped. The set shown in its original box has a mixed and matched combination which is not uncommon: green plates 3¼'', yellow saucers 2¾'', blue covered tea pot 3'' in height, creamer and uncovered sugar 1¼'' in height, and pumpkin colored cups at 1¼'' in height.

"Octagonal Opaque" - This is one of the easiest sets to locate and also one of the most colorful. The opaques were the longest run sets of any in the Akro toy line: green plate 4¼'', white saucer 3¼'', white creamer 1-3/8'', green cup 1-3/8'', complete sugar in blue 2½''. (The colors are given in the text because the photos are in black and white. It needs to be known that sets are complete and original even if they are color-mixed within the same container.)

"Marbelized Interior Panel" - This set comes in blue and white, oxblood and white, and is shown here in green and white in its original container: plate 4¼'', saucer 3¼'', covered tea pot 3½'', covered sugar 1¾'', cereal 3¼'', creamer 1-3/8'', cup 1¾''.

"Stacked Disk" - This water set is green with custard colored tumblers. The water pitchers in the Akro sets are straight sided. This one is 2-5/8'' in height; the tumbler 2'' in height.

"Stacked Disc and Panel" - This water set has straight sides distinguishing it from the curved-sided creamers. This set is azure transparent optic, in the small size. The pitcher is 2-7/8'' tall and the tumblers are 2'' in height.

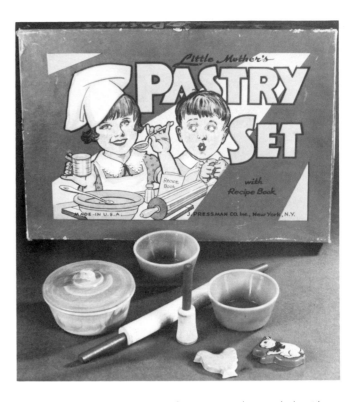

"Lemonade and Oxblood" - These rare pieces come in two basic shapes--the round, large size called "Interior Panel" and the octagonal with closed handles.

Sharon Boren Collection

"Raised Daisy" - The "Raised Daisy" in this publication was taken from a boxed, all blue set which included four cups and saucers, four plates, and a tea pot, all in medium blue. The color photo shows: green tea pot and cup, light blue plate, butterscotch saucer, yellow sugar, creamer and tumbler (see color plate).

Green Collection

"Miss America" - This set from the Green Collection was boxed in a complete transparent green set which included four plates, cups and saucers, tea pot and lid, sugar and lid, and a creamer. This set also comes in white, decal, and orange-white (see color plate).

"Little Mother's Pastry Set" - This set was also made by Akro for J. Pressman. Of all the "Little Mother's Pastry Sets" this is the only one that has a large covered bowl and two small bowls. They are in the typical "Chiquita" green. The contents of the box were removed and pictured in front of the box's lid.

Green collection

"Little Orphan Annie" - This set's photograph was taken in front of the lid to the original box to show Little Orphan Annie and Sandy. The transparent sets were sold as "Little Orphan Annie" tea sets while the baked-on enamel "fat" J. Pressman pieces were sold in a box that says "Chiquita Toy Dishes in Carnival Colors". (Both types of sets were made for J. Pressman by the Akro Agate Company of Clarksburg, West Virginia.)

Green Collection

DEWDROP (DOT)

Collecting companions are rattled from complacency each time there is a new discovery. The "Dewdrop" (Dot) table set has been around for a long time but the pieces have wandered in and out of various sets looking for a home. This four piece table set was made at Factory J, in Findlay, Ohio in crystal, blue, and amber in 1891.

PERTINENT DATA:

Additional pattern names: "Dot"
Pattern pieces: Four piece table set
Pattern colors: Clear, amber, blue
Factory: Columbia Glass, Factory J
Date: 1891
Classification: Difficult to locate in clear, very rare in color
Reproduced: No
Pieces difficult to locate: Butter and sugar in clear, all color

Features attributable to pattern: All over hobnails, plumb appearance

MEASUREMENTS:

Spooner	2-5/8'' ht., 2¼'' wide
Sugar	4'' overall, 3'' wide
Creamer	3¼'' wide, 3'' tall
Butter	2½'' tall, 3¾'' wide

DOYLE'S NO. 500

Doyle and Company of Pittsburgh, Pennsylvania produced a table set and two different sized mugs around 1888. This company further enhanced the table unit by making a matching tray. Actually, there are two sizes of trays, the smaller one's purpose is yet to be determined by ad proof. The tray rarity is found in only two other old toy sets: the "Oval Star" water set is one and the "Hobnail with Thumbprint Base" table set is the other. Collectors of both old and new children's glass are enthralled with the idea of having a tray to give the finishing touch to a set. The tray also helps to keep the unit compacted for display purposes.

Though the tray is unusual, the colors used by the Doyle Company are common to collectors--amber, blue and crystal. A few canary pieces can be found. They might be a result of a single glass batch gone amuck--a situation causing panic at the factory, but delight for the present day collector.

In Heacock's book, *1,000 Toothpick Holders*, he indicated that this set was made in amethyst. If it was made in amethyst, it is the only old toy glass set to have this special treatment.

PERTINENT DATA:

Additional pattern names: "Doyle's Honeycomb"
Pattern pieces: Four piece table set and tray, two sizes of mugs
Pattern colors: Clear, amber, blue
Factory: Doyle & Company
Date: 1888
Classification: Obtainable in clear, amber, blue, very rare if in amethyst
Reproduced: No
Pieces difficult to locate: Butters and sugars
Features attributable to pattern: Honeycomb style motif; tray's base is hobnailed

MEASUREMENTS:

Spooner	2-3/8'' ht., 2¼'' wide
Sugar	2-5/8'' ht. of base only, 2½'' wide
Creamer	2-5/8'' ht. from spout to base, 3½'' width from lip to handle
Butter	1'' base ht., 3-1/8'' width of base, 2½'' overall ht.
Table set tray	6-5/8'' width
Smaller tray	5¾'' across
Mug	2'' ht., 2'' width amber, blue, white
Mug	2½'' ht., 2'' wide

DRUM

One could use several superlatives when describing the enchantment cast by the four piece "Drum" table set and its mug counterparts. The cannon finial atop the covered pieces lends an irresistible charm to this magical set of the 1880's. The clever designer stamped his approval at the bottom of each mould with a unique ridged row of stippled lines not unlike those found in the equally interesting "Bucket" set which was made by the Bryce, Higbee Company within the same time frame.

PERTINENT DATA:

Additional pattern names: None
Pattern pieces: Four piece table set, mugs
Pattern colors: Clear
Factory: Bryce, Higbee
Date: 1880
Classification: Difficult to complete
Reproduced: No
Pieces difficult to locate: Spooner, sugar lid
Features attributable to pattern: Covered pieces have cannon finials, bottoms of the pieces have stippled lines, drum shape (except butter)

MEASUREMENTS:

Spooner	2'' wide, 2-5/8'' height
Sugar	2½'' wide, 3¼'' tall
Creamer	2'' side to side, 3'' across spout to handle, 2¾'' ht.
Covered butter	3½'' width, 1-1/8'' ht. of base, 2¼'' overall ht.
Mugs	2½'' ht. x 2¼''; 2¼'' ht. x 2½''; 1-7/8'' ht. x 2''

DUTCH BOUDOIR

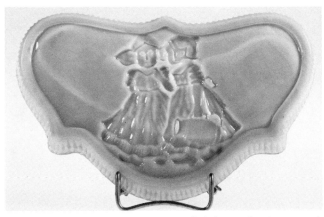

The lucky collector becomes slightly euphoric as each piece of the rare "Dutch Boudoir" unit is carried home and set in place. The maker is unknown, so we must thank the dealer who provides us with this special buy. (There will, in fact, be many dealers to thank for rarely is this pattern bought intact.)

The blue milkglass set easily wins top prize as the most difficult to find, but the white milkglass pieces cause no small amount of sweat and tremble in their acquisiton.

Soon after *Children's Glass Dishes* was published additional pieces to this special unit were discovered. The glass set now consists of: a pitcher and bowl, a glass covered slop jar, a glass covered potty, metal covered pomade jars (two), candlesticks, and a tray with Dutch children imprinted on the underside of the base. Those who have lids for the jars and potty feel

especially content. It has been deduced that the tray should hold two pomade jars and one candlestick because it is not large enough to carry all of the pieces.

PERTINENT DATA:

Additional pattern names: None
Pattern pieces: Covered potty, covered slop jar, candlesticks, two pomade jars, tray, pitcher, bowl
Pattern colors: Blue opaque, blue or white milkglass
Factory: Attributed to United States Glass
Date: Circa 1910
Classification: Rare
Reproduced: No
Pieces difficult to locate: Tray, covered pomades, candlesticks
Features attributable to pattern: Dutch children

MEASUREMENTS:

Potty	Three legged stool with a bucket on it; Dutch girl with long braid, beaded handle; 1-3/8'' ht. without lid, 1-1/8'' wide
Pitcher	Girl with a jug, pastoral scene with a windmill, beaded rim; 2¼'' spout to base, 1-5/8'' side to side
Bowl	Children (three of them on two sides), beaded rim; 3-1/8'' wide, 1½'' ht.
Candlestick	Dog on one side, Dutch boy on the other, beaded socket rim; 3'' ht., 2¼'' across base
Slop jar	Dutch boy with hands in pocket, Dutch boy and girl on the other side, beaded rim; 2-1/8'' ht. without lid
Tray	Beaded rim; irregular shape, Dutch girls impressed on the underside of the tray; 6'' long, 3-5/8'' wide at middle section
Pomade jar	Metal caps with a four petaled flower-shape, cow, Dutch girl, trees, some type of structure between two trees; 1¾'' with cap ht., 1-1/8'' across opening

ENAMELED LEMONADE SETS

form. This set is painted with white enamel in a thistle pattern. The set is shown in the color section of this publication.

A special addition to any collection would be the emerald water set with a pitcher measuring only 1¾'' in height. Great amounts of gold enhance this elegant display of workmanship. The tumblers are 1½'' tall with an opening of only ¾''.

The trinket sized enameled water set seems perfect for little fingers to handle. The pitcher is 3¾'' tall and the tumblers are 1¾'' in height. The enamel paint in high relief sprinkles spring over this five piece toy set. Two pronounced bands capture the pitcher and tumblers sealing in perfection.

MEASUREMENTS:

Ruffled water pitcher	6'' tall, 3¼'' wide
Tankard water pitcher	5¼'' tall, 5'' spout to handle, 3¼'' across bottom
Tumblers for ruffled pitcher and tankard pitcher	2¼'' tall
Cobalt pitcher	4¾'' tall
Cobalt tumbler	1¼'' tall
Emerald pitcher	1¾'' tall
Emerald tumbler	1½'' tall, ¾'' across top
Toy enameled pitcher	3¾'' tall
Toy enameled tumbler	1¾'' tall

EPERGNE AND LUSTERS
Miniature Accessories

E-6   E-2   E-5   E-4

E-1

Certain toy sets evoke special memories for each of us. When I see the three enameled lemonade sets I think of a special apple tree with low hanging branches. From each of those branches hung a pair of chubby sunburned legs whenever a summer occasion called for a tea party. (It was a tea party no matter what was served.) "They're at it again!" Frankie Ransbottom would chortle as he gathered the boys to hassle the little girls who were busy arranging the tea table under the apple tree. How the boys discovered the exact tea-cozy moment is a mystery to this day. (It's been deduced, however, that it was the smell of my mother's famous cinnamon rolls that drew the crowd.)

Frankie, who was reportedly wealthy beyond measure, was fat . . . a constant source of worry to me for he liked sitting on my less than adequate lap! Peter of the short pants was always there. (I was glad, for I admired his bravery . . . he was the only boy brave enough to wear short pants to school.) The dolls were there, each looking as though she'd been hit on the head with a board.

The boys hung upside down like moths and monkeys when they wanted a taste of the sweets; promptly rewarding us by sifting sugar on our dolls and in our hair. Demented bees and racing ants complete that summer memory.

Two of the enameled lemonade pitchers have tumblers in common. The cunningly ruffled pitcher and the tankard style pitcher, usually found in clear or light green, bear either lilies-of-the-valley or forget-me-nots as their painted motif. Whenever the tumblers have the same paint as the pitcher they may be used together, for everything else about them is the same.

The little hostess who spread her tea table with the unique cobalt lemonade set evoked compliments of the highest

E-3

E-7

LUSTERS: chandeliers with drops or pendants--ornamental pieces usually seen on Victorian mantels (see color section)

Note: The lusters are measured from their tallest point; the drops are measured from the top of the glass to the tip with the wire not included in the measurement.

L-1   blue splatter-type glass with petal rim and crystal drops, 5-7/8'' tall, 3'' across rim, 2-3/8'' drops

L-2   grape-colored splatter design, gold petal-type top, slimmer than L-1 . . . but similar in style, 5-5/8'' tall, 2¾'' across, 2¾'' drops (Welker collection)

L-3   amethyst luster with a lush ruffled top and enameled flowers, gold accent paint, 7'' from highest ruffle, 4-3/8'' across the widest ruffled part, 3'' drops

L-4   lavender glass with etching of flowers, jagged rim cuts grace the top, 6½'' tall, 2½'' across, 3-7/8'' drops which may not be original (see color section grouping)

L-5   cobalt with enamel paint, 6½'' tall

EUCLID
REXFORD

''Euclid'' is the factory name for this design encrusted four piece table set. This is a Higbee Company production with similar characteristics which can be found on the following sets: ''Style'', ''Hawaiian Lei'', ''Fine Cut Star and Fan''.

The main design is a rayed figure with grooved outlines crossing one another. The covered sugar has a petaled edge, while the spooner sports beading around the top. A cake salver used by miniature collectors in this pattern makes a nice table setting display.

PERTINENT DATA:

Additional pattern names: ''Rexford''

While epergnes and lusters have yet to be labeled ''toy'', few collectors can deny their ''pixie chattle charm.'' Collectors strive for as many examples as they can acquire of these miniature glass counterparts of adult ware.

EPERGNES: an ornamental piece for the center of the table

E-1   clear with gold trim, ruffles, 5½'' tall

E-2   two-pieced, clear glass with faint etching, bowl is 2-7/8'' high and the stem is 6-7/8'' long

E-3   unusual tiny one-piece epergne, etched design on clear glass, 5'' tall complete

E-4   lush blue with gold white enamel trim, ruffled rims, 7-1/8'' complete

E-5   Bristol glass, enameled flowers inside the ruffled bowl, made (also) without flowers, about 6¼'' complete

E-6   ''Jackson'' miniature epergne, lush blue with opalescent ruffle, four scrolled feet, 6¼'' tall

E-7   blue glass with opalescent ruffles

During the Victorian period in many homes Sunday tea was laid out in the ''front room''. After the tea was cleared the table was covered with a fancy cloth and an epergne was placed in the center of the table with two equally elegant pieces of glass on either side.

Pattern pieces: Four piece table set, cake plate
Pattern colors: Clear
Factory: Higbee
Date: Turn of the century
Classification: Frequently found
Reproduced: No
Pieces difficult to locate: Sugar lid
Features attributable to pattern: Rayed figure with grooved outlines crossing one another; sugar has petaled edge; spooner has beading at the top

MEASUREMENTS:

Spooner	2'' width, 2¼'' ht.
Sugar	2¼'' ht., 2¾'' overall ht.
Creamer	3¼'' spout to handle; 2-3/8'' spout to base
Butter	3-7/8'' width, 1'' ht. of base, 2-5/8'' overall ht.

FENTON'S KITTENS

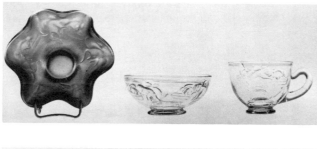

The Fenton Art Glass Company of Williamstown, West Virginia made the "Carnival" Kitten pattern in marigold, cobalt blue and vaseline. The pieces were also made in clear.

There are various kitten groupings but the usual ones are: four groups of kittens on the inside of the spooner, banana dish, and bowls; two gangs of kittens on the outside of the cups; four groups of kittens on the 1'' deep saucer (some rare saucers can be found with only two kittens).

PERTINENT DATA:

Additional pattern names: "Carnival Kittens"
Pattern pieces: Spooner, cup, plain banana, plain bowl, ruffled bowl, vase
Pattern colors: Marigold, cobalt, vaseline, clear, amethyst
Factory: Fenton Art Glass Company

Date: 1912
Classification: Rare other than in marigold
Reproduced: No
Pieces difficult to locate: All in clear; all in colors other than marigold
Features attributable to pattern: Kitten groupings

MEASUREMENTS:

Spooner	2'' ht., 3½'' wide
Cup	2¼'' ht., 2-3/8'' wide
Plain banana	4-5/8'' long, 2¾'' from one turned side to the other
Plain bowl	1-7/8'' ht., 3½'' wide
Ruffled bowl	4'' across longest part, 1½'' across bottom of tiny raised base
Vase	2¼'' tall

FINE CUT AND X'S
No. 379

Although this set was a part of the author's collection in 1976 when *Children's Glass Dishes* was published, it was omitted because catalogue proof was not found to document the set. (Too many sauces and salts have found their way into toy glass collections.)

Indeed this is a toy set produced by the Co-Operative Flint Glass Company as their #379 toy berry set. (The adult salts in this pattern do not measure the same as the berries.)

PERTINENT DATA:

Additional pattern names: "#379"
Pattern pieces: Main bowl, small bowl
Pattern colors: Clear
Factory: Co-Operative Flint
Date: Turn-of-the-century
Classification: Difficult to find the main bowl, small bowls frequently found
Reproduced: No
Pieces difficult to locate: Main bowl
Features attributable to pattern: Fine x's separated by horizontal ribbing

MEASUREMENTS:

Main bowl	4'' wide, 2'' tall
Small bowl	2¼'' wide, 1'' tall

(See Glass Companies and Their Contributions for catalogue proof)

GRAPE STEIN SET
Wabash Toy Series

Stein Set

The grape motif on this toy stein set is attributed to the vast number of vineyards and wineries which were once in Ohio. The absence of these stein sets in nearly every miniature collection in the nation is probably because the Federal Glass Company of Columbus, Ohio was shipping large amounts of glassware to England, Germany, Australia and South America in the early 1900's.

It seems that more attention was given the design than the quality of glass which went into this product. The main stein does not have the convenience of a pouring lip and the glass is murky. The bunches of grapes received the decorators' attention and are tinted purple with green leaves. All pieces are well proportioned and decorated in gold. Barely discernible wording appears on the main stein.

PERTINENT DATA:

Additional pattern names: "Wabash"
Pattern pieces: Seven piece stein set
Pattern colors: Clear glass with purple grapes
Factory: Federal Glass Co.; Columbus, Ohio
Date: 1914
Classification: Very rare
Reproduced: No
Pieces difficult to locate: All
Features attributable to pattern: All have cloudy-gray glass with paneled design and superimposed grape clusters which were appropriately painted, part of a word "shen" is seen in the Federal Glass ad.

MEASUREMENTS: Unavailable

HAWAIIAN LEI

Originally, the Higbee Company produced the Hawaiian Lei four piece table set. At the present time, Tom Mosser of

Cambridge, Ohio is using the moulds which he had made to produce the three piece table set. (The spooner is missing in the Mosser unit for the original was lost on the way to the mould shop.) Mr. Mosser copied the bee in the base of each of his three pieces, but excluded the H I G which is sometimes found on the wings and abdomen of the Higbee company's bee. He has made the new sets in light pink, light blue, clear, and orange-red . . . so far. The old sets were made only in clear.

If you are looking for an old set, your best chance is to get a four piece unit with no bee or one with a bee and the H I G.

PERTINENT DATA:

Additional pattern names: "Daisy and X Band", *Treasury of Canadian Glass*
Pattern pieces: Four piece table set, cake salver
Pattern colors: Clear
Factory: Bryce Higbee and Company
Date: 1900
Classification: Easy to assemble
Reproduced: Yes, Tom Mosser, three pieces; missing spooner
Pieces difficult to locate: None
Features attributable to pattern: Thumbprint design appears at the base of the covered sugar, creamer, spooner; scalloped edges; horizontal band of flowers; lucid glass

MEASUREMENTS:

Spooner	2¼" ht., 2" width
Sugar	3" overall ht., 2¼" ht. of base, 2¾" across base
Creamer	2-3/8" ht. from spout to base, 3-1/8" handle to spout
Butter	2½" overall ht., 7/8" ht. of base, 3¾" across base
Cake salver	3½" ht., 6-5/8" width

Heisey's SAWTOOTH BAND
No. 1225

Mr. Heisey patented the design for this particular pattern in 1898. The set in miniature was made in clear, clear with gold trim, ruby flashed and at times bears an engraved motif of love or travel. The proof of the child's complete lone table set made by the Heisey company is shown in Heisey's First Ten Years catalogue, Book One. A mug #1591 with an elephant head handle was made and is now heavily reproduced for a private distributor. Heisey also made four toy candlesticks: #31, #33, #5 and #30.

The designer of this pattern must have realized that the days of the ostentatious patterns were numbered. The clear, clean, consise lines are comparable to the patterns of today. (Due to the escalated cost of moulds, there will be very few capricous patterns in new lines of the future.)

PERTINENT DATA:

Additional pattern names: "Fine Cut Bands", "Plain Band", "1225"
Pattern pieces: Four piece table set
Pattern colors: Clear, clear with gold trim, clear with ruby flashing
Factory: Heisey
Date: 1898
Classification: Difficult to complete
Reproduced: No
Pieces difficult to locate: Butter, sugar*
Features attributable to pattern: Pure lines, clear glass

*When buying the sugar, make sure you don't have a custard with the child's sugar lid.

MEASUREMENTS:

Spooner	Obscure fine line of jagged ridges are caused by the reflection of the flower-like design in the base; beaded rim; 2½" ht., 2-1/8" side to side
Sugar	Smooth ball finial, subdued bands of ridges around the lids of the butter and sugar; 2-5/8" across base opening, 4-1/8" ht. overall, 2-3/8" base ht.
Creamer	Smooth handle, semi-beaded rim; 2" side to side, 2¾" spout to base, 3½" spout to handle
Butter	Smooth ball finial, conservative row of beading around rim of butter base, 4" ht., 4¾" across base

HOBBS WATER SETS

In 1891 the Hobbs Glass Company, Factory H, of Wheeling, West Virginia conjured the idea of using the toothpick

mould to serve as a child's toy tumbler. In their catalogue proof, they printed the toothpick picture labeling it a toy tumbler and failed to mention its dual use as a toothpick holder for adults. Another omission was the failure to specify which of the five pitchers should serve the toy collector. Collectors have been using the two smallest ones found in the company's lush colors of blue, white opalescent, Rubina (frosted and clear), and Frances Ware (frosted or clear) with amber rims. The hobnails found on these toy sets are the most pronounced of any found to date in children's ware.

PERTINENT DATA:

Additional pattern names: "Frances Ware" ("Dewdrop", "#323")
Pattern pieces: Seven piece water set
Pattern colors: Frances Ware clear and frosted with amber rims; Rubina, clear and frosted with rose red rims; all over blue, all white opalescent
Factory: Hobbs Glass Company
Date: 1891
Classification: Rare
Pieces difficult to locate: All
Features attributable to pattern: Exaggerated hobnails from the base to the top of the pitcher's rim, three pouring areas

MEASUREMENTS:

Pitcher	See features; 4½" spout to base, 4" spout to base
Tumbler	Dual purpose, serving as adult toothpick; 2¼" ht., 1-5/8" width

(See color section)

HOBNAIL WITH THUMBPRINT BASE
No. 150

Doyle and Company, caught in the toy color "lock step" of amber, blue, and clear, created this sparkling table set and added a matching tray between 1880-1895. The otherwise traditional design was further varied by the flat, almost useless finials found on the sugar and butter covers.

Production of this set continued after the company's merger into the United States Glass Company.

Researchers have claimed this set was produced with ruby stain on clear glass, but no evidence of this treatment has been recorded to date in toy glass research.

PERTINENT DATA:

Additional pattern names: "#150"
Pattern pieces: Five piece table set
Pattern colors: Clear, amber, blue
Factory: Doyle and Company
Date: 1885-1891
Classification: Not too difficult to assemble
Reproduced: No
Pieces difficult to locate: Colored trays, butters, sugars
Features attributable to pattern: All over hobnail; flat finials; thumbprints around bases of all pieces except butter and tray

MEASUREMENTS:

Spooner	2-7/8'' ht.''., 2¼'' width
Sugar	2¾'' ht. of base, 2-5/8'' across base, 4'' overall ht.
Creamer	3-3/8'' spout to base, 3¾'' spout across handle
Butter	3-5/8'' across butter base, 2'' ht.
Tray	7¼'' width

HORIZONTAL THREADS

The pellucid glass and the tiny size save this table set from the uninteresting. A certain amount of fervor is involved in finding the butter and sugar while the other two pieces appear a little too frequently. The twelve vertical panels banded by five horizontal lines cut into the glass, relieving its plainness.

Beginning in 1940, to add interest to this set, an occasional painter cut loose and applied a section of ruby stain here and there for relief. Others decided to souvenir various pieces with notes of endearment and proof of travel during their second time around in the 40's. The set was originally made around 1910.

PERTINENT DATA:

Additional pattern names: None
Pattern pieces: Four piece table set
Pattern colors: Clear (originally) and cobalt
Factory: Probably United States Glass
Date: 1910
Classification: Not too difficult to assemble, very rare in cobalt
Reproduced: In 1940 with ruby stain
Pieces difficult to locate: Butter and sugar; all cobalt
Features attributable to pattern: Clear glass, small size; twelve vertical panels banded by five horizontal lines cut into the glass

MEASUREMENTS:

Spooner	2-1/8'' ht., 1¾'' width
Covered sugar	2¼'' ht. of base only, 3¾'' ht.
Creamer	2¼'' spout to base, 2½'' spout to handle, 1-7/8'' side to side
Covered butter	1-1/8'' ht. of base, 2¾'' across top of base

ICE CREAM CONE HOLDER

As the popularity of this item increased, a variety of styles were in evidence. Some of the bases of the holders have hearts encircling the piece (sometimes vivid and sometimes, due to poor moulds, barely discernable). A dealer indicated to me that he read that the Sweetheart company (soda counter supplies) had these holders made.

It came to light that a plainer design was available; one that clearly had no hearts around the base. This plainer version also has a completely plain rim with only the ice cream cone in relief showing on two sides.

The moulds were well designed; one can readily see how it is tapered to accommodate the cone tip. So, rather than being labeled a toy in fact, these items were probably used in soda shops and at birthday parties and then passed on for play.

Additional pattern names: None
Pattern pieces: Single cone holder
Pattern colors: Clear
Factory: Viking
Date: Turn-of-the-century
Classification: Difficult to locate with good mould marks
Reproduced: No
Pieces difficult to locate: Cone holder
Features attributable to pattern: Ice cream cone on each side

MEASUREMENTS:

Ice cream cone holder	2-5/8″ ht., 2-5/8″ across base, 1¼″ across top
Plain rim holder	2½″ tall

ICE CREAM SET
Wabash Toy Series

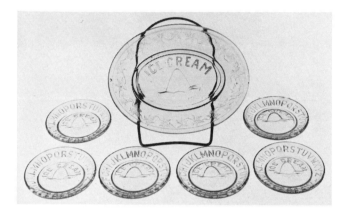

The seven piece dessert set was produced by the now defunct Federal Glass Company in Columbus, Ohio. The ice cream set is a part of the Wabash series, and is not easy to find in Columbus, Ohio or the rest of the nation. The six small round plates have a dish of ice cream in the center with the alphabet rimming each piece. The main oval platter has a leafy border, no alphabet, and a dish of ice cream in its center.

PERTINENT DATA:

(see also Wabash section)
Additional pattern names: "Wabash"
Pattern pieces: Seven piece dessert set
Pattern colors: Clear
Factory: Federal Glass, Columbus, Ohio
Date: 1914
Classification: Rare
Reproduced: No
Pieces difficult to locate: Small round plates
Features attributable to pattern: Dish of ice cream in center of each, leafy border on main dish, alphabet rims on small round plates

MEASUREMENTS:

Oval main plate	5¾″ long, 4½″ wide
Small round plate	2¾″ wide

LACY DAISY

Toy glass collectors are lured by this berry set's octagonal daisies shown in high relief as well as the delicate luminous effect of the well-made glass. Sometimes it is difficult to tell old glass from new when it has been reissued from old moulds. This is not the case in the "Lacy Daisy" toy berry set. Westmoreland is reissuing this set with a 'W' in evidence, at times, on the small berries. They also made the small white milkglass berries, No. 909, to sell as salts. There are teal green small berries which are new as well. The light green and the amber "Lacy Daisy" berry sets are still considered to be old.

PERTINENT DATA:

Additional pattern names: "Crystal Jewel"
Pattern pieces: Seven piece berry set
Pattern colors: (old) Clear, mint green, amber
Factory: United States Glass Company
Date: Turn-of-the-century
Classification: Easy to acquire
Reproduced: Westmoreland
Pieces difficult to locate: Mint green pieces; amber sets
Features attributable to pattern: All over jeweled pattern, octagonal daisies in high relief, star-like figure pressed onto the raised octagons with flat bevelled circle in the center

MEASUREMENTS:

Main berry	4″ wide, 1-5/8″ ht.
Small berry	2¼″ wide, 1″ ht.

LAMB

The balance and grace of the crystal "Lamb" table set attracted the original company into making the same four pieces in a doeskin and white milkglass. The emphasis of production must have been on the two covered table set pieces, for the creamer and spooner are very difficult to find in white milkglass.

In 1981, the Imperial Glass Company* reissued the butter, creamer and spooner in a fractious blue Carnival rendition and in 1982 they made it in "sunburst".

Strangely, this is one of the few old patterns in glass which has not been adversely affected by reissue. The clear and milkglass sets are still persistently pursued.

PERTINENT DATA:

Additional pattern names: None
Pattern pieces: Four piece table set
Pattern colors: Clear, white milkglass, white milkglass with paint
Factory: Imperial (unclear if the "Lamb" moulds were originally from another company)
Date: Clear 1910
Classification: Rare
Reproduced: Dark blue irridescent 1980-81, sunburst 1982
Pieces difficult to locate: Milkglass spooner, creamer, painted pieces, clear spooner, butter, sugar
Features attributable to pattern: Lamb finials, stemmed bases

*In December of 1960, the Imperial Glass Company acquired the moulds of the Cambridge Glass Company. In May of 1958, Imperial had the moulds and equipment of the A. H. Heisey Glass Company. In 1939 it had attained the Central Glass Company moulds.

MEASUREMENTS:

Spooner	1¾" wide, 2¾" ht.
Sugar	4-3/8" overall ht., 2" across base top
Creamer	1-5/8" side to side, 3" ht.
Butter	3-3/8" base to finial, 2-3/8" across top, 1¾" ht. of base

(See color section for "Lamb" in milkglass)

LARGE BLOCK

This turn-of-the-century four piece table set was made in amber, clear, milkglass and sapphire. Because of its comparative age, it is surprising that the pieces are difficult to find.

PERTINENT DATA:

Additional pattern names: None

Pattern pieces: Four piece table set
Pattern colors: Clear, amber, sapphire, milkglass (white or blue)
Factory: Unknown
Date: Early 1900's
Classification: Not easily assembled
Reproduced: No
Pieces difficult to locate: Butter, sugar
Features attributable to pattern: Blocks separated by divided blocks

MEASUREMENTS:

Spooner	Stemmed slender piece, clear base, smooth rim with block division beginning directly under smooth rim; 3-1/8" ht., 2-1/8" across rim
Sugar	Modified stemmed base, indented rosette found in the bottom of each of the pieces; 4¾" base to finial, 3-1/16" tall, 2-3/8" dia.
Creamer	Smooth handle, modified standard; 3" tall
Covered butter	Set pattern is carried to finial, pattern on the inside of butter lid, butter base is scalloped; 2-7/8" overall ht.

LIBERTY BELL

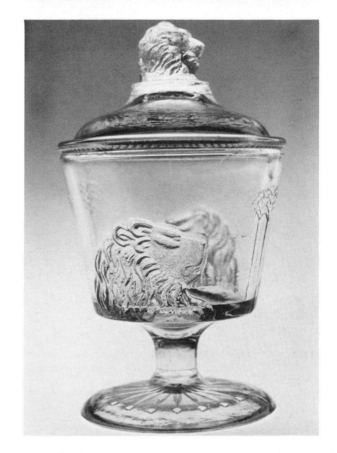

Although beauty and clarity cannot claim to be the superlatives used in describing this four piece table set, it is a known fact that collectors count this among the most important additions to their assemblage.

Gillinder and Sons tapped the pockets of the parents by making their novelties, sold as souvenirs, at the Centennial Exhibition in Philadelphia in 1876. Mugs in clear and white milkglass were also made. Evidence of a milkglass creamer has been claimed, but the rest of the set has not been discovered in this medium.

PERTINENT DATA:

Additional pattern names: None
Pattern pieces: Four piece table set, mug
Pattern colors: Clear, milkglass creamer, clear and milkglass mug
Factory: Gillinder and Sons
Date: 1876
Classification: Rare
Reproduced: No
Pieces difficult to locate: All milkglass, spooner in clear
Features attributable to pattern: Liberty Bell, 100 Years Ago, Declaration Independence, 1776, 1876

MEASUREMENTS:

Spooner	Most difficult piece to locate, pedestal base; scalloped edge, writing and design same on all pieces; 2¼'' ht., 1-7/8'' wide
Covered sugar	Pedestal base; pinched-ribbed finial; 3½'' overall ht., 2-3/8'' across top of bowl
Creamer	Made in milkglass, pedestal base; 1¾'' side to side, 2-5/8'' ht.
Covered butter	Ruffled rim on base; flat-pinched finial to match sugar; 2-3/8'' overall ht., 3-3/8'' base top, 2'' across bottom
Mug	Milkglass or clear; 1-7/8'' ht., 1¾'' wide

This four-piece table set complete with matching cups and saucers rekindles interest each time another sample is encountered from the Philadelphia Centennial in 1876.

Not only was this set made in clear and frosted, but it was also produced in crystal with frosted heads. (The four piece set shown here is from the Lechler collection.) The alleged amber set has not come to light and it is doubtful if it was produced with that treatment.

The thin stemmed spooner, covered sugar, and creamer each have a lion's head on two sides. The butter dish displays three shaggy heads. The "Lion" cup has the same treatment as its counterparts while the saucer has a reclining lion in the middle. When this combination is found in clear with frosting, the reclining lion is all frosted.

PERTINENT DATA:

Additional pattern names: None
Pattern pieces: Four piece table set, cup and saucer
Pattern colors: Clear, all frosted, clear with frosted head
Factory: Gillinder and Sons
Date: 1876
Classification: Rare in frosted, frosted heads on clear are very rare

Reproduced: No (set). There is a new salt-dip-type item with a smudged greenish cast which has nothing to do with the toy set or cup or saucer

Pieces difficult to locate: All clear with frosted heads; butter, sugar

Features attributable to pattern: Lions

MEASUREMENTS:

Spooner	Stemmed base; scalloped rim; lion on each side; 3-1/8'' ht., 2-1/8'' ht.
Sugar	Lion head finial; stemmed; 4-5/8'' ht., 3'' base ht., 2½'' across top of base
Creamer	Stemmed base, smooth rim and handle; 2'' side to side, 3-3/8'' ht.
Butter	Lion head finial; three shaggy lions; beaded edge lid matching that of sugar; 4'' across bowl, 1-1/8'' base ht., 2¾'' overall ht.
Cup	Lion head on each side; 1¾'' ht., 2-1/8'' side to side
Saucer	Reclining lion in center; 3¼'' wide, 7/8'' ht.

LITTLE JO
ARCHED PANELS

A full page ad from an old Westmoreland Glass Company catalogue provided several new bits of information. The one concerned with this set is that "Little Jo" is the correct factory name for the set we've been calling "Arched Panels". In the same ad, it was discovered that "Thumbelina" is the correct name for "Flattened Diamond and Sunburst". To further aid the collector, the set called "English Hobnail" (condiment set) was actually listed as a toy.

Before closing the doors, Westmoreland reached for the tenuous cord binding us to the past by reissuing the "Little Jo" set in clear, cobalt (with or without white painted flowers), canary and orange. A beat has been skipped, however, for the glass quality cannot surpass the old glass sets found in their original colors of clear, amber and cobalt.

PERTINENT DATA:

Additional pattern names: "Arched Panels"
Pattern pieces: Seven piece table set
Pattern colors: (old) Clear, amber, cobalt
Factory: Westmoreland
Date: 1924
Classification: Frequently found in clear; scarce in old amber, rare in old cobalt
Reproduced: Clear, canary, orange, cobalt (with or without flowers)

Pieces difficult to locate: Old amber tumblers, all cobalt (old)
Features attributable to pattern: Pitcher has sweeping handles and eight arched panels

MEASUREMENTS:

Pitcher	Sweeping handle, eight panels with a twenty-paneled figure on the base; 3¾'' ht., 4'' across top
Tumbler	Six to a set, panels matching the pitcher; 2'' ht., 1-7/8'' across

MENAGERIE

Originally, the four piece table set in the "Menagerie" pattern was seen in the 1885 Bryce, Higbee Company catalogue. It was advertised as being made in old gold, blue, and crystal. Nothing was said in the ad about amber; yet most of the sets obtainable in a yellow hue today turn out to be amber rather than old gold. The amber color may be the result of an errant batch of glass or the product of a company other than Bryce Higbee. Walt Oswald, a rare toy glass collector, sent the author two pieces of the Menagerie set in what is believed to be the true old gold color. A comparison of the old gold with the amber pieces can only cause collectors and researchers to deduce that some of the "Menagerie" patterns were copied by other companies. This deduction is supported by the fact that there are some bases in this set which are stippled and some which are plain. Furthermore, alert collectors have noted that the owl's feathers vary in arrangement. There is no question that the owls are found in white or blue milkglass or slag--treatments which were not given the set by the Bryce, Higbee Company.

The hole in the bear's neck causes no small amount of debate among collectors. Some of the bears have holes in the back and some do not. It is difficult to imagine that much factory time was spent in dailogue about what to do with the bears' necks, or, for that matter, what was to go inside the bear container . . . horseradish or sugar. Most collectors are happy to have a bear, hole or no hole.

There is little debate about whether to buy a turtle butter. Some collectors have harbored the turtle base for years waiting for the elusive armored-shell lid to appear. This rarest of the rare commands one of the highest prices (when complete) of any toy glass available to American collectors. (One calloused non collecting observer declared that the only reason only a few turtles are left in existence is because, "Those suckers are ugly and people threw them away!")

PERTINENT DATA:

Additional pattern names: None
Pattern pieces: Four piece table set, horseradish
Pattern colors: Clear, old gold, blue, amber
Factory: Bryce, Higbee
Date: 1885
Classification: Very rare
Reproduced: No
Pieces difficult to locate: All
Features attributable to pattern: Each piece is a different creature having a different function

MEASUREMENTS:

Fish spooner	1-5/8'' side to side, 2¼'' length of the fish mouth, 2-5/8'' base bottom
Bear sugar	4-5/8'' ht., 2¾'' base ht.
Owl creamer	3¾'' spout to base, 2'' side to side
Turtle butter	1-3/8'' ht. of base, 3¾'' length of lid

MICHIGAN
LOOP AND PILLAR
No. 15077

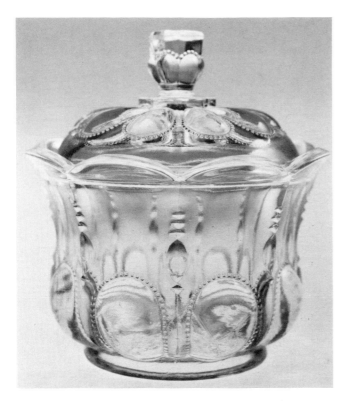

toy steins. The ''purist'' must search, however, for the special candy dips - the ones with a knot of glass at the top and bottom of the handles. The set originally sold for $3.50 a dozen sets.

PERTINENT DATA:

Additional pattern names: ''Loop and Pillar'', ''#15077''
Pattern pieces: #15077 seven piece stein set, seven piece water set, four piece table set, small nappy
Pattern colors: Clear, sunrise, gold decorated ware
Factory: United States Glass Company, (Gillinder; Doyle)
Date: 1902
Classification: Difficult to assemble except for water set
Reproduced: No
Pieces difficult to locate: Correct small steins, butter, nappy
Features attributable to pattern: Table set pieces have scalloped edging, plump finials, smooth loops of glass

MEASUREMENTS:

Spooner	3'' ht., 2-7/8'' width
Sugar	4¾'' overall ht., 2-5/8'' ht. of base, 3-5/8'' across top of base
Creamer	2-7/8'' spout to base, 3-7/8'' spout to handle, 2½'' side to side
Butter	5¼'' across bottom, 4'' across lid opening, 3¾'' approximate overall ht.
Main stein	2-7/8'' spout to base, 2½'' side to side, 3-7/8'' spout to handle
Small stein	2'' tall, 2-1/8'' mid-handle across, 1½'' across base
Small nappy	5-1/8'' across, 4¼'' front to back
Pitcher	4'' spout to base, 3¾'' spout to handle, 2-3/8'' side to side
Tumbler	2-1/8'' ht., 1¾'' width

MONK STEIN SET

The ''Michigan'' sets are products of the United States Glass Company. A table set, a water set, and a stein set were all made around the turn of the century.

In the catalogue proof, the table set is shown with the small print indicating that the sets were made in crystal, sunrise, and gold decorated ware. The picture on the same page has the following items: a butter, a covered sugar, a creamer, a spooner, an uncovered-ledged 3½'' sweetmeat, and the actual adult toothpick which is not to be used interchangeably with the spooner.

A later discovery showed catalogue proof of a toy ''Michigan'' stein set which is nothing more than the creamer from the table set with four familiar root beer and candy dip

Large stein	4″ ht.
Small stein	2-1/8″ ht.
Banana dish	6½″ long, 4½″ wide

MUGS

M-1   "Little Bo-Peep", etched, 3″ x 3½″

Quality control was not in evidence when the "Monk" stein sets were being made around the turn of the century. The 1910 Butler Brothers catalogue pictured these thickly made sets along with the equally thick "Wild Rose" punch and table sets. Catalogue groupings such as this have led researchers to believe that all items in the group came from the same factory origin for normally the distributors did not separate the barrels of glass products for their advertising trade journals.

The "Monk" stein sets came in clear and white milkglass. At times, the milkglass sets have a blue tinge. It is believed that these strays are a part of a wandering batch of glass. This color oddity is not uncommon because at times the caustic milkglass was used to clean out tanks in preparation for another glass color.

A dozen sets of the mixed variety of "Wild Rose" and the "Monk" ware sold for a staggering $2.10. A variation in the steins has been noted by alert collectors. Some pieces have a rim of lines encircling the top of the steins and some are without the rings.

The embellishments found on the "Monk" items and the "Wild Rose" sets are carelessly added and are shown with all over vivid pink, green, blue, matt silver, matt gold, and red.

There is a clear glass Monk-style banana dish with the same ale drinking "Monk" as is found on the stein set.

PERTINENT DATA:

Additional pattern names: None
Pattern pieces: Seven piece stein set
Pattern colors: Clear, milkglass
Factory: United States Glass Company
Date: Turn of the century
Classification: Obtainable
Reproduced: No
Pieces difficult to locate: Clear stein set
Features attributable to pattern: Embossed monk medallion on the front and back of each piece; monk holding stein of foaming ale

M-2   HMS Pinafore - "Little Buttercup", 3″ x 3½″

M-3 "Monkeys and Vines", 2½" x 2½"

M-5 "Santa Claus", 3" x 3½"

M-4 "Fighting Cats", 1-7/8" x 2-1/8"

M-6 "Plain Monkey", 3-1/8" x 3¾"

M-7   "Cat In a Dress and Hat", clear, milkglass, 2-3/8" tall

M-9   "Westward Ho", clear, 2" tall

M-8   "Cat In a Tangle", clear, 2" tall

M-10   "Dog and Quail", 2¾" x 3¼"

M-11   "Swan", 2-3/8" x 2-3/8"

M-12   "Blue Rabbit", 3" x 3-3/8"

M-12   "Blue Wolf", 3¾" x 3-7/8"

M-13   "Stag & Deer", clear, cobalt, 2" x 2"

M-14   ''Feeding Deer'', 2-3/8'' x 2-5/8''

M-16 ''Baby Animals'', 2½'' x 2¾'', 3¼'' x 3'', reproduced

M-15 ''Chicks and Pugs'', clear, amber, 1-7/8'' x 2'', U. S. Glass
          Co., Bryce

M-17   ''Squirrel'', 2'' x 3''

M-18 "Butterfly and Log", 2-3/8" x 2", child's tumbler also available in this design

M-20 "Pointing Dog", 2-5/8" tall, Bryce (U. S. Glass Co.)

M-19 "Bird on a Branch", 2¾" x 2¾", Bryce (U. S. Glass Co.)

M-21 "Waterfowl", clear, blue and cobalt, 2" tall, Bryce (U.S. Glass Co.)

M-22 "Birds at Fountain", clear, soft blue, 1¾" x 2"

M-24 "Robin", 3¼" x 3½" milkglass, 2¼" x 2¾" blue opaque, 2" x 1¾" amber

M-23 "Heron and Peacock", clear and cobalt, 2¾" x 2½"

M-25   "Begging Dog", clear, cobalt, 2¼" tall

M-26   "Dutch Mill", clear, 2¾" x 3"

M-28 King Co. "Grape Vine", 3" x 3", clear, cobalt, amber
                (comes in three sizes)

M-27   "Heart and Vines", 2½" x 2½"

M-29   "Winding Vine", 1¾" x 2¼"

M-30 "Vine With Stippling", clear, cobalt, 2" x 2-3/8", King Sons Co. #198

M-32 "Butterfly", 2" x 2", 2½" x 2¾", third size unavailable, Bryce Higbee

M-31   "Banded Stalks", clear, 2½" x 2¾"

M-33   "Diamond With Circle", blue, 2¾" x 3"

M-34 ''Hobnail and Bar'', amber, clear, 2½'' x 3-1/8''

M-36   ''Stars and Stripes'', 2¼'' x 3-1/8''

M-35 ''Stump and Vine'', blue opalescent, 2-5/8'' x 2-7/8''

M-37 ''All Over Stars'', with seven stars in bottom, 2½'' x 3¼''
similar to ''Effulgent Star''

84

M-38   ''Clear Diamond'', 2¼'' x 3-3/8''

M-40   ''Our Girl'', 3'' x 3½'', McKee, 1887

M-39 ''A Good Girl - A Good Boy'', 3'' x 3½'', reproduced

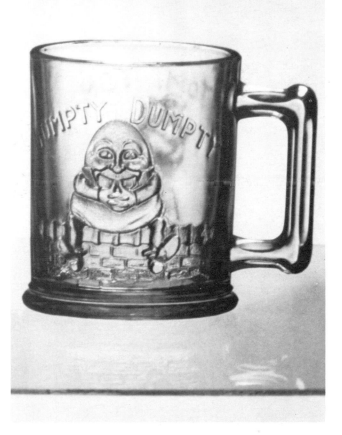

M-41 ''Humpty Dumpty - Tom Thumb'', 2¾'' x 3½''

M-42 ''Lighthouse and Sailboat'', Canadian, 2-1/8'' x 2-5/8''

M-44 ''Captain Hook'', 1-7/8'', has a second mug which comes with this . . . in an original box

M-43 ''Little Bo-Peep'', blue on white, 3-1/8'' x 3''

M-45   ''By Jingo'', 2½'' tall

M-48 "Ceres" ("Medallion", "Cameo"), crystal, turquoise, mosaic, opal, amber, dark amethyst, 1-7/8" x 1-7/8", 2½" x 2-1/8", Atterbury & Co., 1870,

M-46   "Small Flowered Tulips", 1-5/8" x 1-7/8"

M-47   "McKee New York", 2¼" x 3½"

M-49 "Block" (No. 1220), 1½", Alexander J. Beatty & Sons after 1891, creamer available also

M-50   "Daisy Pleat", 2¼" x 2½"

M-52 "Divided Block With Sunburst", 2¼" x 3-3/8", note low handle

M-51 "New York Honeycomb", clear, flint glass, applied handle, 2½" x 2-7/8"

M-53   "Paneled Cane", clear, blue, cobalt, 1¾" x 2-3/8"

M-55   "Vandyke", blue, canary, clear, amber, 2'' x 2¼'', 2½'' x 3'', 2-5/8'' x 3-1/8'', Alexander J. Beatty Sons, after 1891, reproduced

M-56   "Beaded Circles", clear, green, 2'' x 3¼''; "Pleated Skirt" clear, cobalt with or without paint, green, 2'' x 3¼'', American and Canadian

M-57   "Leaf & Triangle", 3-1/8'' x 3¼'', 2-3/8'' x 2-3/8''

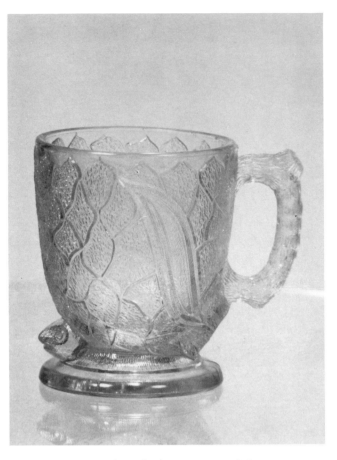

M-54 "Grape & Festoon With Shield", 1¾'' x 2'', 2-3/8'' x 2½''

M-59   "Garden of Eden'', 3'' x 3-5/8''

M-58   "Stippled Arrow'', 1¾'' tall

M-60 "Alphabet and Children'', 2¼'' x 2¾'', U. S. Glass Co., Adams Division

M-61 "Birds and Harp", 2½" x 2½", McKee Brothers

M-63 "Beads in Relief", clear, milkglass, blue opaque, 1¾" x 1¾", Atterbury and Co.

M-62 "Gooseberry", blue milkglass, milkglass, soft blue, clear

M-64   "Acanthus Leaves", 1¾" x 2"

M-65 "Opalescent Rib" ("Ribbed Opal"), 2½" x 3¼", Beatty & Sons, (No. 87) 1888

M-67   "Lighthouse", 2" x 2½"

M-66   "Lamb", clear, blue, 2¾" x 3"

M-68 "Pert" ("Ribbed Forget-Me-Not"), clear (dimensions unavailable) Bryce, McKee & Co. 1880

M-69   ''Rea'', 1½'' x 1¾'', 2'' x 3¼'', Beatty & Sons after 1891 (large size can be found with a tin lid)

M-70   ''Cupid and Venus'', clear, 2'' tall

M-71   ''Dart and Ball'', clear, cobalt, 2'' tall (possibly new)

M-72   "Ribbed Leaves", clear, 2½" x 2½"

NORTHWOOD HOBNAIL

This table set pattern has been attributed to Northwood by collectors. No catalogue proof has come to light to indicate that this is a Northwood product, however. The complete four piece table set has turned up in Virginia, Pennsylvania and California to date, with little known about its true origin or date.

The quality of the glass is excellent and the attention to detail is evident in all four pieces. The ruffled rims are pinched with the added attraction of delicate beading surrounding the modified pleats.

PERTINENT DATA:

Additional pattern names: None
Pattern pieces: Four piece table set
Factory: Northwood (perhaps)
Date: Unknown
Classification: Very rare
Reproduced: No
Pieces difficult to locate: All

Features attributable to pattern: Beaded handles, hobnails on the bases, pleated ruffles which are beaded

MEASUREMENTS:

Spooner	2-7/8" tall, 2-1/8" across
Covered sugar	3¾" to top of finial, 2-5/8" lid diameter, 2-5/8" base height without lid
Creamer	3" to highest point (lip to base)
Covered butter	2-5/8" overall ht., 3¾" lid diameter, 3-15/16" base diameter

NURSERY RHYME

94

it was "assumed" that this pattern was made strictly for children because of the design. The 1908-1919 United States Glass Company catalogue, found in the Corning Glass Museum Library, showed an adult water set with running bears in a wooded area, complete with the "Nursery Rhyme" motif of leaves and berry clusters. Also, an adult berry set shown in this catalogue had the message: "1 (4") bowl and six (2½") and 6 (2½") berry (sic) in paper box. Illustrations half the size. $1.60 per dozen sets. Also made 8" size, $1.60 per dozen. Also made 4" size, $3.30 per gross." So, a child's "Nursery Rhyme" berry set and an adult set exists. The 8" bowl is the main adult bowl and six of the toy 4" main bowls are the small dessert bowls.

At the top of this interesting, but poorly written ad is: "Toy water, berry and tea sets to please the little folks at very little cost. Large water and berry sets for the home, proportionately low in price."

The punch sets come in clear, medium blue glass, and white or blue milkglass. The medium blue set is quite rare. It has been deduced, due to the absence of the punch sets in ads containing the pattern counterparts that the punch sets were produced by a different company--probably the Gas City connection.

An oddity noted by an alert dealer was that some of the water tumblers had handles added, turning them into tiny mugs.

PERTINENT DATA:

Additional pattern names: None
Pattern pieces: Four piece table set, seven piece punch and berry sets, seven piece water sets
Pattern colors: Clear table, water, and berry sets, clear and white or blue milkglass, medium blue glass punch set
Factory: United States Glass Company
Date: 1908-1919
Classification: Rare in either blue
Reproduced: No
Pieces difficult to locate: Blue pieces
Features attributable to pattern: Leaf and fruit clusters; children

MEASUREMENTS:

Spooner	Some with smooth rim--some with scalloped rims; Puss In Boots and Mary and a Little Lamb, 2" across, 2½" ht.
Sugar	Wooden shoe and drum on lid; base has cat with umbrella, 4" overall ht.
Creamer	Jack and Jill; scalloped rim; 1-7/8" side to side, 3¼" spout to handle, 2½" spout to base
Butter	Children holding hands, also a rake, 3¼" width of top of base, 2-5/8" overall ht.
Water pitcher	See-saw scene, 4¼" ht.
Tumbler	Boy with a hoop and a bear, 1-3/8" width, 2" ht.
Large berry	Grape and leaf border, children holding hands ring the dish, 4½" wide, 1-3/8" ht.
Small berry	Grape and leaf cluster on base, 2½" wide, 1-1/8" ht.
Punch bowl	Red Riding Hood tale, 4-5/8" width, 3-3/8" ht.
Punch cup	Repeated motif, 1-5/8" wide, 1-3/8" ht.

One of the most complete packages in toy glass collections is the pattern called "Nursery Rhyme". A toy water set, a berry set, a tea table set, and a punch set complete the selection.

When dealing with the subject of children's glass, one learns to assume nothing. In the book, *Children's Glass Dishes*,

OVAL STAR
CRYSTAL NO. 300

65¢ Post paid

Imitation Cut Glass Water Set

These pieces look exactly like mother's and it will make you feel happy to have them. in your little buffet, ready to serve your guests. Consists of **four** 2-inch high cut glass design glass tumblers, 7½-inch glass tray with beautiful cut glass style design and a 4⅝-inch heavy glass pitcher.

49D1904
Postpaid **65c**

The Indiana Glass Company of Dunkirk, Indiana produced a rare toy glass catalogue which is as much of a collector's item as the pieces of glass. The Corning Glass Museum Library staff was kind enough to permit excellent copies of this publication. The absence of the water set tray in this publication suggests that the Sears Roebuck Company placed the "Oval Star" water set on a matching tray to enhance sales. This is a welcome combination, however, making it only one of three sets in the toy glass category to claim a tray. The complete water set with the tray sold for 65¢ in the 1927-30 Sears Roebuck and Company catalogue.

PERTINENT DATA:

Additional pattern names: "Crystal No. 300"
Pattern pieces: Four piece table set, seven piece water set and tray, seven piece berry set, seven piece punch set (two sizes in the water pitchers)
Pattern colors: Clear, clear with gold
Factory: Indiana Glass Co.
Date: 1920
Classification: Not too difficult to assemble
Reproduced: The toy plates are reproduced for a "home party" company
Pieces difficult to locate: Tray, main berry

Features attributable to pattern: Rosettes, ribbed design between the star motif

MEASUREMENTS:

Spooner	2½'' ht., 2¼'' across top
Covered sugar	4¼'' overall ht., 2-3/8'' ht. of base only, 5'' handle to handle
Creamer	2-5/8'' spout to base, 4 1/8'' spout to handle back
Covered butter	3½'' overall ht., 5¼'' diam. of base, 3'' ht. of lid, 3¾'' diam. of lid
Water pitcher	4¼'' ht., 4½'' spout to handle, 2¾'' side to side, 3-1/8'' base
Tumbler	2-3/8'' ht. (will vary slightly), 1¾'' width, 1-3/8'' width of bottom
Water pitcher	4'' spout to base, 4'' spout across handle, 2-3/8'' side to side, 2-7/8'' across bottom
Tray	7¼'' width, ¼'' ht.
Large berry	4¼'' width, 2'' ht.
Small berry	2¼'' width, 1'' ht.
Relish dish	4-1/8'' length, 2¾'' side to side

(See Glass Companies and Their Pattern Contributions for complete catalogue proof identification.)

PATTEE CROSS
BROUGHTON

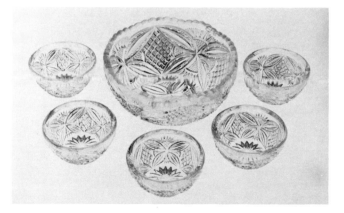

The pattern called "Pattee Cross" by collectors and dealers was made by several different factories within the United States Glass Company. It was given many different names by the various factories . . . and Pattee Cross is one of them.

Two of the known producers were the Richards & Hartley Company in Tarentum, Pennsylvania, and Bryce Brothers in Pittsburgh, Pennsylvania. The "Pattee Cross No. 15112" sets were issued in the late 1800's and early 1900's. There is an ad in the 1910 Butler Brothers catalog showing a dozen sets selling for $2.20. The sets are also shown in catalogue proof in Revi's *American Pressed Glass and Figure Bottles* publication. All of the sets in the toy ad have a lined Sawtooth design rather than the plump, smoothed petal appearance. It is fair to say, however, that the pieces to this pattern served a dual purpose many times as seen in various ads . . . the water pitcher was a toy, but it was also an adult creamer, the main toy bowls were adult small sauces. The small toy berries were used as adult salts. No toy table set was made in this pattern.

Although no ad proof justifies their choice to date, collectors use the bowl shown in the publication as a punch bowl. Any punch bowl chosen to represent this set can be proven to have another purpose -- such as a jelly compote.

PERTINENT DATA:

Additional pattern names: "Broughton", "15112"
Pattern pieces: Seven piece berry set, seven piece punch set, seven piece water set
Pattern colors: Clear or clear with gold trim
Factory: United States Glass Company (Bryce Bros.; Richard Hartley)
Date: 1890's, also 1909
Classification: Punch set is difficult to locate
Reproduced: No
Pieces difficult to locate: Punch set, all lined sawtooth designs
Features attributable to pattern: Three flower design, flowers have four petals with petals outlined with ridged design, dotted diamonds separate the flowers

MEASUREMENTS:

Tumbler	1¾'' ht.
Water pitcher	4¼'' spout to handle, 4-5/8'' spout to base
Large berry	2'' ht., 4'' width
Small berry	1-1/8'' ht., 2 1/8'' wide
Punch bowl	2-5/8'' ht., 4-3/8'' wide
Cup	1¼'' ht., 1-3/8'' wide

(See Glass Companies and Their Pattern Contributions for catalogue proof)

PENNSYLVANIA
BALDER
No. 15048

97

This United States glass product (#15048) is of the 1897 vintage and is a well-proportioned example of excellent workmanship. It is desirable in clear with or without gold trim and is difficult to locate in the emerald shade which also may be seen with or without the gold. Ruby stained pieces in the "Pennsylvania" pattern are scarce in adult ware and virtually nonexistent in the toy series.

The deeply scalloped covered butter of this imitation cut glass design has a base with an eight-pointed figure. The lovely cut-type pattern is repeated in the ball finials of both covered pieces.

Butler Brothers sold these sets from their distributing company for 18½ cents per set.

PERTINENT DATA:

> **Additional pattern names:** "Balder", "#15048"
> **Pattern pieces:** Four piece table set
> **Pattern colors:** Clear, clear with gold, green, green with gold
> **Factory:** United States Glass Company (Central Glass, Gillinder & Sons in Greensburg, Pennsylvania)
> **Date:** 1897
> **Classification:** Rare in green
> **Reproduced:** No
> **Pieces difficult to locate:** All green, clear butter, sugar
> **Features attributable to pattern:** Imitation cut glass; sparkling glass; scalloped edges on creamer, spooner and sugar; patterned ball finials

MEASUREMENTS:

Spooner	2½" ht., 2½" wide
Covered sugar	4" overall ht., 2-3/8" ht. of base, 3" width
Creamer	2½" ht. from spout to base, 2¼" side to side, 3½" across spout to handle
Covered butter	3½" overall ht., 4¾" width of base

PERT

"Pert" is the collector's name for this heart embellished table set which has a tiny butter much out of proportion to the rest of the pieces. The butter base has twelve rows of two hearts placed in an upside down position, while the lid has six rows of hearts on its high rising dome. The sugar, creamer, and spooner stand on pedestal bases. Each of the four pieces has a row of little teeth racing around the top.

"Pert" is a name also given to a set which is sometimes mistaken for a child's set. The so-called "Ribbed Forget-Me-Nots" breakfast set carried the factory name of "Pert" from the United States Glass Company, Factory B.

No other toy counterparts are known in this prim design.

PERTINENT DATA:

> **Additional pattern names:** None
> **Pattern pieces:** Four piece table set
> **Pattern colors:** Clear
> **Factory:** Unknown
> **Date:** Unknown
> **Classification:** Obtainable
> **Reproduced:** No
> **Pieces difficult to locate:** Spooner, creamer
> **Features attributable to pattern:** Hearts design (upside down)

MEASUREMENTS:

Spooner	Pedestal base, row of teeth around rim; arched panels with four hearts each; 2-7/8" wide, 3½" ht.
Sugar	Pedestal base, dome lid; 5-1/8" overall ht., 3½" base ht., 3-1/8" across top of base
Creamer	Pedestal base, row of teeth, same heart design as spooner; 2" side to side, 3-5/8" ht., 4" spout to handle
Butter	Mushroom type finial; twelve rows of two upside down hearts with six rows of the same design on the lid; 2-7/8" overall ht., 1-1/8" base ht., 3-1/8" across top of base

PETITE HOBNAIL

This is one of the rarest water sets in toy form to be collected. It comes with a matching tray and may be seen in complete form, in blue, at the Mary Merritt Museum in Pennsylvania.

PERTINENT DATA:

> **Additional pattern names:** Unknown
> **Pattern pieces:** Eight piece water set (tray)
> **Pattern colors:** Clear, amber, blue
> **Factory:** Unknown
> **Date:** Unknown

Classification: Very rare
Reproduced: No
Pieces difficult to locate: All
Features attributable to pattern: Thin glass, hobnails, clear rims, smooth handle

MEASUREMENTS:

Pitcher	4¾'' tall, 3'' across
Tumbler	2-3/16'' tall, 1¼'' diam.
Tray	6½'' x 7¾'' (irregular shape)

(Photograph by David Grim.)

PETITE SQUARE

Since the tumbler to this newly discovered set is the exact match for the "Petite Hobnail's" water set, the two sets must have come from the same point of origin. The pitcher to this set has a square mouth, a rough pontil and an applied handle. It is smaller than the "Petite Hobnail" pitcher.

PERTINENT DATA:

Additional pattern names: None
Pattern pieces: Seven piece water set (the tray to "Petite Hobnail" might serve a dual purpose); vase
Pattern colors: Known in clear only . . . so far
Factory: Unknown
Date: Unknown
Classification: Very rare
Reproduced: No
Pieces difficult to locate: All
Features attributable to pattern: Thin glass, hobnails

MEASUREMENTS:

Pitcher	3¼'' tall, 3'' diameter, 1¾'' from top diagonal point to diagonal point
Tumbler	1¼'' across the top, 2-3/16'' tall

PLAIN PATTERN NO. 13 FROSTED RIBBON DOUBLE BAR

The King Glass Company showed pattern No. 13 in plain and with frosted ribbon. The table set was made in cobalt as well. Even though the pieces are, indeed, plain in looks they are very difficult to locate in clear, and nearly impossible to find in either cobalt or with frosted-ribboned double bars.

The spooner, covered sugar, and smooth-rimmed creamer are on modified stemmed bases. The spooner has a scalloped rim. A finial design of vertical ribs adorns the shallow covered butter.

PERTINENT DATA:

Additional pattern names: "King's Ribbon"
Pattern pieces: Four piece table set
Pattern colors: Clear, frosted bars, cobalt
Factory: King Co.
Date: 1875
Classification: Difficult to locate in clear, very rare in frosted and cobalt
Reproduced: No
Pieces difficult to locate: All frosted, all color
Features attributable to pattern: Scalloped spooner, covered sugar; smooth rimmed creamer; all but butter on modified stemmed bases

MEASUREMENTS:

Spooner	2¼'' ht., 1¾'' width
Sugar	3-3/8'' overall ht., 2¼'' ht. of base, 2-1/8'' width of base top, 1-7/8'' width across bottom
Creamer	2½'' ht., 2-7/8'' across spout to handle
Butter	2-1/8'' overall ht., 1'' ht. of base, 3-1/8'' width of base

(See Glass Companies and Their Pattern Contributions for catalogue proof)

PLATES

Indiana Glass Company	No. 1, Little Bo-Peep No. 2, Hey! Diddle Diddle No. 3, This Little Pig Went to Market No. 4, (See catalogue reprint) Three bears: all 6½'' each; now being reproduced for a "home party" company; originally in crystal with gold trim or plain. (See Glass Companies and Their Pattern Contributions)
"Clock" (scalloped border)	Rising and falling looped border with alphabet, three rows of blocks circling the numerals, hands pointing to Roman Numerals, 6'' across, U.S. Glass co. (Ripley and Co. 1891). Not pictured here.
"New Martinsville No. 10" plate	(Not shown) open work on rims forming lace, plain center, souvenir plate
"New Martinsville No. 530" plate	(Not shown) Star A B C; star center, scalloped alphabet border

"Rooster"

King Company, 6'' across, chicken in barnyard, brick wall background; two styles, 6'' across

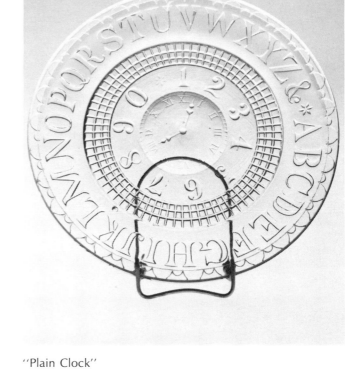

"Plain Clock"

"Christmas Eve"

Stippled rim with alphabet, words ''Christmas Eve'', Santa climbing down chimney, 6-1/8'' across, frosted picture center.

"Old Independence Hall"

1876, stippled alphabet, picture of Independence Hall in center, 6-7/8'' across scalloped edge.

100

"Elephant"   Alphabet on rim of plate, elephant with riders, 6" across.

"Seated Dog"   King Glass Company, numeral border, 4-1/8" across.

"Flower Bouquet"   Alphabet on stippled background, frosted flowers, 6" across.

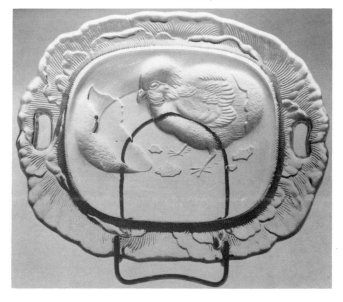

"Chick and Shell"   May be a miniature bread plate in clear or milkglass OR a bone dish, 5-1/8" long. (No ad proof to show it to be a toy.)

101

"Boy #531 A-B-C"

Also called Emma; clear, blue, amber; alphabet rim, 6½", Bryce Higbee, 1893; New Martinsville #531. Now being reproduced.

"Quilted Center"

Alphabet rim on stippled background, 7" across, roping of beads with numerals from zero to nine, quilted center.

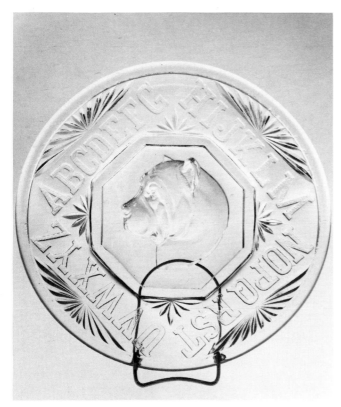

"Dog's Head A-B-C"

New Martinsville #532, blocked off textured alphabet, 6½" (reproduced)

"Iowa City" Plate series

Four sizes, two of which are 5-3/8", 6½"; Be True, Be Affectionate, Be Gentle, Be Playfull (sic). (Two plates from the series shown in this text.)

"Iowa City"

This company also produced the "Elaine" plates.

POINTED JEWEL

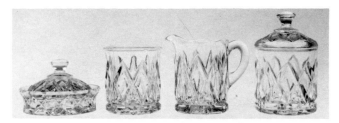

"Pointed Jewel" is an adult pattern which collectors enjoy adding to their assemblage. In 1891, its toy counterpart was made in a four piece table set at Factory J of the United States Glass Company. A set has been found in its original carton labeled "15006".

The distinguishing features of this set consist of the thickly notched bases and nine long bevelled diamonds on the creamer, spooner, and covered sugar. The butter base has twelve elongated diamonds with a deeply set lid. The creamer carries a ripple of a ruffle around its top.

PERTINENT DATA:

Additional pattern names: "Long Diamond"
Pattern pieces: Four piece table set
Pattern colors: Clear
Factory: United States Glass Co., Findlay, Columbia Glass Co. (J)
Date: 1891
Classification: Difficult to assemble
Reproduced: No
Pieces difficult to locate: Butter
Features attributable to pattern: Bases notched, nine long bevelled diamonds creamer, spooner, sugar; twelve elongated diamonds on butter base

MEASUREMENTS:

Spooner	2¼" width, 2½" ht.
Covered sugar	3-7/8" approx. overall ht., 2½" ht. of base, 2-3/8" across base top
Creamer	2-7/8" ht. from spout to base, 3" across spout to end of handle, 2-1/8" side to side
Covered butter	1" ht. of base, 3-1/8" across top of base, 2-7/8" across bottom of dish

PORTLAND

The "Portland" pattern is shown in a 1909 United States Glass Company catalogue. The tumblers to this water set served a dual purpose -- at times they were advertised as toy tumblers, at other times they were in ads to promote shot glasses. This exchange was prominent in the "Michigan" and the "Galloway" water sets, as well as in the "Mirror and Fan" decanter set -- although the latter had smaller tumblers.

The "Portland" pitcher's panels are scalloped on the top while the bottom of the panels flair to a graceful conclusion. Some pitchers have an all over gold embellishment and are usually found with gold rimmed tumblers. The all crystal sets are in evidence rather frequently.

PERTINENT DATA:

Additional pattern names: None
Pattern pieces: Seven piece water set
Pattern colors: Clear, gold trim, all over gold on pitcher
Factory: United States Glass Company
Date: 1909
Reproduced: No
Pieces difficult to locate: None
Features attributable to pattern: Scalloped panels on top of pitcher; flairing base

MEASUREMENTS:

Pitcher	4" spout to base
Tumblers	2-1/8" ht., 1¾" wide

REPRODUCTIONS AND REISSUES

Reproductions of children's glass sets are, to date, limited to less than a dozen PATTERNS which are reissued from old moulds.

People who say that there are too many reproductions in the toy glass realm may be term-confused. Very few patterns have been copied, but a wide range of colors has been used to produce the copied patterns.

Glassmakers of the past made it very easy to spot reproductions or new toy glass items. Most of the old ware was pressed crystal (clear). The producers made a bit of amber, blue and green glass and some white or blue milkglass. Therefore, if the old toy glass color range is remembered, the collecting "purist" will have little cause for alarm. Some collectors, however, wish to have samples of all toy glass history. Their displays are startling and splendid.

"Chimo" — Spooner and creamer have been made in clear, green, amber, blue, orange . . . various trims are employed depending on the reproducer (L.E. Smith is one reproducing firm.)

"Lacy Daisy" — Berry set made in clear with a W; small salts in white milkglass and in teal green (see regular text for pattern identification)

"Little Jo" ("Arched Panels") Water set reissued in cobalt (with or without white flowers), clear, orange, canary

"Lamb" — Imperial Glass Company reproduced the butter, spooner, and creamer. They call the spooner a "sugar". Reproduced in blue and sunrise.

"Inverted Strawberry" — New sets made by Tom Mosser are marked with his M; found in red, carnival shades, custard, clear, pink, blue

"Buzz Star", "Whirligig" — Punch cups in clear and cobalt; punch bowl is not from original mould

"Tappan"   See old glass text

"Wheat Sheaf"   Punch bowl made in a pinkish hue, no cups, made originally only in clear (see regular text for pattern identification)

Pattern identification examples have usually been limited to one item due to space limitation.

The mug and candlestick reproductions will be noted in the regular text to alleviate duplication of photographs.

Plates   Indiana glass Company series: "Little Bo-Peep", "Cat and Fiddle", "Three Bears", "Little Pig" (see Glass Companies and Their Pattern Contributions)

"Little Emma" (or Boy) has been reproduced . . . also "Dog's Head"

—End of Reproductions—

REX
FANCY CUT

"Thumbelina" ("Flattened Diamond and Sunburst")   Both the table set and the punch set have been heavily reproduced in carnival colors; with opalescent trims; milkglass; and regular colors by Westmoreland.

New Mould Based on Old Pattern   "Hawaiian Lei"; three pieces, no spooner, light pink, light blue, orange, clear; bee in base with the exclusion of the Higbee mark of H I G

"Rex" is the proper name, but "Fancy Cut" burbles from the lips of toy glass collectors. It certainly is an apt, descriptive name for the three children's sets in this cut-glass type pattern.

The punch set, most difficult of the three sets to attain, is shown with four cups in an ad from the Co-Operative Flint Glass Company's 1911 catalogue. (Many collectors continue the tradition of buying six cups for their punch sets, for that is the way most of the toy sets were sold.)

The "Fancy Cut" water set is the second most difficult to locate of the pattern. The four piece table set is quickly found for most collections.

PERTINENT DATA:

>**Additional pattern names:** "Fancy Cut"
>**Pattern pieces:** Four piece table set, seven piece water set, seven piece punch set
>**Pattern colors:** Clear, clear with gold trim
>**Factory:** Co-Operative Flint Glass Company
>**Date:** 1911
>**Reproduced:** No
>**Pieces difficult to locate:** Punch set pieces
>**Features attributable to pattern:** Cut glass type motif

MEASUREMENTS:

Spooner	2¼" ht., 2" side to side
Covered sugar	2¼" ht. of base, 2-5/8" across base top
Creamer	2-7/8" spout to base, 2" side to side
Covered butter	3-5/8" across butter base, 2-7/8" across butter lid opening
Water pitcher	2-1/8" side to side, 3-5/8" spout to handle, 3½" spout to base
Tumblers	1¼" width, 1½" ht.
Punch bowl	4-3/8" width, 4¼" ht.
Punch cup	1¼" ht., 1-3/8" side

ROOSTER

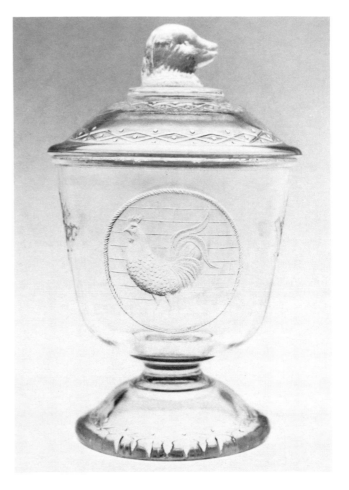

An unsurpassed table set created expressly for children has been dubbed "Rooster" by collectors and "No. 140" by the company that produced it. The King Glass Company pictured the Rooster table set with an extra three-inch toy nappy in their 1890-1891 trade catalogue. The ad was so poorly executed that it is impossible to tell what objects appear under the rick rack rim of this newly discovered three-inch rarity. Since no collector has claimed having this item, one can only guess that the same rooster image found on the other four pieces is repeated on the toy nappy.

In another King Glass Company ad there is a toy glass plate with the same motif as the "Rooster" table set -- a chicken with a brick wall background. In the same ad is a small number plate with a seated dog in the center. The dog may have been posing, for his likeness appears in finial form on the lids of the "Rooster" table set.

PERTINENT DATA:

>**Additional pattern names:** "#140"
>**Pattern pieces:** Four piece table set, toy nappy, plates
>**Pattern colors:** Clear
>**Factory:** King Glass Company
>**Date:** 1890-1891
>**Classification:** Rare
>**Reproduced:** No
>**Pieces difficult to locate:** Nappy, good sugar bases, butter
>**Features attributable to pattern:** Chicken on all the pieces, brick wall background, dog head finials; butter has a spider in the base.

106

Spooner	3-1/8'' tall, 2'' wide
Covered sugar	4½'' overall ht., 3-1/8'' base ht., 2-5/8'' width of base
Creamer	1¾'' high, 3-3/8'' spout to handle
Covered butter	3'' overall ht., 1-1/8'' ht. of base, 3-5/8'' across base toy
"Rooster" nappy	3'' across
Plate	6'' across

SANDWICH

This publication shows but a few examples of Sandwich glass which were made in Cape Cod, Sandwich, Massachusetts. The following is a list of toy glass, as described by the Cape Cod Glass Company, office no. 102, Boston and Sandwich Glass Company:

tumblers (two are shown in this text), lemonades, cups and saucers (one set is shown in cups and saucers section), sugars, creamers (one shown here), butters (see figure #33 in Singles, Paris and Possibilites section), candlesticks (see also candlestick section), four bottle caster sets (see caster set section,) caster bottles, oval dishes (see Singles, Pairs and Possibilities section for example), flat irons, nappies, decanters (one shown here with the wrong stopper), pitchers (one shown in this text) and ewers. (Circa 1835-1855.)

MEASUREMENTS:

| Miniature tumbler | Modified pleated base, 1¾'' tall, 1½'' across |
| Miniature tumbler | Arrow-style band around base; 1-3/8'' tall, 1'' across |

Candlestick   Clear or color, 1-5/8'' tall

Mug   With hand painting, 2¼'' tall

Goblet   Flared lip, 2½'' tall

Covered dish   Paneled sides and lid, measurements unavailable

Decanter   Blown three-mould, approx. 2½'' to 3'' tall

Pitcher   Sunburst and diamond in blown three-mould; approx. 2-3/8'' tall

Caster set   Blown bottles, pewter holder; 1-5/8'' tall bottles, 3¼'' tall pewter holder

SAWTOOTH

Several companies began making the sawtooth pattern in 1860. This four piece toy table set bears the name of its pattern "Sawtooth".

The design is carried out from the base to the rim on all of the pieces except the creamer, in which the pattern ends midway. The pieces have a murky appearance as a result of poor glass quality.

At times, this set is confused with another sawtooth patterned set which is called "Amazon" by collectors. Several differences exist between the two table sets. The Amazon is a sparkling creation with jagged teeth carried to the rims of the butter and spooner. Unlike the "Sawtooth" butter and sugar the "Amazon" creations must have mitered lids which rest with precision on the jagged bases. (Even though the name Mitered Sawtooth is more exact, collectors and dealers still refer to this brilliant table unit as "Amazon".)

Little is known about the "Sawtooth" set as far as the factory, but it has been attributed by glass researchers to the United States Glass Company. It is known, however, that lead was used in the batches of glass because the pieces have great resonance when lightly tapped.

PERTINENT DATA:

Additional pattern names: None
Pattern pieces: Four piece table set
Pattern colors: Clear
Factory: Attributed to United States Glass Company
Date: 1870
Classification: Not too difficult to find
Reproduced: No
Pieces difficult to locate: Sugar, butter
Features attributable to pattern: Murky glass; flint glass; sawtooth motif

MEASUREMENTS:

Spooner	Sawtooth design carried to the top; 3-1/8'' ht., 2-1/8'' ht.
Sugar	Edges of the covered pieces are smooth; 3-1/8'' width of base, 2-7/8'' base ht., 5'' overall ht.
Creamer	Sawtooth motif ends half way with a clear rim section; 2-1/8'' side to side, 3½'' spout to handle, 3½'' spout to base
Covered butter	Smooth rim, sawtooth motif; 3-1/8'' overall ht., 4'' across top of base, 1-5/8'' base ht.

SINGLES, PAIRS AND POSSIBILITIES

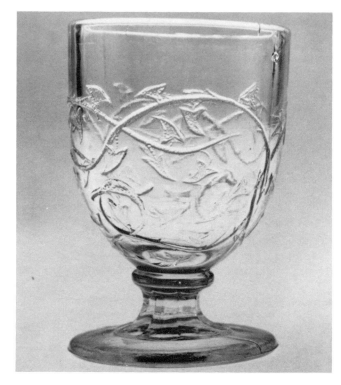

Figure #1 — King Company's footed vine goblet (also comes without vines); listed as a toy in a trade catalog.

Figure #2 — "Button and Arches" toy butter dish; Duncan and Miller pattern; 3¾'' tall, 5'' across base.

Figure #3 — Three cut glass miniature nappies or relish dishes; not listed as toy; one on the right measures 3½'' long and 1¾'' across.

Figure #4 — "Baby Swirl" butter 2¼'' tall and 2½'' across base, creamer 2-3/8'' tall; "Baby Plain Panels" pieces measure the same. There is a known butter, creamer and sugar in these patterns . . . the mystery is their age.

Figure #5 — Depression glass type miniature butter; origin and date unknown; no proof as a toy; 3½'' tall, 4¾'' across base.

Figure #6   Possibly "Baccarat" pieces; blue compote, and candy stand; compote 3'' tall and 3½'' wide; candy 2-1/8'' tall, 5'' wide; not listed as toys.

Figure #7   Correction: figure #190 in *Children's Glass Dishes* (so called goblet, shown here) is really a stickpin holder (needs a metal lid with holes); nut dish (so called compote).

Figure #8   "Banded Leaves" goblet 2-1/8'' and 1-1/8'' across; matching compote style piece 2'' tall and 2¼'' across; no toy proof to date.

Figure #9 ''Beaded Forget-Me-Not'' sherbet set possibility; underplate 2-7/8'' across; sherbet 1-7/8'' tall and 1½'' wide. No toy proof to date.

Figure #11 Sunny Suzy Glass Baking Set No. 261 Wolverine Supply and Mfg. Co., Pittsburg, Pennsylvania. Marked Fire-King Oven Glass; mixing bowl 5-3/8'' across, covered dish 4-5/8'', 4 custard cups 3¾'' (Oswald collection).

Figure #10 McKee's ''Betty Jane'' nine piece Glasbake (sic) Baking Set; oval bowl 6-3/8'' x 4¼'' #075, round covered 4½'' #064, bread pan 4½'' x 3'' #025, pie plate 4½'' #07, custard cups 3¾'' #58 (Oswald collection).

Figure #12 ''Block and Rosette'' table set possibility; no proof to indicate this is a toy. Sugar shown here for pattern identification. (See regular text).

Figure #13   Bell Mason jar (miniature); toy, about 2¼"
                    tall.

Figure #16   Spiraled goblet (possible toy); 2½" tall and
                    1½" across bowl top.

Figure #14   "Stippled Hearts" butter dish, 2½" across
                    base, 1½" tall. "Stippled Hearts" compote
                    (not pictured) 2-1/8" tall and 2-3/8" wide.

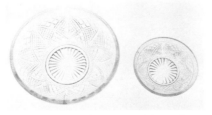

Figure #15   "Peaks and X's" possible toy berry set; main
                    bowl 4½" across, 1¼" tall, small berry bowl
                    ¾" tall and 2¾" wide.

Figure #17   Miniature tumbler, possibly Sandwich;
                    measurements will vary due to excess glass,
                    about 1½" tall and 1½" across.

Figure #18   Miniature celery, possibly Sandwich; 1-5/8″ long and 1″ wide.

Figure #21   "Rippled Arrows" compote; no toy proof; 1½″ and 2-3/8″ across top.

Figure #19   Miniature compote; possibly Sandwich; (opalescent) 1¾″ tall, 2½″ across; no toy proof.

Figure #22   Cranberry milk and mush set; child-sized; no toy proof; creamer 3″ spout to base; bowl 2-1/8″ tall and 4-1/8″ across (possibly Czechoslovakian)

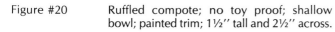

Figure #20   Ruffled compote; no toy proof; shallow bowl; painted trim; 1½″ tall and 2½″ across.

Figure #23   "Rick Rack" butter; no toy proof, 3″ overall height, 4-7/8″ diameter.

Figure #24   Toy Loving Cup; toy proof; 3½'' tall and 2''
across bowl's rim.

Figure #26   Lutz miniature compote; 2'' tall and 2-5/8''
across.

Figure #25   Miniature Heisey ice cream holder or violets
holder, #352; not a toy. (Largent collection).

Figure #27   "Sisters" rose bowl; Kate Greenaway style,
etched design of children on clear glass, 5''
across. (Also called "Two Sunbonnet Girls"
from "Three Little Girls Were Sitting On A
Rail").

Figure #28   Salt dip; ¾'' tall and 1'' across, spoon accessory 1½'' long.

Figure #29   Relish dish; 4-1/8'' long and 2¾'' side to side.

Figure #30   Group shot: Hook mug and creamer, spiraled goblet, Vine goblet, toy tumbler called "Prism".

Figure #31   Ruby tea pot with white enamel (part of a complete glass tea set), the pot is 5'' tall.

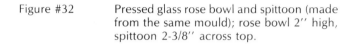

Figure #32   Pressed glass rose bowl and spittoon (made from the same mould); rose bowl 2'' high, spittoon 2-3/8'' across top.

Figure #33   Goblet and butter having wide vertical panels and narrow bands of closely spaced ribbing; spooner is 1¾'' tall, butter is 2-1/8'' across the base and 1½'' high to the top of the finial (attributed to Sandwich).

Diamond Ridge, a Duncan Miller product, was made in a toy pair . . . a creamer and a sugar. (This pattern was unavailable at the time the book's photos were being taken.)

SOWERBY GLASS WORKS
Sowerby & Co., Gateshead-on-Tyne, England
Sowerbys Ellison Glass Works

Even though most of the glass found in this publication is of American origin, collectors find the "Sowerby" glass products with nursery rhyme characters and children to be of value in their collection. Fortunately, there are generous people in this country who share their knowledge with researchers and Mr. Charles W. Funaro of California kindly supplied the information (catalogue proof) of the Sowerby products.

Book VIII, Vitro-Porcelain Etc. by Sowerby and Co., Gateshead-on-Tyne, England, Offices 6, Coleman St. Bank, London 10, Broad St. - Birmingham, shows the following:

Vitro-Porcelain   Turqoise, #1232, "Old King Cole" (vase, spill, or match holder), (opaque glass) shown in clear in this publication.

Vitro-Porcelain	Turqoise, "#1234", Shepherd vase
Vitro-Porcelain	Turqoise, #1263, "Little Bo-Peep" spill or match holder

Vitro-Porcelain	Turqoise, #1219, "Birds' Nest" posy holder
Vitro-Porcelain	Gold color, #1219, #1232
Vitro-Porcelain	Opal, #1225, "Witch and Caldron" posy holder
Vitro-Porcelain	Opal, #1226, "Girl on the Bench" (rough game on the reverse side)
Vitro-Porcelain	Opal, #1227, "Mary Had A Little Lamb" (boy with flowers on reverse side)
Vitro-Porcelain	Opal, #1220, "Mary, Mary Quite Contrary"

Vitro-Porcelain	Opal, #1260, "Lavender Blue", shown in this publication

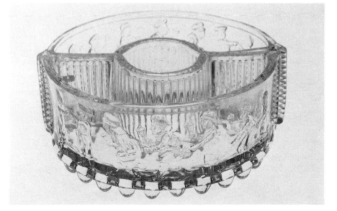

Vitro-Porcelain	Clear, #1293, "Lemons and Oranges", semi-circle to so-called "London Bridge" centerpiece

Vitro-Porcelain	Opal, #1281, "Jack and Jill", posy holder
Vitro-Porcelain	Opal, #1294, "Ma Mammy Dance a Baby", posy holder or match holder
Vitro-Porcelain	Opal, #1285, "Little Jack Horner", bellows style posy holder
Vitro-Porcelain	"Lemons and Oranges", "Arrangements for table decorations, made in flint & col. glass, also Vitro-Porcelain, from Nos. 1293 & 1293½"
Vitro-Porcelain	#1293 A, two semi-circular pieces shown together serving as a candle cup . . . shown in this publication

Vitro-Porcelain	#1293 B, two rectangular pieces with two semi-circular pieces . . . shown in this arrangement in this text

Vitro-Porcelain	#1293 C, all six pieces . . . shown in this arrangement in this text

(Vitro-Porcelain is similar to milkglass products.)

Book IX, Pattern Book of Fancy Goods, Manufactured in Glass by Sowerbys Ellison Glass Works, Limited, Gateshead-on-Tyne, England shows the following vases, spills baskets, and match holders in flint, opal, turqoise, malachite, Patent Queen's Ware and Blanc de Lait:

#1219, "Birds' Nest" posy holder or match holder

#1220, "Mary, Mary Quite Contrary" posy holder

#1224, "Witch and Caldron" or "Old Woman Spinning" posy holder

#1226, 'Cinderella" match holder, posy holder, or spill

#1227, "Little Bo Peep" vase

#1232, "Old King Cole" vase, spill, or match holder, shown here

#1234, "Shepherd" vase

#1260, "Lavender Blue" shown in this publication

#1263, another version of "Little Bo-Peep" spill, vase or match holder

#1261, "Jack and Jill" vase

#1265, bellows shape, "Little Jack Horner"

#1293, 1293½, "Lemons and Oranges" centerpiece parts

#1294, "Ma Mammy Dance a Baby"

Sowerby's Colors:

Flint	A word used to describe a heavy glass containing lead oxide and usually used, indiscriminately, to describe clear glass products
Opaline	This is an opalescent glass made with the addition of cryolite or arsenic to the glass batch. It appears milky by reflected light, showing many blue and golden tints.
Blanc de Lait	One unkind account given of this color of Sowerby's "newest" glass technique suggested it resembled the "cow with the iron tail". The color of the glass was a milky version showing sky blue tints in the thinner portions . . . similar to the color of watered-down milk. (Farmers once pumped water into their milk supply to make more to sell at market.)
Queen's Ivory	This is an ivory version of vitro-porcelain which resembles present-day milkglass to a degree.
Sorbini	This is blue and white marbling.
Rubine	This color is a deep red.
Malachite	This is a green and white marbling treatment.

Some of the vases, spills and match holders with the nursery rhymes and children were also done with a marbling treatment in various colors. This is often referred to as "slag" glass which is not an appropriate title for this type of glass. The "Lemons and Oranges" centerpiece items have been seen in several colors of "marbling". Unfortunately, the design is lost with this special treatment.

The Sowerby firm was responsible for the new invention called vitro-porcelain which had the dual qualities of glass and china. It is like glass because of the manufacturing process and similar to china because of its appearance and composition. This special glass discovery was introduced in 1877. This opaque glass lends itself to many varieties of colors and combinations.

In 1876, John G. Sowerby registered his famous trademark, the peacock's head crest. This mark is found on the interior or exterior of Sowerby articles and is sometimes so indistinct as to resemble a worm or a performing seal rather than the head of a peacock.

STANDING LAMB

The name "Standing Lamb," was chosen for this set long before its counterparts came to light. "Animal Farm" might have been a better choice.

117

The butter dish has a well-formed lamb in a stand of grass on the lid. The sugar is the famous "Dog Holding The Bowl" which several authors shown uncovered and call a salt or toothpick. This sugar is indeed covered and has another animal in a sitting position, guarding the contents of the bowl. The creamer is distinguished by a snake handle with a bunny carrying the bowl's weight. The spooner, which is in existence, has never been kept by one dealer long enough for them to be able to describe it to this author.

A willowy flower design is found on these pieces in an all-over pattern, with the sets coming in clear or with frosting.

This set, no doubt, equals the "Menagerie" set's turtle in its rarity.

PERTINENT DATA:

Additional pattern names: "Animal Farm"
Pattern pieces: Four piece table set
Pattern colors: Clear or frosted
Factory: Unknown
Date: Unknown
Classification: Very rare
Reproduced: No
Pieces difficult to locate: All . . . with the spooner heading the list
Features attributable to pattern: Over all willowy flowers; animals on all the pieces; heavy glass

MEASUREMENTS:

Spooner	Unavailable
Sugar	Dog holding the bowl; animal finial; 3'' base bottom ht.
Creamer	Snake handle; bunny carrying the bowl; 5¾'' overall ht.
Butter	Standing lamb finial; 3¾'' overall ht., 4'' width of base, 1¼'' ht. of base

STIEGEL-TYPE LEMONADE SET

William Henry Stiegel worked with the most fragile material as well as the most durable. "Baron" Stiegel made stoves which he signed and glass which he rarely claimed in written form.

This unpretentious tiny water set is very thin and full of bubbles. The handle is hand applied.

MEASUREMENTS:

Pitcher	Applied handle mould lines, 3'' tall
Tumbler	Mould lines, 1¼'' tall

STIPPLED DEWDROP AND RAINBOW

Amber, clear, and cobalt are the colors for this hard-to-find table set. The creamer, covered sugar, and spooner are on a raised base; the spooner has a scalloped top.

Each piece carries the design of a column of stippling, alternating with an unadorned panel. A band of balls secures the design at the top and bottom.

PERTINENT DATA:

Additional pattern names: None
Pattern pieces: Four piece table set
Pattern colors: Amber, clear, and cobalt
Factory: Unknown
Date: Unknown
Classification: Rare
Reproduced: No
Pieces difficult to locate: All in color, clear sugar and butter
Features attributable to pattern: Columns of stippling alternating with plain panels; band of balls around the top and bottom

MEASUREMENTS:

Spooner	Modified stemmed base, scalloped rim; 2¼'' ht., 1¾'' wide
Sugar	Ribbed finial, puffy lid, modified stemmed base; 3-1/8'' overall ht., 2-1/8'' base ht., 2'' across top, 1¾'' across bottom
Creamer	Plain rim, pointed spout, smooth handle; 2-3/8'' ht., 3'' width from handle to spout
Butter	Ribbed finial; 2'' overall ht., 7/8'' base ht., 2-7/8'' width of base

STIPPLED DIAMOND
STIPPLED FORGET-ME-NOT

The design in the "Stippled Diamond" set consists of a double row of diamonds with overall dense stippling on each of the pieces. It is believed to achieve the "Forget-Me-Not" design, the delicate flowers were embedded on the stippled surface.

The sets are rare in clear and nearly impossible to locate in amber and blue.

PERTINENT DATA:

Additional pattern names: None
Pattern pieces: Four piece table set in each pattern, mugs
Pattern colors: Clear, amber, blue
Factory: Findlay Flint
Date: Circa 1891
Classification: Rare
Reproduced: No
Pieces difficult to locate: All
Features attributable to pattern: All over stippling with diamonds on the "Stippled Diamond" set; stippling and Forget-Me-Nots on the set that bears the name

MEASUREMENTS:

Spooner	2-1/8'' ht., 1-7/8'' width
Sugar	3¼'' overall ht., 2-1/8'' ht. of base, 2'' width
Creamer	2¼'' spout to base, 1-7/8'' side to side
Butter	1-1/8'' ht. of base, 2-7/8'' across top of base
Mug	1¾'' x 2½''

STIPPLED VINE AND BEADS

The coarse stippling, raised leaves, and inter-twining vines, topped by a cascading beaded chain, all serve to create interest in this table set. The colors, however, are the real claim to fame. A sapphire set of "Stippled Vine and Beads" is breathtaking, the amber set is lovely, and the teal treatment is extremely rare . . even the crystal rendition is seldom refused by a collector of toy glass dishes.

The elongated pouring lip of the creamer leads a tenuous existence; it's just asking for a cracking. Positioned for disaster, the creamer takes the prize for the hardest to find member of the unit.

PERTINENT DATA:

Additional pattern names: None
Pattern pieces: Four piece table set
Pattern colors: Clear, teal, amber, sapphire
Factory: Unknown
Date: Unknown
Classification: Very rare in color, difficult to complete in clear
Reproduced: No
Pieces difficult to locate: Creamer, all color
Features attributable to pattern: Coarse stippling; raised leaves; twining vines; beaded rim

MEASUREMENTS:

Spooner	2-1/8'' wide, 2¼'' tall
Sugar	Ribbed short finial; 2-1/8'' ht. of base, 3-1/8'' overall ht., 2¼'' across base
Creamer	Elongated pouring lip; 2-1/8'' side to side, 3-3/8'' spout to handle, 2½'' spout to base height
Butter	Ribbed finial, deep base; 3½'' width of base, 1-1/8'' ht. of base, 2½'' overall ht.

119

STYLE
ARROWHEAD-IN-OVALS

SULTAN
WILD ROSE WITH SCROLLING

The caper between the centuries is illustrated by the fluctuation in pattern styles and taste from the very fussy to the austere. Because the original name "Style" falls short in exactness, collectors continue to revert to the more descriptive name of "Arrowhead-in-Ovals".

PERTINENT DATA:

Additional pattern names: "Arrowhead-in-Ovals", "Beaded Oval and Fan No. 2" in Canadian glass
Pattern pieces: Four piece table set, small adult counterpart cake salver
Pattern colors: Clear
Factory: Higbee
Date: 1900's
Classification: Frequently found
Reproduced: No
Pieces difficult to locate: None
Features attributable to pattern: Notched handles; four ovals with fans in between

MEASUREMENTS:

Spooner	Rim two handles, notched, and a scalloped; 2" wide, 2¼" ht.
Sugar	Covered base with four ovals and a vertically ribbed finial; 3-1/8" complete, 2¼" base ht.
Creamer	Notched handle, plain rim, four ovals; 2-3/8" high, 3-3/8" spout to handle
Butter	Vertically ribbed finial on lid, four ovals on lid and base; 2½" complete ht., 3¾" across base

The "Sultan" four piece table set comes with a variety of trims and treatments. There are frosted sets (white, green); there are clear sets with or without stippled backgrounds; there are four piece sets in green with or without the stippled treatment . . all three types have been seen with or without painted flowers (see color section).

It's the chocolate glass set, however, that commands the largest price. Even though chocolate glass is thought of simultaneously with Greentown glassware, no shards of the "Sultan" toy pattern have been dug at the Greentown site. The "Sultan" chocolate set is on display at the Greentown Glass Museum in Greentown, Indiana out of respect to its developer, Mr. Jacob Rosenthal. It is not thought of as a Greentown product.

Only two chocolate toy glass sets are known . . . the "Austrian #200" table set which is a Greentown product and the "Sultan" table set which is a McKee Glass Company issue.

The pattern of "Wild Rose With Bowknot", which is sometimes confused with the toy Sultan pattern is exclusively an adult pattern.

PERTINENT DATA:

Additional pattern names: "Wild Rose With Scrolling"
Pattern pieces: Four piece table set
Pattern colors: Chocolate, clear, green, frosted white, frosted green
Factory: McKee
Date: 1915-1925
Classification: Rare
Reproduced: No
Pieces difficult to locate: Sugar, all chocolate pieces, all frosted green
Features attributable to pattern: Open roses with scrolling around the top and bottom; scrolling appears vertically between the roses and on the finials

120

MEASUREMENTS:

Spooner	2-5/8'' ht., 2¼'' width
Sugar	3'' ht. of base only
Creamer	2¾'' ht., 3-5/16'' across top, lip to handle
Butter	5-1/8'' across base, 3¼'' across lid opening

(See color section)

SUNBEAM
TWIN SNOWSHOES
No. 15139

This is a misunderstood set on two counts. The four piece table set was given the name of "Twin Snowshoes" before the factory name came to light. The set is also mistaken to be an easy acquisition. (It took this author fifteen years to finally put this unit in order). Although the design is typically Victorian and interesting, the sets were produced by the Gas City factory in a poor grade of glass.

The design is a petal-type series of ellipses joined at the bottom, giving a snowshoe effect. The petals are filled with diamond points which would have sparkled nicely if the glass had been pure. The rims of the sugar and spooner are both scalloped.

It must have been the thick, imperfect glass that caused the decision to limit the production of these tiny table sets.

PERTINENT DATA:

Additional pattern names: "Twin Snowshoes", "15139"
Pattern pieces: Four piece table set
Pattern colors: Clear
Factory: Gas City, Indiana; McKee 1894-1908
Date: 1912
Classification: Very difficult to complete
Reproduced: No
Pieces difficult to locate: Butter, sugar
Features attributable to pattern: Petal-like ellipses joined at the base to give snowshoe effect; petals are filled with diamond points; caning at bottom; elongated ridges inside lids with bands of diamond points above ridges.

MEASUREMENTS:

Spooner	Scalloped rim; 2¼'' ht., 2'' side to side
Sugar	Scalloped rim; ribbed finial; inside lid are 32 elongated ridges; 3-1/8'' overall ht., 2-3/8'' ht. of base, 1-7/8'' across lid opening
Creamer	Smooth handle; 2¾'' ht.
Butter	32 inside ridges on lid; 2'' tall, 3-5/8'' across

TAPPAN

This pattern was produced by the McKee Glass Company in clear glass about 1890. The crystal sets were in their catalogues until 1925. Mr. John Kemple attained the McKee moulds and made miniature sets in milkglass until fire destroyed the factory in East Palestine, Ohio in 1956. The Kemples resumed work on January 21, 1957 at Kenova, West Virginia, where the three piece miniature sets were reissued in milkglass, cobalt, black and light amethyst, light green, honey, amber, and aqua. In 1963 Old Virginia blue and West Virginia red were developed especially for the state's centennial. The pattern was called "Button and Waffle" and was made in a butter, creamer, and covered sugar. The sugar was also sold uncovered as a toothpick for the convenience of people who collected individual pieces for adult tableware use.

Octagonal buttons hem a textured set of plain squares which alternate with lovely diamond pointed squares. All of the pieces except the butter are on modified stemmed bases with the pattern of the glass carried to the finial atop the butter and sugar dishes.

The picture of the Tappan set is from an old catalogue. It was produced by the National Glass Company while they were operating McKee & Brothers Glass Works in Jeannette, Pennsylvania (circa 1892).

PERTINENT DATA:

Additional pattern names: "Button Waffle"
Pattern pieces: Four piece table set
Pattern colors: Clear, milkglass, cobalt, black, amethyst, green, honey, amber, aqua, Old Virginia blue and West Virginia Centennial red. (Some rare four piece table sets have been reported in light blue, amber, light blue milkglass.)
Factory: McKee 1890-early 1900's; Kemple 1950's-1963
Classification: Depending on color--clear and milkglass frequently found
Reproduced: Not after 1963
Pieces difficult to locate: Spooner
Features attributable to pattern: Octagonal buttons hem in a textured set of plain squares which alternate with diamond point squares

MEASUREMENTS:

Spooner	Modified stemmed base; 2-5/8'' ht., 2'' wide
Covered sugar	Patterned finial, modified stemmed base; 2-5/8'' ht. of base, 4'' overall ht., 2-1/8'' across base
Creamer	Modified stemmed base; 2¾'' ht., 2½'' from spout to handle
Covered butter	Patterned finial, domed lid; 3-1/8'' overall ht., 1¼'' ht. of base., 3-5/8'' width of base

THUMBELINA
FLATTENED DIAMOND

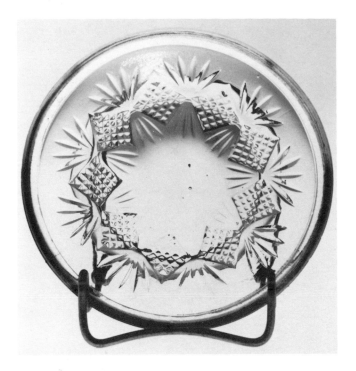

The Westmoreland Glass Company has made good use of the beautifully proportioned moulds which were designed about 1890. They have reissued the punch and table sets in a multitude of colors which were never used originally. The clear punch unit was advertised in a 1910 edition of the Butler Brothers catalog; a dozen sets sold for 94¢. The ad described the design as a deep strawberry, fan and diamond pattern.

In 1950 the milkglass three piece table sets appeared and were still available in 1958. In the 1960's amber, blue and green glass sets were advertised, some with opalescent edges. In the last few years several additional colors have appeared, making collectors of old toy glass shy away from this excellent design.

The miniature cake plate, which is a true toy cake salver, and the tray, which probably served a dual purpose for the adult wine set, are the only pieces in miniature collections which have not been reproduced in the "Thumbelina" pattern.

In the 1925 catalogue proof, the table set, which collectors have been calling "Flattened Diamond", is called by the factory name "Thumbelina", and while the sugar and spooner appear occasionally without handles, this particular publication shows both pieces with notched handles.

PERTINENT DATA:

Additional pattern names: "Flattened Diamond and Sunburst", "Pineapple and Fan" "Strawberry and Fan"
Pattern pieces: Seven piece punch set, table set, cake plate, tray
Pattern colors: (old) Clear, green, sapphire, amber
Factory: Westmoreland Glass Company
Date: Circa 1924
Classification: Easy to find
Reproduced: Yes
Pieces difficult to locate: Toy cake plate, tray
Features attributable to pattern: Diamond pattern alternating with a star design, sunburst effect protrudes at the top, sawtooth edges, handles have cross-ribbing bars; handles are shown on sugar and spooner in the 1925 edition

MEASUREMENTS:

Spooner	2¼" ht.
Sugar	2¼" ht., 1-7/8" width
Creamer	2-3/8" spout to base, 3" spout to handle
Butter	2½" approx. ht., 3½" across base
Small cake	2-7/8" across top, 2" across standard, 7/8" ht.
Tray	7-3/8" width, 3/8" ht.
Punch bowl	4¼" ht., 4½" width
Punch cup	1-3/8" width, 1¼" ht.

TULIP AND HONEYCOMB
Wabash Toy Series

The so-called "Tulip and Honeycomb" table set, punch unit and serving pieces are a part of the Federal Glass Company's 1914 "Wabash" toy series.

PERTINENT DATA:

Additional pattern names: "Wabash"
Pattern pieces: Four piece table set, an extra butter dish, four vegetable servers, a punch set
Factory: Federal Glass Co., Columbus, Ohio
Date: 1914
Classification: Obtainable
Pieces difficult to locate: Vegetable servers
Features attributable to pattern: Murky glass, tulip and honeycomb motif

MEASUREMENTS:

Spooner	2½" ht.
Sugar	3-7/8" overall ht.
Creamer	2-5/8" ht.
Large butter	3¼" ht. of lid, 4-5/8" across base
Small butter	2-1/8" ht. of lid, 4" base length
Open square dish	2½" wide
Open ruffled dish (oblong)	3¼" longest part, 2-5/8" wide, 2" high
Round covered dish	3-5/8" overall ht
Oblong covered dish	2½" ht., 4-1/8" handle to handle

TUMBLE UPS

Persistence is the key when collecting or writing about miniature tumble ups. It took 15 years to find a bit of information about these delicate objects from the past which were produced in America as well as abroad.

Tumble ups are water carafes or decanters or pitchers with a single tumbler turned over the neck of the carafe or decanter, or more rarely, fitting down inside the neck of a pitcher. Tumble ups were placed beside the bed as recovery units or placed in the home wherever a nip of refreshment was required. (Usually holding water, they were at times used for something a shade stronger.)

In the search for documentary evidence, permission was granted and the opportunity given to crawl around under the tables in a booth at an Indianapolis Antiques Show. Having spotted a stack of children's magazines written in 1888 called *Our Little Men and Women* caused this author to crawl a little faster. Wonder of wonders---all 12 magazines in the series were present and accounted for . . . a subscription cost of $1.00 a year or 10 cents a number, as advertised on each cover. The series was produced by the D. Lothrop Company of Boston.

SUSANNA'S AUCTION.

SUSANNA YIELDS.

Everything was sold.

Uncle Eugene had just bought the last — a whole lot of toys for three cents, to give to the poor children in that part of the city — when Susanna's nurse discovered another doll tucked away in a corner of the closet where Susanna's playthings were kept. She brought her out and gave her to Uncle Julius.

It must be owned that she was a very shabby doll. She had, however, seen better days. She had been given to Susanna by her friend Joseph. And Susanna had been so much pleased with her — for she was then a beautiful creature — that she had named her Josephine as a compliment to the giver.

PARDON, PAPA!
PARDON, MAMMA!

But of late Susanna had been so taken up with her other children that she had allowed poor Josephine to be knocked about, until she had lost first an arm, then a leg, then an eye, and at last more than half her hair. Yes, she was a very shabby child — a poor useless invalid. But, shabby as she was, she must be sold with the rest of the family.

Uncle Julius held her up that all might see her, and said, "We will now sell a sick doll, which " —

But his sentence was never finished. Susanna, struck with shame and sorrow at the thought of having her sick child sold, threw

herself upon Uncle Julius and tried to seize hold of Josephine, crying out : "No! no! it is Josephine! I can't have Josephine sold!"

Then came a great flood of tears. As her papa and mamma hastened to her, she cried again : "Pardon, papa! Pardon, mamma! It is Josephine! I can't have Josephine sold. Pardon! pardon!"

The auctioneer arose from his chair with dignity. "Do you ask pardon, Miss?" he said.

"Yes. I want Josephine," was the answer.

"That is sufficient," said Uncle George. "The auction is over. Uncle Julius, return Josephine to her mother."

Uncle Julius did so, and Susanna hugged her and covered her with kisses. And at the same time her papa and mamma kissed Susanna, who promised to be a good child in the future.

"And so I suppose they gave back to her all her playthings," somebody says. By no means. You forget that Uncle George said the sale was a real one. So, of course, the things were really sold, and could not be taken back.

But to keep Susanna in mind of her promise to be a good child, her papa and mamma bought a set of bedroom furniture for Josephine. Still, although her little mother now loves her dearly, and with constancy, Josephine can never regain the leg and arm and eye which she has lost. But Susanna tells her that if she is obedient her hair will grow again. *— From the French.*

JOSEPHINE IN HER BEDROOM.

Frugality was not reserved for the Mother Country when it came to making the most of a printed page or an opportunity for preachment. D. Lothrop made sure that everything from Electric Soap to social etiquette was present in those monthly volumes. Moral certainty was shared and lessons were taught in uncompromising terms. Thanks to one of these lessons and poor Susanna's imprudent behavior we are blessed with tumble up proof . . . of sorts. Part of a continuing series in Vol. IX, No. 3, March, of *Our Little Men and Women* was concerned with a naughty THREE year old girl who broke a vase and failed to show proper humility. She said she could pay for it . . . and pay she did! Every toy she owned was sold at auction for three pennies and the pennies were given to the poor. The obstinate hooligan had, however, neglected to include Josephine, a favorite doll who had lost a leg, an arm, one eye, and half her hair . . . a condition not uncommon to collectors of miniature tumble ups. It was Josephine who saved our day and helped Susanna a bit, too. The story on the subject is reprinted here along with the picture proof for your enjoyment. (Notice the decanter and glass on the table beside the doll.)

TUMBLE UPS:

Five of the old miniature tumble ups shown in this publication are Bohemian style ranging from 3-3/8" to 4-7/8" in height. This special treatment employed a decorative technique practiced by the ancients and is also one which was popular in France and England. This technique made the Austrian factories in Bohemia famous before the mid-19th century. It is doubtful if Bohemian glass was produced in America before the 1840's for it was not taken too seriously by our glass manufacturers until after the French and Austrian displays at New York's Crystal Palace in 1853. That display proved a tremendous stimulus to its popularity in this country. The peak of its production was in the 1860's. The manufacturer's trade name for the ware was "Bohemian Glass", also covering all types borrowed from Bohemia.

This cased or overlay glass is a decorative device combining the use of different colored metals in layers. After the finished article has been annealed, it passed to the hands of a glass cutter who cut a design through the casing so as to show the various colors and the inner clear glass body.

Two of the old miniature tumble ups are in the Mary Gregory style. Mary Alice Gregory lived her life on Summer Street in Sandwich, Cape Cod, Massachusetts. She never married but loved children and decorated her glass to prove it. She was a great admirer of Kate Greenaway, the famous English illustrator whose representations of children grace many miniature pieces. Miss Gregory worked only at the Boston and Sandwich Glass Company, decorating little figures of boys and girls in white enamel with much finesse. A European "Mary Gregory" style can be found produced in the same time frame, but it often has gold florals, scrolls, and tinted flesh, the people are in costumes of obvious European design.

Another famous person, Nicholas Lutz, worked for Deming Jarves at the great Boston and Sandwich Glass Company.

He was famous for glassblowing during the late Victorian era. At the age of ten he was apprenticed in St. Louis, Lorraine, France where he made many of the finest paperweights ever produced. In 1869 he left the Dorflinger factory and went to work at the Boston and Sandwich Glass Company where he stayed until it closed. His name is particularly associated with delicately blown glass, in the Ventian style, in what is known as "Striped glass". Pieces of bright colored rods or canes were encased in a gather of clear glass which was rolled on a marver and then expanded to produce this special treatment which is found in miniature tumble up #6.

Tu-1, 5-3/8'' tall   This tumble up is unusual because of the color. It seems that amethyst was not often used in miniature glass.

Tu-2, 4-7/8'' tall   This clear paneled tumble up has gold trim and green leaves with white flowers. The glass is very clear and thin.

Tu-3, 5'' tall   This green opaline tumble up is a lovely color, but has no design.

Tu-4, 5'' tall   This is the most unusual tumble up in the author's collection. Adult tumble ups such as this have been seen, but this style rarely appears in miniature. The main body of the unit is a blue pitcher with etched flowers and a smooth yellow handle. The matching blue tumbler fits down inside the neck of the pitcher. A charming flower was etched in the bottom of the tumbler completing the picture.

Tu-5, 4-7/8'' tall   This tumble up is not a true Bohemian type, rather it is more a decorative flashing imitating the style in order to economize.

Tu-6, 3-7/8'' tall   This blue and white tumble up in miniature has been attributed to Nicholas Lutz.

Tu-7, 3-1/8'' tall   This is an example in cranberry of the Mary Gregory style. This was also produced in an apple green. Gold trim graces the rim.

Tu-8, 4-3/8'' tall   The clear glass in this set is thin, having gold trim around the tumbler top, around the base of the decanter neck and around the bottom of the decanter. The white enamel is a chain of circles on both the tumbler and decanter bottom. There are vertical decorations in the white enamel as well.

Tu-9, 1½'' tall   A tumble up in miniature is rare enough, but when it is only 1½'' tall and done in cobalt glass with the Mary Gregory style, it becomes outstanding.

Tu-10, 3¾'' tall   This ornate tumble up was bought in England. It is cranberry with enameled flowers and butterflies. Large amounts of gold enhances the design of this miniature.

Tu-11, 4¼'' tall   This miniature has a grape, flower, and leaf design etched on its graceful body. The bases of the decanter and tumbler are cut in a honeycomb design. This tumble up has a stopper.

Tu-12, 3'' tall   Blue opaline glass with fancy gold and white enameled scrolls and flowers complete this miniature tumble up.

Tu-13, 4¼'' tall   This miniature carries a wooded scene with dogs and birds etched into the glass. The stopper to this set is ruby, matching the rest of the set.

Tu-14, 3-3/8'' tall   The smallest of the Bohemian tumble ups has pictures and writing from its native land. It also has a stopper.

Tu-15   This unusual tumble up (pictured in black and white) has the addition of an underplate. This blue glass tumble up, from the Largent collection, is decorated with swimming fish in gold, 5'' complete, 4'' across.

Tu-16, 17, 18   The three tumble ups shown in the black and white group shot are as follows:

Tu-16 has a band of six closely spaced lines. There is a zig-zag design as well. The base is 3½'' high, the tumbler is 2¼'' high, and together the total measurement is 4''.

Tu-18 is a crystal tumble up with black silhouettes of a little boy petting his dog (decanter); the tumbler shows the same child playing a horn. Vines and flowers complete the toy tumble up. The base is 3½'' high, the tumbler is 2-1/8'' high and together they are 3-7/8'' tall.

Tu-17 is a crystal set with enameled decorations of trumpet flowers and trefoil leaves which band each of the two pieces. The flowers are orange, blue and cream with gold highlights. The base is 3¾'' tall, the tumbler is 2-3/8'' high and together they are 4¼'' high.

Tu-19, 5''   This Bohemian tumble up is on a modified stem. It is etched all over with wooded scenes and deer. This 5'' beauty has a matching mushroom style stopper.

Tu-20, 4''   This 4'' tall art glass miniature tumble up changes its swirls as this cased glass beauty is turned in the light. It is embellished with peach enamel over the rich yellow and cream glass.

TWIST

The "No. 137 Model Swirl" set, a late 1800's product, is common to the Findlay and Albany factories.

The lovely opalescent and frosted "Twist" sets are expensive and difficult to locate, while the clear sets are frequently found. The frosted sets with the added attraction of pink, blue, green or yellow on the rims command the largest price of all.

The miniature vase was made in the Twist-type pattern and has been seen in bluish-white, light yellow and white (See color secion).

PERTINENT DATA:

Additional pattern names: "Swirl", "Model Swirl", "No. 137"
Pattern pieces: Four piece table set; vase
Pattern colors: Clear, plain frosted, frosted with colored rims, opalescent yellow, white, blue
Factory: Findlay, Albany
Date: Before 1893
Classification: Rare in color and frosted, frequently found in clear
Pieces difficult to locate: All color, frosted
Features attributable to pattern: Twisted swirled effect

MEASUREMENTS:

Spooner	2½" ht., 2¼" wide
Sugar	3-7/8" overall ht., 2-3/8" ht. of base, 2-5/8" width
Creamer	2-7/8" ht. from spout to base, 3½" spout to handle back, 2-1/8" side to side
Butter	2½" overall ht., 3-5/8" width
Vase	3½" ht.

TWO BAND

The pattern name, derived from the two different bands encircling the pieces of this four piece table set, is also claimed by the adult table unit.

The top band consists of a chain of alternating shapes, one being a stippled octagon--the next, a plain hexagon. The lower band has only four of the octagon-hexagon arrangements.

The handles are the set's most outstanding feature--two pieces of extended glass on each side, interrupted by a vertical third piece.

This set is known only in clear in adult and toy ware.

PERTINENT DATA:

Additional pattern names: None
Pattern pieces: Four piece table set
Pattern colors: Clear
Factory: Unknown
Date: Unknown

Classification: Obtainable
Reproduced: No
Pieces difficult to locate: Spooner
Features attributable to pattern: Two different bands encircling the pieces, extended glass handles interrupted by vertical third piece of glass

MEASUREMENTS:

Spooner	1-7/8" width, 2¾" ht.
Covered sugar	2¼" width of base top, 2¾" ht. of base, 3-7/8" overall ht.
Creamer	1¾" side to side, 2-5/8" spout to handle, 2¾" spout to base
Covered butter	3½" width of base top, 2" overall ht.

WABASH TOY SERIES
TULIP AND HONEYCOMB
FISH SET
GRAPE STEIN SET
A B C ICE CREAM

The Federal Glass Company of Columbus, Ohio created a surprise by recording in a 1914 catalogue proof a series of items made expressly for children. The series was named the "Wabash" and consists of: a seven piece ice cream set, a seven piece fish unit, a seven piece grape stein assemblage, and a table set replete with two butters and four odd-shaped vegetable servers. A punch set also matches the pattern of the table set and server.

The ice cream set has an oval main platter with a leafy border showing a dish of ice cream in the center. The six smaller plates have the same center but there is a rim difference. The small round plates have the alphabet racing around the rim in place of the leaf motif. This set is difficult to complete. The Fish set, however, seems impossible to assemble for it appears to have been an export item as was the "Grape Stein" set. (No complete sets of either have been reported to date.) The Wabash series is done in a poor grade of glass, but that does not mean the "Fish" set, the "Grape Stein" set and the four servers to the "Tulip and Honeycomb" pattern are not chased with zeal. (The small butter to the "Tulip and Honeycomb" pattern is difficult to locate at times as well.)

Fred Bickenheuser reported the Wabash toy series in a series of Federal Glass Company articles. He kindly loaned me the valuable catalogue to be pictured in this publication. Mr. Bickenheuser reports that this series was found only in the 1914 Tableware Catalogue, leading him to believe these sets were made for only a short period of time.

PERTINENT DATA:

Additional pattern names: Table and punch sets and servers were called "Tulip and Honeycomb", "Fish" "Grape Stein" and "Ice Cream" sets

Pattern pieces: Four piece table set, two covered servers, two uncovered servers, small covered butter, seven piece ice cream set, seven piece fish set, seven piece grape stein set

Pattern colors: Clear; Grape set clear with paint

Factory: Federal Glass Company, Columbus, Ohio

Date: 1914

Classification: "Fish" and "Grape Stein" sets very rare, "Ice Cream" set rare, servers and small butter difficult to locate, punch and table set frequently found

Reproduced: No

Pieces difficult to locate: All of the "Fish" set, the "Grape Stein" set, the servers, the small butter, and the small ice cream plates

MEASUREMENTS:

Spooner	2½" ht., 1-7/8" side to side, 4" handle to handle
Sugar	3-7/8" overall ht., 2½" ht. of base
Creamer	2-5/8" ht., 2" side to side, 3-3/8" spout to handle
Large butter	3¼" ht. of lid, 3½" length across lid opening, 4-5/8" across base
Tiny butter	2-1/8" ht. of lid, 3" across lid opening, 4" length of base
Open square compote, ruffled	2½" width, 1¾" longest part
Open ruffled oblong dish	3¼" longest part, 2-5/8" width, 2" ht.
Main platter	5¾" long ("Fish" and "Ice Cream" sets)
Small plate	2¾" wide
Punch bowl	4" ht., 4½" width
Round covered dish	1¾" ht. of base, 3-5/8" overall ht., 3-1/8" handle to handle
Oblong covered dish	4-1/8" handle to handle, 2½' approx. ht.

The Wee Branches table set has counterparts uncommon to most sets included in the toy tea set category. This pattern has the added rarity of cups, saucers, and plates to complete the table set unit. The butter, sugar, creamer, and spooner are difficult to locate while the plates, cups, and saucers command a high price and are rarely found with the normal four piece assemblage. At least four cups, four saucers and four plates would accompany a complete collection of the "Wee Branch" set.

The mugs in this pattern are more readily located and are displayed in several collections (in three sizes) in white or blue milkglass, opaque soft blue, cobalt, and crystal. Unfortunately, the table set was made only in clear.

The mottled leaves found on this set appear on the "Nursery Rhyme" and "Rooster" pieces, which leads one to believe the "Wee Branches" set might have been a United States Glass Company product.

The vines, leaves, and berries are repeated on all of the "Wee Branches" pieces while the butter exclusively claims the added "alphabetical value" -- a much sought after addition to any toy glass item.

A lucky acquisition by the author was a "Wee Branches" set in its original box which read "Engraving, Half size, 1 set, 20 cents". The set was pictured on the top of the box lid.

PERTINENT DATA:

Additional pattern names: None
Pattern pieces: Four piece table set, cup and saucer, plate, mug
Pattern colors: Clear for the table set, cup, saucer, plate; mugs are white or blue milkglass, opaque soft blue, cobalt, clear
Factory: Attributed to the United States Glass Company
Date: Unknown
Classification: Difficult to locate
Reproduced: No
Pieces difficult to locate: Cups, saucers, plates, spooner
Features attributable to pattern: Mottled leaves, berries, branches

MEASUREMENTS:

Spooner	Smooth rim, rayed base, repeated design, 2'' wide, 2-3/8'' tall
Sugar	Stemmed base, tiny handles, repeated design, flat sided finial; 3'' ht., 2¼'' base ht.
Creamer	Vines, leaves, and fruit, smooth handle, rayed base; 1 5/8'' side to side, 2½'' across spout to handle; 2¼'' in ht.
Butter	Alphabet on a stippled background circling the rim; three stars between the A and Z; flat sided; 2'' total ht., 3-1/8'' wide
Cup	1¾'' tall, 2-3/8'' across
Saucer	3'' across, ½'' deep
Plate	Has a raised rim; ½'' border design, 2½'' across
Mug	1-7/8'' x 2''

WILD ROSE

The pattern of "Wild Rose" is festooned with flowers, scrolls and scallops. The toy punch set was cast in crystal or wandering shades of white milkglass. Its fine lines are design-marred due to the excess glass which was left "as is" when the pieces were lifted from the mould.

The ungainly table set is collected only in milkglass. The butter dish is the set's one redeeming feature with the well designed rose impressed in the butter's base. The lidless sugar bowl and spoon holder have abnormally large handles which are often cracked due to their precarious position.

The trim on the punch and table sets is enough to knock a canary from its perch . . . wild pink or red, bilious blue or green, flat silver or gold, with the yellow trim doing little to enhance the appearance.

The crystal candlesticks are rare and noticably absent in most toy glass collections.

The "Wild Rose" sets and the "Monk Stein" sets were sold together in the Butler Brothers catalogue in 1910.

PERTINENT DATA:

Additional pattern names: None
Pattern pieces: Four piece table set, seven piece punch set, candlesticks
Factory: Attributed to U.S. Glass Co.
Date: Turn of the century
Classification: Clear punch set and candlesticks rare
Reproduced: No
Pieces difficult to locate: All clear pieces, milkglass creamer
Features attributable to pattern: Scrolls, scallops and roses

MEASUREMENTS:

Spooner	1-7/8'' high side, 4'' handle to handle
Open sugar	2¼'' side to side, 4-5/8'' handle to handle, 1-7/8'' ht. from side
Creamer	3½'' from handle to spout, 1-7/8'' side to side, 2'' spout to base
Covered butter	3-7/8'' overall ht.
Punch bowl	4'' width, 4¼'' ht.
Punch cup	1½'' side to side, 1¼'' ht.
Candlestick	4-1/8'' ht.

NEW TOY GLASSWARE

Thin Glass Epergne

"Lechler Heirlooms" (Cranberry Opalescent)

Contemporary toy glass emerging from newly designed moulds has punched the collecting market with a sudden burst of color. At the time of this publication the new lines of children's glass were produced in very limited editions; five hundred sets per color seemed to be the magic number, with a limited number of mould uses. Due to the glass producer's pride in their 20th century products, the sets have been marked as new.

The deftness with which a glass craftsman wields, turns and shapes the molten glass looks effortless, but it is part of a rhythm born of long practice and attuned to an innate artistry. It is an ancient craft that cannot be duplicated by a machine nor imitated by a semi-skilled person. Above all, it will not be hurried . . . without jeopardizing the final product.

The new toy glassware seen in this section is done privately. No two pieces are exactly alike, that is the true worth and beauty of hand-crafted glass; every piece is unique because it is measured by the eye and fashioned by the hand and embellished by an artist.

There is no "faster" way of making these tiny hand-crafted jewels. No assembly line can be speeded up to deal with an unexpected spurt of orders . . . no extra labor can be rushed in for emergencies . . . no additional materials and equipment that can be put to work suddenly. Production is governed by the time taken by the craftsman. This is the costliest, most precious ingredient in every piece of the ware shown in this section.

Glass making, blowing and designing are now and always have been patient, painstaking operations which call for years of apprenticeship before a person is qualified to perform these rites. Take note of the ruby over-lay tumble-up in the line of Lechler Heirlooms of Tomorrow . . . it look 24 men to make each one of the decanters rendered from batches of glass containing gold. Gold was also used in the Burmese lemonade set shown in the same color photo.

"Wetzel" Water Set

"Encore" Glass by the Taylors

"Encore" Miniatures by the Taylors

130

A BRIEF DESCRIPTION OF THE
GLASSMAKING PROCESS

ACTIVITY	AT WHAT TEMPERATURE	REQUIRES HOW MUCH TIME?
Ingredients weighed and mixed	at room temperature	approximately 30 minutes
Loaded into melting furnace	approximately 2000° F.	approximately 5 minutes
Melting and refining takes place	approximately 2500° F.	10 to 35 hours, depending on type of glass and type of furnace
A group of men make glassware. They draw the glass from the furnace in gobs ranging in size from 3 oz. to 90 oz. In some factories the glass flows from the furnace into forming machines on a lower level.	approximately 2000° F.	Men work 8 hour shifts
Each gob is formed into a basic shape by a man using air or mechanical force. In factories making less complicated shapes or higher quantities, this forming is performed by machines.	approximately 2000° F.	5 to 50 seconds
The basic shape is reheated and changed to the final shape.	1800° F.	20 to 60 seconds
The piece is put in an annealing lehr to strengthen the glass and to cool it off.	1000° F. to room temperature	1 hour to 6 hours or longer
The piece is then inspected, packaged and shipped.	room temperature	1 day to weeks

The main ingredients used and their approximate percentage of the total batch are:

Sand (SiO_2)	75%
Soda Ash (Na_2CO_3)	15%
Lime $(CaCO_3)$	9%

Some manufacturers substitute potash for soda ash, and barium or borax for lime. In some opaque glasses fluorspar and feldspar are substituted for lime.

The color controlling ingredients are mixed in with the main ingredients before melting. Some of the materials used to create certain colors are:

MATERIALS	COLOR PRODUCED
Uranium	Yellow
Cobalt	Blue
Sugar and Iron	Amber
Neodymium	Pink
Iron	Green
Gold	Red
Selenium and Cadmium	Orange
Selenium and Manganese	Crystal
Alumina and Fluorine	White

COLOR	GENERAL COLORANT
Burmese	Pure gold and Uranium Oxide
Custard	Uranium Oxide
Amethyst	Manganese Dioxide
Ruby Overlay	Gold and Crystal Glass
Blue Satin	Copper Oxide
Cranberry Opalescent	Gold and Calcium Phosphates
Colonial Blue	Copper
Colonial Amber	Sugar

Art Edwards
Fenton Art Glass Co.

SECTION II: CHINA

China To A Tea

The subject of antique toy china is a dark pocket of confusion in the history of children's chattel. Shiploads of tiny ware have landed in American ports over the last two hundred years, yet a prudent poke is all that has been given the subject by authors from the exporting countries. This is not surprising, for researching porcelain is something akin to cutting capers in a minefield; the topic nearly defies analysis. While some artists initiated, departing from old forms while expressing things in a new way, some followed and imitated, and still others instinctively selected the best of the past and fused it with perfection. The cycle of effort was then recommenced, sometimes only after perfection had deteriorated into decadence. The application of delicate incongruities by the decorating masters, however, caused the most confusion in the toy china classification. It seems that complete toy china sets were rarely decorated in exactness even though style-repeated "blanks" were used. The decorator's mark and the potter's mark, if placed at all, were usually given to only one member of a unit. Through the years the sets have been separated and reassembled countless times with the result being that some collectors have sets with no marking at all. All of these problems were compounded by the fact that every country gave and every country received. Innumerable exchanges occurred on the technical side, the aesthetic side, and on the personal level. This complex interplay of persons and forces resulted in a many-sided contribution in miniature form which is enjoyed by today's collectors.

Toy china casts light on the timber of the times in which it was produced. Examples of mid-Victorian frugality and Rousseau influence shine in preachment form on the English toy ware. The plates and mugs are rife with moral and educational platitudes while the tea and dinner sets pose excellent botanical lessons--proving that the mind and stomach were served in sync. Historical scenery, both English and American, is in evidence--the latter being less than perfect in specifics since most designs were made from memory or hear say. Preachment and frugality took to the air and flapped away, however, when the German decorators stroked the tiny ware. Even though the English embellishers pulled an occasional monkey shine, it was the German decorators who had the fun bedecking toy china with scenes of rhymes, animals, children and overblown lusty floral scenes. Paint, decals and luster were used in abundance, streaking the ware with slashes of humor and signs of love.

Since the vogue of drinking tea, coffee and chocolate gained popularity with amazing rapidity, the impetus to an introduction of porcelain was quick to follow. The afternoon tea was a social revivifying ritual in the days before hollandaise sauce ran its slick fingers across menus. Anna Duchess of Bedford secretly combated the sinking five o'clock feeling with tea before she had the idea of inviting a few of her friends into her chamber for tea and cakes. The fashion caught on and the tea party with its sticky buns and elaborate equipage came out of the boudoir and into the drawing room.

Americans were not one whit behind the Mother Country in the elegancies of domestic appointment; therefore, much adult and toy china arrived in the Boston Harbor. Opaque blue and white (earthenware) toy sets looking as though the Mad Hatter had a hand in decorating them, sold for $1.10 in Boston around 1816. Crooked decals, bumps and ridges and ill fitting lids are a few of the examples of neglect . . . untidy, interesting, and highly collectible in the 20th century. As interest in the child as a consumer escalated, so did the quality of the tea sets. (Collections of today are graced by some very fine examples of R.S. Prussia and Staffordshire ware.)

Visual satisfaction cannot be explained and for some collectors seeing and owning these china gems from the past is enough. Others, wishing to be fact-blinded, will find interest in the following section which includes identifying clues, countries of origin, and dates.

Chinaware is porcelain, usually translucent, and is not to be confused with pottery even though it evolved from pottery. Porcelain, which has a clay paste base is beyond and apart from pottery, for it is the highest, most precious, and the most highly organized expression of the potter's art which first originated in China.

132

The glaze is an important identifying factor. When the ware is glazed, it is really another form of the word "glass". The glaze gives the body a glass transparent coat which reflects the light and makes the surface smooth and soft as a shell's lining. When the paste body is unglazed, it is called biscuit.

The "body" of the ware is another identifying clue: HARD PASTE was introduced to Europe in the early 1700's by Johann Bottger at the Meissen factory. This porcelain is distinguished by hardness, by the high impermeability to fluids that stain and by resistance to heat. The close, compact texture, translucence, and bell-like note when struck, indicate that the thoroughly blended and compacted elements of Kaolin (china clay) and petunste (china stone) gives an elegant, mellow and satisfactory product when covered by the skin or glaze. The decorations of the ware rest on top of the glaze and do not merge as they do in soft paste products.

SOFT PASTE was introduced by France but became a chiefly English product. It is sometimes called artificial porcelain because some of the materials used in the composition were substitutes for the materials used in the original Oriental porcelain. Soft paste is distinguished by the soft creamy tones with the decorations tending to sink slightly into the glaze. When soft paste is chipped or broken the unglazed portion of the exposed ware is granular and chalky. The soft paste body is not as resistant to heat as the hard paste ware.

BONE PORCELAIN is a middle ground, combining the qualities of hard and soft paste. The materials of bone porcelain consists of Kaolin, felspar, petuntse, and bone ash. If bone porcelain fractures, it has more qualities of the hard than of the soft paste. It has the durability of the hard with the softer, warmer, appearance of the soft paste.

English ware has "color" clue. Most printed English earthenware of the early 1800's is found in the typical "Blue Willow" blue. In general, the blue of the 1810-1820 period was a medium dark shade; 1820-1830 the blue was a darker shade, but after 1830 it came to be noticably lighter. The plates, platters, dishes, tureens, jugs and tea services with American buildings, views, and public figures printed in blue as decorations were made at Liverpool or in the countless side street potteries of the nine main china producing areas of Staffordshire, England.

Pertinent information for collectors of English ware:

1. "England" was added to marks from 1891 to comply with the American McKinley Tariff Act.

2. "Made in England" signifies a 20th century dating.

3. "Limited" (Ld., Ltd.), indicates a date after 1860 and was not in ceramic marks before the 1880's.

4. "Trade-Mark" signifies a date subsequent to the Trade-Mark Act of 1862 and the words denote a date after 1875.

5. The occurrence of "Rd. No." followed by a number, dates it after 1884; if the number is above 360,000 the date is subsequent to 1900.

6. Any printed mark using the Royal Arms or versions of the Arms are 19th century or later.

7. Any printed mark using the name of the pattern is subsequent to 1810.

8. If "Royal" is in the manufacturer's title, it may be dated after the middle of the 19th century.

9. If the words "Bone China" or "English Bone China" are used it denotes a 20th century date.

10. English earthenwares are opaque and prior to 1770. They are usually unmarked.

11. English delft-type earthenwares with a coating of tin glaze are usually unmarked as are the salt glazed wares.

12. Porcelain was not made in England before the 1740's.

13. Porcelains are normally translucent, while earthenwares are opaque.

14. The pottery centers in Staffordshire England were centered in: Lane End; Longport; Burslem (B) the largest; Cobridge (C); Hanley (H); Stoke, Fenton (F); Longton (L). . .those initials in ( ) indicate the example way of marking: E. & B. L. was Edwards & Brown of Longton.

15. The main London pottery centers were Bow, Chelsea, Fulham, Lambeth. . .all locations had countless side street potteries.

16. Incised marks are scratched into the body before the first firing and before decoration. (Signatures are often done in this way.) Applied marks, which are rare, are impressed marks on a raised pad.

17. Impressed marks are made by applying a metal die to the ware before the first firing and before the decorating.

18. Seal-type marks are made up of initials or monograms in a shaped-outline, common to seal devices.

19. Printed marks came into use about 1800 and were applied over the glaze during or after the decoration. The mark is transferred to the item from engraved copper plates by means of special paper.

20. There are three typical china ware handles: the crabstock, the foliated scroll, and the double interlaced.

21. Gaudy Dutch (1800-1820) is a soft paste pottery with blue under the glaze and other colors on top. Gaudy Dutch has no luster trim.

22. Gaudy Welsh (Swansea 1830-1845) is a translucent porcelain with luster (an application of gold that turns coppery when fired on a dark clay base) included with the decorations.

23. Gaudy Ironstone (1855-1865) is a heavy ware that is a mixture of pottery and porcelain clay. It has a blue under the glaze and other colors on top. It was made with or without luster trim.

24. Gaudy Staffordshire (1820-1850) was made with the regular opaque Staffordshire clay having different hand decorations which occasionally included luster.

25. Spatter (1820-1860) is a type of decoration rather than a special ware. English potters used Spatter on much of the early soft paste pottery. Spatter decorations were made with a sponge, a brush end or with a cloth or stick dabbed into paint.

Three excellent books to aid researchers, collectors and dealers are: Geoffrey A. Godden's *Encyclopedia of British Pottery and Porcelain Marks*, Robert E. Rontgen's *Marks on German, Bohemian and Austrian Porcelain 1710 to the Present* and Sam Laidacker's *Anglo-American China Part I*.

Pertinent information for collectors of German Ware:

Nearly half of all European porcelain in existence was made in Germany, Bohemia and Austria. A slim strip of land from Bavaria to Bohemia became the center of continental porcelain after 1708. (European porcelain was first developed commercially at Meissen, Germany by Johann Bottger in the early 1700's.) Family bonds, technical methods and circumstances of history interrelate, making this still a highly productive porcelain area.

Since the literature about porcelain concerns itself mainly with the one hundred and twenty years between the invention of the European porcelain and the beginning of industrilization, little is written about toy china. Scant reference is made to children's ware in research from the exporting countries. Therefore, this section of the text is not complete, but to wait until the last question has been answered and the last picture taken would have meant that the book would never have been published. . .so a preliminary line has been drawn with some contributors listed.

ALTWASSER
Silesia, Germany (now Walbrzych, Poland; Tielsch & Co., 1845-1945). Products--household, decorative porcelain, coffee and tea sets

Text example--"Little School Teacher"
Markings--Altwasser, Germany; a flying horse, C.I. all in green on the bases

BAYREUTH
Bavaria, Germany (presently Federal Republic of Germany, 1899-1920). Company name changed from Siegmund Paul Meyer 1899-1920 to Erste Bayreuther Porzellanfabrik "Walkure" 1920-present day

Text example--"Bayreuth Children", "Royal Bayreuth Nursery Jingles"

BEYER & BOCK (1853-1960)
Nationalized and named VEB Porcelain; also produced Rudolstadt-Volkstedt and Royal Rudolstadt from 1890

NIEDERSALZBRUNN
Silesia, Germany (presently Franz Prause Porcelain Factory, Poland, 1894-1936). Products were household ware, table products, coffee and tea sets.

Text example--"Princess Driving A Bird"

REINHOLD SCHLEGELMILCH
Suhl and Tillowitz (1869-circa 1938)

Text examples--"Green And Yellow Luster Twig Finials"
"Prussia Poppies"
"R.S. Prussia Blue Luster With Pink And White Roses"
"Baby Red Roses With Gold Draping"
"R.S. Prussia Cream And Tan Roses"
"Four Seasons"
"Petite R.S. Prussia"

RUDOLSTADT (1854)
Thuringia, Germany (now German Democratic Republic) see also Volkstedt; Ernst Bohne Sons; 1920 factory became a branch of Bros. Heuback in Lichte; sold to Stahl & Co. in 1937

Text examples--"Happifats"
"Golliwags" (Creatures)

VILLEROY & BOCH (1836)
See next entry

WALLENFANGEN
Saarland, Germany (Nicolas Villeroy, 1789-1836) Products--household ware (earthenware)
Company merged with Boch in Mettlach becoming a branch (Villeroy & Boch 1836-1931)

Text example--"Paula"
Markings--Vaudrevange (impressed on earthenware) Villeroy & Boch (impressed or stamped overglaze)

Pertinent information for collectors of American ware:

Mr. William Ellis Tucker of Philadelphia, was the first to supply the home with a purely American china product of quality. Mr. Tucker set to work, unaided and uneducated in the fine art of china's hidden mysteries, succeeding in perfecting a porcelain equal to the best which England had produced after more than eighty years of trial and error. (Mr. Tucker accomplished his task in only a few years.) His ware, which is collected today with unequaled zeal, resembles a hard porcelain. He created his work from new and untried materials. After Mr. Tucker's death in 1832 his work and methods were carried on by a partner, Judge Joseph Hemphill.

It is not known by this author if any children's ware was produced in Mr. Tucker's factory or in subsequent years by those who suceeded him; this material is included out of respect for the gentleman who began quality production in the field of china in America.

America was the stepchild when it came to producing china as far as the rest of the world was concerned. Writers have more or less neglected this country since nothing resembling porcelain was produced until Tucker's work in the late 1820's. In the little town of East Liverpool, Ohio, however, several of the twenty-nine potteries with their nine decorating works, managed to produce toy tea sets which are neither insignificant nor devoid of interest. East Liverpool is a pottery city and nearly half of its people are connected in some manner in the potting business. The workers have caused establishment of many potteries in every section of the nation.

In 1854 the works owned by the Knowles, Taylor, & Knowles Company was established in East Liverpool, Ohio. They started their business with yellow ware in a single kiln and added bisque and glost-ware and later they added Rockingham. In 1872 they produced ironstone china or white graniteware. Their vitreous-translucent china is found in this text. It is marked K., T. & K. vitreous.

CHINA

Other East Liverpool works are listed here to aid the collector:

Harker Pottery (Harker and Taylor)
C.C. Thompson Pottery Company (The C. C. T. P. Co.)
Laughlin Brothers
The Dresden Pottery Works of the Potters' Co-operative Co.
Industrial Pottery Works
The Standard Pottery Company
Messrs. Wallace & Chetwynd (Mr. Joseph Chetwynd was employed in a Staffordshire pottery in England prior to coming to America.)
Messrs. Rowe & Mountford
The American Pottery Works
Riverside Knob Manufacturing Co.
Burford Brothers
Burgess & Co.
J. W. Croxall & Sons (Successors to Croxall & Cartwright)
Eagle Pottery Works
Great Western Pottery Works (John Wyllie & Son)
Globe Pottery Co.
Novelty Pottery Works (McNicol, Burton & Co.)

The Centennial Exhibition in 1876 not only stirred the glass world in America, but set our potters to thinking as well, stimulating them to greater competition. The best productions of the nation were produced after the Centennial because of the exhibition of the world's best efforts which were displayed next to our modest accomplishments. Prominent American exhibitors at the Centennial Exhibition in 1876 were:

Empire China Works, Greenpoint, N.Y.
Issac Davis, Trenton, N.J.

Messrs. Yates, Bennett, & Allen, Trenton, N.J.
Brunt, Bloor, Martin, & Co., East Liverpool, Ohio
American Crockery Co., N.J.

Key To Using The China Section:

TITLE - Most china sets were not factory named; to aid the collector and dealer, a descriptive title has been given
SERIES - The china section has been divided into four categories: ANIMALS; PEOPLE; FLOWERS AND FANCY TRIMS; RHYMES, JINGLES AND TALES (the name of the series appears under the descriptive title)
PERTINENT DATA - Includes: identical blanks, known pattern pieces, point of origin, date, classification and features attributable to the set
    Identical blanks--if the word "none" appears, this indicates that the author (who has not seen everything) has not found identical blanks with different decorative treatment to include in this text
    Known pattern pieces--tea, coffee and chocolate sets usually had from four to six settings; dinner sets, chowder and fish and fowl sets had from six to twelve settings plus additional serving pieces
    Point of origin--a country is given if it is known, as well as any company information and markings.
    Date--a date is given when possible
    Classification--all toy china is difficult to locate-some being harder to find than others
    Features attributable to the set--this section is meant to aid the picture
MEASUREMENTS - Sizes are given when possible; sets and pieces will naturally vary to some degree in size
COMMENT - This section is meant to clarify a point and to give added bits of interesting information

AMERICAN KITTENS AND CHARIOT
(Animal Series)

PERTINENT DATA:

Identical blanks: None; same decals on German set
Known pattern pieces: Large dinner set for children
Point of origin: W.K.C. Co., East Liverpool, Ohio
Date: Circa 1900
Classification: Rare
Features attributable to pattern: Gold roping tied with a bow; kittens in a chariot, in a boat and in a wheelbarrow

MEASUREMENTS:

Tea pot	4 1/8" tall
Creamer	3 5/8" tall
Sugar	3 7/8" tall
Cup	2" tall
Saucer	5" across
Dinner plate	7¼" across
Fruit dish	5 3/8" across
Butter pat	3 3/8" across
Oval server	5½" long

Small platter	7 3/8'' long
Large platter	9 5/8'' long
Tureen	9'' handle to handle

CAT TEACHING THE RABBITS
(Animal Series)

PERTINENT DATA:

Identical blanks: None
Known pattern pieces: Tea and dinner set
Point of origin: America (Knowles, Taylor & Knowles Co., East Liverpool, Ohio)
Date: Circa 1890
Classification: Difficult to complete
Features attributable to the set: Dressed cat reading to bunnies with a switch in one hand and a book in the other; children
Color: Variety of vivid colors on white, crazed blank

MEASUREMENTS:

Tea pot	4-1/8'' tall
Creamer	2¼'' tall
Sugar	3¼'' tall
Cup	2¼'' tall
Saucer	4½'' across
Plate	6'' across
Oval vegetable dish	6'' long
Platter	8'' long

COMMENT:

This semi-vitreous porcelain is marked K.T. & K S-V (See color plate).

DOG AND CAT IN THE CREAM PITCHERS
(Animal Series)

PERTINENT DATA:

Identical blanks: "Bridesmaid"; "Germany Houses"; "Gold Flowers"
Known pattern pieces: Tea set and mug
Point of origin: Germany
Date: Late 1800's
Classification: Available
Features attributable to the set: Cat in pitcher that says "Forget Me Not"; dog in pitcher that says "Think of Me"

MEASUREMENTS:

Tea pot	5¼''
Creamer	3½''
Sugar	2¾''
Cup	2½''
Saucer	4¾''
Plate	6½''

COMMENTS:

The measurements are the same for the "Bridesmaid" set and the set showing thatched homes in Germany.

DRESSED ANIMALS AND VERSES
(Animal Series)

PERTINENT DATA:

Identical blanks: "Easter"; "Kittens And Puppies"; "Carts And Sled" (handle variations on the cups)
Known pattern pieces: Tea set
Point of origin: Germany
Date: Late 1800's
Classification: Available
Features attributable to the set: Dressed animals and verses; other sets feature children
Color: Luster trim in various shades

MEASUREMENTS:

Tea pot	5¼" cat with a whip riding a dressed lion
Creamer	2½" strolling animal with a hoop
Sugar	3¼" elephants
Cup	2" repeated animal scenes
Saucer	4¼"
Plate	5¼" one animal giving another animal a hair cut

COMMENTS:

The "Easter" set consists of pictures of a chicken selling decorated eggs to a rabbit; a rabbit leading a lamb laden with baskets of colored eggs; an elf wiping his brow after loading a large egg on a wheelbarrow; a girl carrying a bunny in her apron. The sizes are the same as on the "Dressed Animals And Verses" set and the "Kittens And Puppies" set.

FISH
(Placed In Animal Series)

PERTINENT DATA:

Identical blanks: None
Known pattern pieces: Fourteen piece fish and game set
Point of origin: England (Empire Works, Stoke on Trent)
Date: Circa 1896
Classification: Very rare
Features attributable to the set: Six different fish represented including: pike, pickeral, trout, salmon

MEASUREMENTS:

Platter	6" wide x 12" long
Plates	5" across
Sauce boat	4½" long x 2" wide

COMMENTS:

This set was made in a smaller size and in other colors. In this photo, the transfers and the spatter type edges are in blue. The blue seems to "flow" on some pieces.

GROUP OF FIVE
(Placed In Animal Series)

138

PERTINENT DATA:

Identical blanks: "Water Hen", "Stag", "Apple Blossom", "Child And Dog", "Blue Leafy", "Punch And Judy"
Known pattern pieces: Tea sets
Point of origin: England (marked Hanley Staffordshire); also Allerton (Park Works, Longton, Staffordshire)
Date: Late 1800's
Classification: This blank is easier to find than those sets with other shapes
Features attributable to the set: "Water Hen" has a tea and coffee pot; "Stag" set comes in other shapes; "Child And Dog" found in other shapes

MEASUREMENTS:

Tea pot	5''
Creamer	3¼''
Sugar	4½''
Cup	2''
Saucer	4¼''
Plate	5''

COMMENTS:

These sets are found in brown, blue or rose. The "Punch And Judy" motif is found on this blank as well as others.

HUNTER AND DOG
(Animal Series)

PERTINENT DATA:

Identical blanks: None
Known pattern pieces: Tea set

Point of origin: Bavaria
Date: 1874-1944
Classification: Rare
Features attributable to the set: Hunter and dog

MEASUREMENTS:

Tea pot   6''
Other pieces not available for measurement.

JAPAN'S MICKEY MOUSE
(Animal Series)

PERTINENT DATA:

Identical blanks: Other Disney characters
Known pattern pieces: Tea set
Point of origin: Japan
Date: 1930's
Classification: Available
Features attributable to the set: Mickey Mouse;
luster trim

MEASUREMENTS:

Tea pot	3¾'' tall
Creamer	2'' tall
Sugar	2¾'' tall
Cup	1¼'' tall
Saucer	3¼'' across
Plate	3¾'' across

KITTENS IN A BOAT
(Animal Series)

KITTENS, PUPPIES, MUSICIANS
(Animal Series)

PERTINENT DATA:

Identical blanks: "Capering Elves" (with handle variations); "Roosevelt Bears" (without foliated scroll handles); "Santa On The Move"; "Industrious Maid"; "Girl, Dog, Chickens And Lambs"
Known pattern pieces: Tea sets
Point of origin: Germany
Date: Circa 1900
Classification: Difficult to complete with matching cup handles
Features attributable to the set: Kittens in a boat

MEASUREMENTS:

Tea pot	5-3/8" tall
Creamer	3" tall
Sugar	3" tall
Cup	2¼" tall
Saucer	4½" across
Plate	5¼" across

COMMENTS:

Some of the same pictures are found on the "American Cats In A Chariot" dinner set.

PERTINENT DATA:

Identical blanks: None
Known pattern pieces: Tea set
Point of origin: Germany (marked in black in a circle)
Date: Circa 1910
Classification: Difficult to find complete
Features attributable to the set: Kittens singing and playing instruments

MEASUREMENTS:

Tea pot	5½" tall
Creamer	3" tall
Sugar	3-5/8" tall
Cup	1¾" tall
Saucer	3¾" across (no picture)
Plate	5¼" across

PETER RABBIT
(Animal Series)

PERTINENT DATA:

Identical blanks: None
Known pattern pieces: Tea set
Point of origin: England
Date: 1981
Features attributable to the set: The rabbit family with the Peter Rabbit story written in parts on the set's pieces

MEASUREMENTS:

Tea pot	4½''
Creamer	2½'' tall
Sugar (open)	2½'' across
	1½'' tall
Cup	1½'' tall
Saucer	3¼'' across
Plate	4¼'' across

RABBIT PULLING A CART
(Animal Series)

PERTINENT DATA:

Identical blanks: None
Known pattern pieces: Complete dinner and tea sets
Point of origin: East Liverpool, Ohio (H.R. Wyllie marked on bases)
Date: 1900's
Classification: Difficult to find complete

Features attributable to the set: Rabbit pulling a cart filled with flowers and butterfly passengers

MEASUREMENTS:

Tea pot	3½'' tall, 7'' wide
Creamer	3'' tall, 4½'' wide
Sugar	3'' tall, 5½'' wide
Cup	2'' tall
Saucer	5'' across
Plate	6'' across
Fruit dish	5'' across
Round bowl	6'' across
Oval server	6-1/8'' long
Platter	9-5/8'' long
Tureen	9'' long handle to handle

ROOSEVELT BEARS
(Animal Series)

MEASUREMENTS:

Tea pot with
foliated handles   5-3/8″ tall
Creamer with
foliated handles   3″ tall
Sugar with
foliated handles   3-7/8″ tall
Cup   2¼″ tall
Saucer   4¼″ across
Plate   5¼″ across

COMMENTS:

The measurements for the "Roosevelt Bears" tea set without the foliated handles are given in the "Kittens In A Boat" text.

SINFUL PIGS
(Animal Series)

PERTINENT DATA:

Identical blanks: "Clown On Pig"
Known pattern pieces: Tea sets
Point of origin: Germany
Date: Circa 1910
Classification: All children's sets with bears are highly collectible and difficult to locate

PERTINENT DATA:

Identical blanks: None
Known pattern pieces: Tea set
Point of origin: Germany
Date: Late 1800's
Classification: Difficult to locate
Features attributable to the set: Pigs drinking beer, smoking, gambling; pink luster trim

MEASUREMENTS:

Tea pot	6'' tall
Creamer	3½'' tall
Sugar	3-7/8'' tall
Cup	2¼'' tall
Saucer	3¼'' across
Plate	5'' across

SPORTS MINDED BEARS
(Animal Series)

PERTINENT DATA:

Identical blanks: None
Known pattern pieces: Tea set
Point of origin: Unknown
Date: Circa early 1900's
Classification: Difficult to locate
Features attributable to the set: Bears playing, golf, baseball, and skating

MEASUREMENTS:

Tea pot	3¾'' tall
Creamer	2''
Open sugar	1½'' tall
Cup	1¾'' tall
Saucer	3¾'' across

SWAN ON THE LAKE
(Animal Series)

PERTINENT DATA:

Identical blanks: "Ducks"; "Pink Roses And Bands"
Known pattern pieces: Tea set; "Pink Roses And Bands" dinner set
Point of origin: Japan (Noritake)
Date: 1918-1930
Classification: Difficult to find
Features attributable to the set: Rich sunset colors; swan on the lake

144

MEASUREMENTS:

Tea pot	3¾'' tall
Creamer	2½'' tall
Sugar	3'' tall
Cup	1¼'' tall
Saucer	3¾'' across
Plate	4¼'' across
Platter	7'' long
Tureen	6'' long

COMMENTS:

The set "Swan On The Lake" is much more difficult to find than "Ducks" or "Pink Roses And Bands".

APPLE BLOSSOMS From Japan
(Flowers And Fancy Trims Series)

BIRDS AND FOLIAGE
(Flowers And Fancy Trim Series)

PERTINENT DATA:

Identical blanks: "Azalea"
Known pattern pieces: Tea set
Point of origin: Japan
Date: Circa 1930
Classification: Rare in "Azalea"; obtainable in other patterns on this blank
Features attributable to the set: Hand painted flowers
Color: Blue trim; pink flowers; gold accent

MEASUREMENTS:

Tea pot	3¼'' tall
Creamer	2'' tall
Sugar	2¾'' tall
Cup	1¼'' tall
Saucer	4'' across
Plate	4½'' across

PERTINENT DATA:

Identical blanks: None
Known pattern pieces: Tea set
Point of origin: England (marked J & RG) Staffordshire
Date: 1840
Classification: Rare
Features attributable to the set: Beautiful handles; squash blossom finial
Color: Brown on cream

MEASUREMENTS:

Tea pot	4'' tall
Creamer	2½'' tall
Sugar	3¾'' tall
Cup	1¾'' tall
Saucer	4½'' across
Plate	5'' across

BLUE BANDS
(Flowers And Fancy Trims Series)

PERTINENT DATA:

Identical blanks: None
Known pattern pieces: Tea set
Point of origin: Prussia
Date: 1870
Classification: Difficult to locate
Features attributable to the set: Sugar has grips instead of handles; typical Prussia finials and handles

MEASUREMENTS:

Tea pot	5¼'' tall
Creamer	3¾'' tall
Sugar	3¾'' tall
Cup	2'' tall
Saucer	4¼'' tall

BROWN-MAROON FLOWERS
(Flowers And Fancy Trims Series)

PERTINENT DATA:

Identical blanks: None
Known pattern pieces: Tea set
Point of origin: Unknown
Date: Unknown
Classification: Difficult to obtain
Features attributable to the set: Grips instead of sugar handle; unusual color combination on child's set

MEASUREMENTS:

Tea pot	4'' tall
Creamer	2½'' tall
Sugar	2½'' tall
Cup	1¼'' tall
Saucer	2¾'' across
Plate	3'' across

CASTLE STAFFORDSHIRE
(Flowers And Fancy Trims Series)

PERTINENT DATA:

Identical blanks: None
Known pattern pieces: Tea and dinner set
Point of origin: England
Date: Circa 1800
Classification: Very rare
Features attributable to the set: Cups without handles; short tipped spout; no handles or grips on sugar bowl; sipping saucer

MEASUREMENTS:

Tea pot	3½''tall
Creamer	2½''tall
Sugar	2¾'' tall
Cup	1½'' tall
Saucer	3¾'' across

CHOWDER
(Flowers And Fancy Trims Series)

PERTINENT DATA:

Identical blanks: None
Known pattern pieces: Chowder set
Point of origin: Unmarked
Date: Unknown

Classification: Difficult to locate
Features attributable to the set: Deep plates
Color: Cornflower blues and plum

MEASUREMENTS:

Three covered	
tureens	3'' tall
	5'' long
	3'' tall
	3½'' tall with attached plate
Sauce with	
attached plate	4½'' long
	1-7/8'' tall
Six plates	5'' across

CHRISTMAS HOLLY
(Flowers And Fancy Trims Series)

PERTINENT DATA:

Identical blanks: None, decals used on smaller blanks
Known pattern pieces: Tea set with serving bowls
Point of origin: England
Date: 1914
Classification: Rare
Features attributable to the set: Christmas Holly; open work on lattice bowls

MEASUREMENTS:

Tea pot	5½'' tall
	5½'' wide
Creamer	3'' tall
	3'' wide
Sugar	3½'' tall
	4½'' wide
Saucer	3-7/8'' across
Two bowls	1½'' x ½'' open lattice work around rim

MEASUREMENTS: (smaller set with variations; not shown in text)

Tea pot	3¾'' tall
Creamer	1¾'' tall
Sugar	1¾'' tall
Cup	1½'' tall
Saucer	2½'' across

CRUSADE
(Flowers And Fancy Trims Series)

PERTINENT DATA:

Identical blanks: "Chelsea"
Known pattern pieces: Tea set
Point of origin: England (marked CRUSADE B and A)
Date: Circa 1840
Classification: Rare
Features attributable to the set: Soft paste; green leaves

MEASUREMENTS:

Tea pot	4¾'' tall
Creamer	2¼'' tall
Sugar	3-3/8'' tall
Cup	1¾'' tall
Saucer	4½'' across
Plate	5'' across
Waste	2¾'' tall

COMMENTS:

The same blank was used for the very collectable "Chelsea" tea set, blue and white Grecian.

DAUPHINE'S WEDDING RING
(Flowers And Fancy Trims Series)

Identical blanks: "Pink And White Roses" (with mustard luster)
Known pattern pieces: Tea set
Point of origin: Germany
Date: 1910
Classification: Difficult to assemble
Features attributable to the set: Ruffle-footed main pieces; good gold band

MEASUREMENTS:

Tea pot	6-1/8'' tall
Creamer	3¼'' tall
Sugar	3-7/8'' tall
Cup	2¼'' tall
Saucer	4½'' across
Plate	5'' across

DAVENPORT MALTESE CROSS
(Flowers And Fancy Trim Series)

PERTINENT DATA:

Identical blanks: None
Known pattern pieces: Tea set
Point of origin: England (Davenport)
Date: 1860-73
Classification: Rare
Features attributable to the set: Comes in brown and in gray-green

MEASUREMENTS:

Tea pot	4½'' high
Creamer	3'' high
Sugar	4¼'' tall
Cup	1¾'' tall
Saucer	4½'' across
Waste bowl	2½'' tall
	3¾'' across

DE JEUNER
(Flowers And Fancy Trims Series)

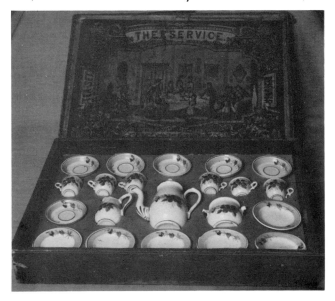

PERTINENT DATA:

Identical blanks: None

Known pattern pieces: Tea set
Point of origin: France
Date: 1880
Classification: Difficult to locate
Features attributable to the set: Three right handed cups and three left handed cups; violets with blue trim; pictured in original box

MEASUREMENTS:

Tea pot	5'' tall
Creamer	3'' tall
Sugar	3¼'' tall
Cup	1½'' tall
Saucer	3'' across
Plate	3½'' across

DELHI
(Flowers And Fancy Trim Series)

PERTINENT DATA:

Identical blanks: Not in this text
Known pattern pieces: Tea set
Point of origin: England
Date: Circa 1860
Classification: Difficult to obtain
Features attributable to the set: Brown and cream flowers

MEASUREMENTS:

Tea pot	4½'' tall
Creamer	2-5/8'' tall
Sugar	4¼'' tall
Cup	2'' tall
Saucer	5'' across
Plate	5-5/8'' across
Waste bowl	2½'' tall
	4'' wide

EGG SHELL
(Flowers And Fancy Trims)

PERTINENT DATA:

Identical blanks: None
Known pattern pieces: Tea set
Point of origin: Unknown
Date: Unknown
Classification: Rare
Features attributable to the set: Excellent quality; translucent; pastel flowers in relief; footed ware

MEASUREMENTS:

Tea pot	4-1/8'' tall
Creamer	2¼'' tall
Sugar	2-3/8'' tall
Cup	2'' tall
Saucer	4¼'' across

COMMENTS:

The tea set in the group photo is old and rare. The miniature egg creation is new. . .by Mar-Hil from Munster, Indiana.

ENAMELWARE
(Flowers And Fancy Trim Series)

PERTINENT DATA:

Identical blanks: None
Known pattern pieces: Large dinner set
Point of origin: Unknown
Date: Unknown
Classification: Difficult to assemble
Features attributable to the set: Red and green decoration with gold line trim

MEASUREMENTS:

Six plates	3½'' across
Six soups	3½'' across

Soup tureen with	
lid	3-7/8'' across handles of base
	3½'' tall complete
Vegetable dish	4'' across handles; ladle is 6'' long
Oval platters	5¼'' x 3¼''
Round servers	5¼'' x 3¼''
Gravy boat	3½'' long, lip to handle
Center handled	
items	2-5/8'' long
	1½'' high

COMMENTS:

The turk's head mold is pictured at the right of the photograph. It is 3¼'' in diameter and is not a part of the dinner set.

ENGLISH COTTAGE
(Flowers And Fancy Trims Series)

PERTINENT DATA:

Identical blanks: None
Known pattern pieces: Tea set
Point of origin: England
Date: Late 1800's
Classification: Rare
Features attributable to the set: Shaped to fit the name

MEASUREMENTS:

Tea pot	3½'' tall
Creamer	1-7/8'' tall
Sugar	1-5/8'' tall
Rest of set unavailable	

FEATHERY FERNS
(Flowers And Fancy Trims Series)

PERTINENT DATA:

Identical blanks: None
Known pattern pieces: Tea service
Point of origin: S.P. Co. (two lions holding a crown)
Date: Unknown

Classification: Blank available with different decorations
Features attributable to the set: Ironstone china
Color: Green on white

MEASUREMENTS:

Tea pot	5-3/8'' tall
Creamer	3½'' tall
Sugar	4¾'' tall
Cup	2-1/8'' tall
Saucer	4½'' tall
Plate	4½'' tall

FLOWER POTS
(Flowers And Fancy Trims Series)

PERTINENT DATA:

Identical blanks: None
Known pattern pieces: Tea set; baking series
Point of origin: Japan
Date: Circa 1900-1930
Classification: Difficult to complete
Features attributable to the set: Batter pitchers and other unusual items for the toy kitchen such as the pancake warmer
Color: Caramel with bright flower pots

PHOTO CONTENTS:

(Front row)	Four piece canister set
(Row 2)	Covered dish, trivet, spade-shaped cake server, cake plate, rare pancake warmer
(Row 3)	Cookie box with reed handle, salt box, cookie basket with reed handle, chocolate pot, tea pot, syrup pitcher, batter pitcher (both on tray)

COMMENTS:

The toy reamer and mixing bowl are missing from the photo.

FLOWERS AND CARAMEL LUSTER
(Flowers And Fancy Trims Series)

PERTINENT DATA:

Identical blanks: None
Known pattern pieces: Tea set and dinner set
Point of origin: Japan
Date: Circa 1930
Classification: Available
Features attributable to the set: Caramel luster

MEASUREMENTS:

Tea pot	4¼'' tall
Creamer	2¼'' tall
Sugar	3'' tall
Cup	1½'' tall
Saucer	4'' tall
Plate	4½'' across
Vegetable	5-3/8'' long
Gravy	4-1/8'' long

FLOWERS AND VINES
(Flowers And Fancy Trims)

PERTINENT DATA:

Identical blanks: None
Known pattern pieces: Tea set
Point of origin: France
Date: 1830-1845
Classification: Rare
Features attributable to the set: Translucent porcelain with luster; flowing cobalt blue leaves; orange-red berries

MEASUREMENTS:

Tea pot	3-7/8'' tall
Creamer	3¼'' tall
Sugar	3¼'' tall
Cup	1¾'' tall
Saucer	3¼'' across
Waste	1½'' tall
	3'' across

PERTINENT DATA:

Identical blanks: "Floral Rust And Tan"; "Kate Greenaway"
Known pattern pieces: Tea set
Point of origin: England
Date: 1880
Classification: Available
Features attributable to the set: Delicate flowers and leaves

Color: Tan, brown, cream

MEASUREMENTS:

Tea pot	4½'' tall
Creamer	2¾'' tall
Sugar	3¼'' tall
Cup	2'' tall
Saucer	4¾'' across

FLOWING BLUE AND BERRIES
(Flowers And Fancy Trims Series)

GAUDY STAFFORDSHIRE (Dahlia)
(Flowers And Fancy Trims Series)

PERTINENT DATA:

Identical blanks: "Little Mae"; "Girl With Dog"; "Punch And Judy"; "Stag"; "Water Hen"; "Goat"; "Persian"; "Crescent"; "Wagon Wheel"; "Tulip"; "Oyster"; "Stick Spatter" series; "All Over Spatter"
Known pattern pieces: Tea set
Point of origin: England
Date: 1820-1860
Classification: Very rare
Features attributable to the set: Dahlia flower with flowing blue style and luster trim

MEASUREMENTS:

Tea pot	5'' tall
Creamer	3'' tall
Sugar	4-3/8'' tall
Cup	2'' tall
Saucer	4-5/8'' across
Plate	5½'' across

COMMENTS:

Gaudy Staffordshire is the correct category for the "Dahlia" set because Gaudy Dutch has no luster trim; Gaudy Welsh was translucent porcelain; and Gaudy Ironstone was too heavy a ware. The blank was a typical Staffordshire shape and happened to be used in many tea sets for children.

GOLD AND ORANGE BUDS
(Flowers And Fancy Trims Series)

PERTINENT DATA:

> **Identical blanks:** None
> **Known pattern pieces:** Tea sets
> **Point of origin:** France
> **Date:** Circa 1890
> **Classification:** Difficult to locate in original box
> **Features attributable to the set:** Poor quality; hand painted; gold trim; crooked shapes; interesting boxes

MEASUREMENTS:

Tea pot	3½'' tall
Creamer	2½'' tall
Sugar	2-7/8'' tall
Cup	1½'' tall
Saucer	3¼'' across
Plate	3¼'' across

GOLD CORN DECORATION
ON WHITE
(Flowers And Fancy Trims Series)

PERTINENT DATA:

> **Identical blanks:** None
> **Known pattern pieces:** Coffee set
> **Point of origin:** Possibly American
> **Date:** Unknown
> **Classification:** Difficult to locate
> **Features attributable to the set:** Leaf-shaped saucers; grain and corn motif on a baroque-style blank

MEASUREMENTS:

Coffee pot	6'' tall
Creamer	3'' tall
Sugar	3¼'' tall
Cup	2'' tall
Saucer	4¾'' across

GOLD FLOWERS ON WHITE
(Flowers And Fancy Trims Series)

PERTINENT DATA:

> **Identical blanks:** None
> **Known pattern pieces:** Chowder set
> **Point of origin:** England
> **Date:** Unknown
> **Classification:** Difficult to assemble
> **Features attributable to the set:** Delicate flowers with gold enhancement

MEASUREMENTS:

Tureen	4'' (has a matching ladle)
Sauce	3¼'' long
	1¼'' tall
Deep plates	3½'' across
Double dip	2½'' long
	1'' tall (original spoon)
Bread plate	5¼'' across

GOLD TEA LEAF
(Flowers And Fancy Trims Series)

PERTINENT DATA:

> **Identical blanks:** None

152

Known pattern pieces: Tea set
Point of origin: Mellor, Taylor & Co. (marked warranted stone china; crown and four squares)
Date: 1880-1904
Classification: Rare
Features attributable to the set: Gold tea leaf on ironstone

MEASUREMENTS:

Tea pot	5-5/8'' tall
Creamer	3½'' tall
Sugar	5¼'' tall
Cup	2¼'' tall
Saucer	4½'' across
Plate	5'' across
Waste	2'' tall
	3'' across

GRAY WITH BLUE LEAVES
(Flowers And Fancy Trims Series)

PERTINENT DATA:

Identical blanks: None
Known pattern pieces: Tea set
Point of origin: Unknown
Date: Circa 1800
Classification: Rare
Features attributable to the set: Soft paste; cups without handles

MEASUREMENTS:

Tea pot	4¼'' tall
Sugar (open)	1¾'' tall
	2¼'' wide
Cup	1½'' tall
	2¼'' across
Saucer	1'' tall
	3¾'' across

LAVENDER AND RED
(Flowers And Fancy Trims Series)

PERTINENT DATA:

Identical blanks: None

Known pattern pieces: Tea set
Point of origin: France
Date: Circa 1900
Classification: Difficult to complete in tact
Features attributable to the set: Poorly made; thin body

Color: Lavender and red

MEASUREMENTS:

Tea pot	3'' tall
Creamer	1-7/8'' tall
Sugar	2½'' tall
Cup	1½'' tall
Saucer	2¼'' across
Plate	2½'' across
Cake plates	4½'' handle to handle

LEA FLOWER
(Flower And Fancy Trims Series)

PERTINENT DATA:

Identical blanks: Adult set is identical
Known pattern pieces: Tea and dinner set
Point of origin: England
Date: 1840
Classification: Very rare
Features attributable to pattern: Original name on bases; dimity type motif; no sugar handles

Color: Blue and white

MEASUREMENTS:

Tea pot	4¼'' tall
Creamer	unavailable
Sugar	3-5/8'' tall
Cup	1½'' tall
Saucer	4½'' across
Plate	4-7/8'' across

Waste bowl	4¼'' across
	2½'' tall
Platters	5¼'' long, 5¾'' long, 4¼'' long,
	6½'' long
Serving bowl	3½'' across
	2'' high
Large tureen	4-5/8'' tall
	5-7/8'' long
Covered tureen	3-5/8'' tall
	4'' long
Covered	
vegetable	3'' tall

LILAC AND BEGONIA
(Flowers And Fancy Trims Series)

PERTINENT DATA:

Identical blanks: None
Known pattern pieces: Tea set
Point of origin: Germany
Date: Late 1800's
Classification: Obtainable
Features attributable to the set: Over blown, lusty flowers

MEASUREMENTS:

Tea pot	5½'' tall
Creamer	3½'' tall
Sugar	3¼'' tall
Cup	1¾'' tall
Saucer	4-1/8'' across
Plate	5¼'' across

LITTLE PINKS
(Flowers And Fancy Trims Series)

PERTINENT DATA:

Identical blanks: None
Known pattern pieces: Tea set
Point of origin: England
Date: Unknown
Classification: Difficult to assemble

Features attributable to the set: All over "little pinks" with fern type leaves; bud finials

MEASUREMENTS:

Tea pot	5½'' tall
Creamer	3½'' tall
Cup	2'' tall
Plate	5'' across

MAJOLICA
(Flowers And Fancy Trims Series)

PERTINENT DATA:

Identical blanks: None
Known pattern pieces: Tea set
Point of origin: Italy
Date: Eighteenth century
Classification: Very rare
Features attributable to the set: Tin enameled glaze; blue, gray, green leaves with pink interior; handleless cups; probably oldest set in this publication

MEASUREMENTS:

Tea pot	3'' tall
Creamer	1¾'' tall
Sugar	2¾'' tall
Cup	1'' tall
Saucer	2½'' across
Plate	2¾'' across

MEISSEN STYLE
(Flowers And Fancy Trims Series)

PERTINENT DATA:

Identical blanks: None
Known pattern pieces: Tea set
Point of origin: Germany
Date: Circa 1894
Features attributable to the set: Delicate translucent ware in blue and white

154

MEASUREMENTS:

Tea pot	2¾'' tall
Creamer	1¾'' tall
Sugar	2¼'' tall
Cup	1½'' tall
Saucer	2½'' across
Plate	unavailable
Waste bowl	1'' tall

NIEMAN-MARCUS
(Flowers And Fancy Trims Series)

PERTINENT DATA:

Identical blanks: The ''Leaf'' design and the ''Pink Roses'' design are the second and third designs for the Nieman-Marcus (store) blank; also bought in plain blank

Known pattern pieces: Tea sets

Point of origin: England

Date: Circa 1976; 1977

Classification: Difficult to obtain

Features attributable to the set: Autumn tones on the ''Leaf'' set; ''Pink Roses'' design

MEASUREMENTS:

Tea pot	6'' tall
Creamer	3'' tall
Sugar	3¼'' tall
Cup	1½'' tall
Saucer	4¼'' across

OLD MOSS ROSE
(Flowers And Fancy Trims Series)

PERTINENT DATA:

Identical blanks: None in this publication; sets are available plain and with other decorations

Known pattern pieces: Tea set

Point of origin: America and abroad; this set, Knowles, Taylor and Knowles

Date: Circa 1886

Classification: Obtainable

Features attributable to the set: Ironstone china; different finials on sugar and tea pot

MEASUREMENTS:

Tea pot	5¼'' tall
Creamer	3½'' tall
Sugar	4-1/8'' tall
Cup	2½'' tall
Saucer	4¼'' across
Plate	4½'' across

OLD PARIS
(Flowers And Fancy Trims Series)

PERTINENT DATA:

Identical blanks: None

Known pattern pieces: Tea service with strainer

Point of origin: France

Date: Made in the 18th and 19th centuries

Classification: Very rare

Features attributable to the set: Cobalt handle, finial and flowers; gold

enhancement; toy
china tea strainer
with the set; hand
painted

MEASUREMENTS:

Tea pot	6'' tall
Creamer	4'' tall
Sugar	4'' tall
Cup	2¼'' dia.
	2'' high
Saucer	4¾'' dia.
Plates	4½'' dia.
Cookie plates	6'' dia.
Tea strainer	1¾'' dia.

ORANGE POPPIES
(Flowers And Fancy Trims Series)

PERTINENT DATA:

Identical blanks: None
Known pattern pieces: Two pot sizes; tea set
Point of origin: Unknown
Date: Unknown
Classification: Difficult to obtain
Features attributable to the set: Soft paste body

MEASUREMENTS:

Coffee pot	6½'' tall
Tea pot	4½'' tall
Creamer	3-1/8'' tall
Sugar	2¾'' tall
Cup	2'' tall
Saucer	3½'' wide
Plate	3½'' wide

OYSTER STEW SET
(Flowers And Fancy Trims Series)

PERTINENT DATA:

Identical blanks: Known with pink luster trim
Known pattern pieces: Thirteen piece oyster set
Point of origin: Unknown
Date: Unknown
Classification: Difficult to assemble
Features attributable to the set: Unusual serving
pieces and set's
function
Color: Blue trim on white blank

MEASUREMENTS:

Stew pot	5-1/8'' handle to handle
	3¼'' tall
Serving piece	2½'' x 2-3/8'' x 7/8'' tall
Platter	4-5/8'' x 3-1/8'' x 5/8'' tall
Server	3'' diam. x 7/8'' tall
Double dip	2-3/8'' long
Sauce boat	2½'' x 1-5/8'' x 1-1/8'' tall
Plates	3-1/8'' in dia.

PAULA
(Flowers And Fancy Trims Series)

PERTINENT DATA:

Identical blanks: None in this publication
Known pattern pieces: Tea set
Point of origin: Germany (Villeroy & Boch [V&B])
Date: Circa 1870
Classification: Obtainable
Features attributable to pattern: Blurred, delicate
flower pattern in old
blue

MEASUREMENTS:

Tea pot	5¼'' tall
Creamer	3½'' tall
Sugar	4½'' tall
Cup	2¼'' tall
Saucer	4½'' across
Plate	5'' across

PEACH AND PINK ROSES
(Flowers And Fancy Trims Series)

PERTINENT DATA:

Identical blanks: None

Known pattern pieces: Tea set
Point of origin: Germany
Date: Circa 1900
Classification: Difficult to assemble
Features attributable to the set: Pink roses; unusual handles; sloped finials

MEASUREMENTS:

Tea pot	6-1/8'' tall
Creamer	3¼'' tall
Sugar	4'' tall

Rest of the set unavailable

PERIWINKLE ENAMELWARE
(Flowers And Fancy Trims Series)

PERTINENT DATA:

Identical blanks: None
Known pattern pieces: Tea set
Point of origin: Europe
Date: Circa 1880's
Classification: Difficult to obtain
Features attributable to the set: White bow design on periwinkle colored enamelware

MEASUREMENTS:

Tea pot	5½'' tall
Creamer	2½'' tall
Sugar	1½'' (open and on a standard)
Cup	2'' tall
Saucer	4'' across

PETITE WHITE WITH GOLD TRIM
(Flowers And Fancy Trims Series)

PERTINENT DATA:

Identical blanks: None

Known pattern pieces: Tea set
Point of origin: Germany
Date: Unknown
Classification: Difficult to complete
Features attributable to the set: Interesting shape; fancy handles and finials

MEASUREMENTS:

Tea pot	4½'' tall	
Creamer	3'' tall	
Sugar	3'' tall	
Cup	1½'' tall	
	2'' across	
Saucer	3½'' across	

PINK CHINTZ
(Flowers And Fancy Trims Series)

PERTINENT DATA:

Identical blanks: ''Maidenhair Fern'' (green)
Known pattern pieces: Tea set
Point of origin: England (Ridgway)
Date: 1881
Classification: Difficult to obtain
Features attributable to the set: ''Pink Chintz'' has butterflies, flowers and ferns in the busy design; ''Maidenhair Fern'' has a ginkgo leaf appearance

MEASUREMENTS:

Tea pot	3-1/8'' tall
Creamer	2'' tall
Sugar	2-5/8'' tall
Cup	1¾'' tall
Saucer	3½'' across
Plate	4½'' across
Waste bowl	3¼'' across

PINK, GOLD AND BLACK BANDED
(Flowers And Fancy Trims Series)

PERTINENT DATA:

Identical blanks: None
Known pattern pieces: Dinner set
Point of origin: England
Date: 1890
Classification: Difficult to assemble
Features attributable to the set: Pink and white bands outlined with black bands

MEASUREMENTS:

Three covered pieces	4½'' tall
	3'' tall
	3½'' tall
Open sauce with plate	6'' long
	3'' at tallest point
Compote	2'' tall
	3¾'' across
Nest of platters	7-7/8'' long
	5-5/8'' long
	4¾'' long
Soups	4¾'' across
Plate	4¾'' across
Plate	4½'' across

PINK SPRING
(Flowers And Fancy Trims Series)

PERTINENT DATA:

Identical blanks: None
Known pattern pieces: Tea set
Point of origin: Germany
Date: Circa 1880-1900

Classification: Difficult to locate
Features attributable to pattern: Daisy pattern on spring pinks and blues; gold trim; delicate and fine

MEASUREMENTS:

Tea pot	6'' tall
Creamer	3½'' tall
Sugar	3½'' tall
Cup	2'' tall
Saucer	4¼'' across
Plate	4½'' across

R.S. PRUSSIA
(Flowers And Fancy Trims Series)

''Green And Yellow Luster'' (pink roses, beading with gold trim)

MEASUREMENTS:

Tea pot	5'' tall
Creamer	2¼'' tall
Sugar	3'' tall
Cup	1¾'' tall
Saucer	3¾'' across

"Twig Finials"

MEASUREMENTS:

Tea pot	5½'' tall
Creamer	3'' tall
Sugar	3-3/8'' tall
Cup	2'' tall
Saucer	4¼'' across
Plate	4½'' across

"Prussia Poppies"

MEASUREMENTS:

Tea pot	4-7/8'' tall
Creamer	2¼'' tall
Sugar	2-7/8'' tall
Cup	1¾'' tall
Saucer	3¾'' across

R.S. Prussia "Blue Luster With Pink And White Roses"

MEASUREMENTS:

Tea pot	4¾'' tall
Creamer	2¼'' tall
Sugar	2¾'' tall
Cup	1¾'' tall
Saucer	3¾'' across

R.S. Prussia (red mark) "Baby Red Roses With Gold Draping"

MEASUREMENTS:

Tea pot	4'' tall
Creamer	2½'' tall
Sugar	2¾'' tall
Cup	1-1/8'' tall
Saucer	3'' across
Plate	3'' across

R.S. Prussia "Cream And Tan Roses" (like the red marked Baby Roses set, without the red mark)

COMMENTS:

There are at least four differently decorated treatments for the same blank. (Baby Red Roses and Cream And Tan Roses.) Only one set, so far, has been marked with the red mark.

R.S. Prussia "Four Seasons" (see color plate)

MEASUREMENTS:

Tea pot	6'' tall
Creamer	3½'' tall
Sugar	3½'' tall
Cup	2'' tall
Saucer	4¼'' across
Plate	5½'' across

R.S. Prussia "Petite" (see color plate)

MEASUREMENTS:

Tea pot	4'' tall
Creamer	2'' tall
Sugar	2¼'' tall
Cup	1½'' tall
Saucer	3'' wide

RED ROSES PETITE
(Flowers And Fancy Trims Series)

PERTINENT DATA:

Identical blanks: None
Known pattern pieces: Tea set
Point of origin: Unknown
Date: Unknown
Classification: Difficult to complete
Features attributable to the set: Delicate panels with petite roses; gold trim; medallion face handles on sugar

MEASUREMENTS:

Tea pot	2¾'' tall
Creamer	2¾'' tall
Sugar	3'' tall
Cup	1'' tall
Saucer	½'' across
Plate	2-7/8'' across

SHAGGY ASTERS
(Flowers And Fancy Trims Series)

PERTINENT DATA:

Identical blanks: None
Known pattern pieces: Tea set
Point of origin: Austria (Crown Imperial Victoria; Carlsbad Austria; Porcelain Factory Victoria)
Date: After 1900-1918
Classification: Difficult to locate

Features attributable to the set: Purple asters; crabstock handles; odd shaped saucer; tea pot lid bell pepper shape; all pieces are pleated

MEASUREMENTS:

Tea pot	4'' tall
Creamer	2-3/8'' tall
Sugar	unavailable
Cup	1¾'' tall
Saucer	4-1/8'' across

SPATTER TEA POTS
(Flowers And Fancy Trims Series)

PERTINENT DATA:

Identical blanks: Used with various decorations
Known pattern pieces: Tea and coffee sets
Point of origin: England (Allerton)
Date: 1859
Classification: Very difficult to obtain
Features attributable to the set: Decorations were accomplished by using a sponge, a brush end, a cloth or a stick dabbed into paint and then applied to the soft paste pottery

PLACEMENT IN COLOR PLATE:

Back row: Three tea pots, 5'' tall
Middle row: Two tea pots, 5'' tall
Front row left to right: Bulge-bottomed tea pot, 5-1/8'' tall; small red and green pot (unmarked), 3½'' tall; red and green (bud finial) tea pot, 5'' tall

COMMENTS:

Eight stick spatter tea pots were taken from their complete sets to show some of the variations in color, shape and design placement. All tea pots in this photo are Allerton with the exception of the two with red and green designs; those are unmarked.

STAFFORDSHIRE CHOWDER
(Flowers And Fancy Trims Series)

PERTINENT DATA:

Identical blanks: None

Known pattern pieces: Tea set; possible dinner set
Point of origin: England
Date: Circa 1880
Classification: Rare
Features attributable to the set: Bands of rose designs; matched ladle

MEASUREMENTS:

Tureen	5'' tall
Under plate for tureen	5'' across
Bowls	4½'' across
Ladle	4½'' long

"Blue And White" (with gold trim)

MEASUREMENTS:

Tea pot	2'' tall
Creamer	1'' tall
Sugar	1½'' tall
Cup	½'' tall
Saucer	1¼'' across
Tray	4¼'' long
	3¼'' wide

TETE-A-TETE SERIES
(Flowers And Fancy Trims Series)

"Pink Rose Buds" (with gold trim)

MEASUREMENTS:

Tea pot	3'' tall
Creamer	2½'' tall
Sugar	3'' tall
Cup	1'' tall
Saucer	2¾'' across
Square tray	5½'' x 5½''

"Japanese Dragons" (gray, blue, white)

MEASUREMENTS:

Tea pot	5'' spout to handle
Sugar	2'' handle to handle
Cup	1'' tall
Saucer	2'' across
Tray	5'' across

"Gold And Roses"

MEASUREMENTS:

Tea pot	2'' tall
Creamer	1-1/8'' tall
Sugar	1'' tall (missing lid)
Cup	7/8'' tall
Saucer	1½'' across
Tray	7'' long
	4'' wide

"Shell" (blue, pink, yellow)

MEASUREMENTS:

Tea pot	4'' tall
Creamer	2¼'' tall
Sugar	3'' tall
Cup	1½'' tall
Saucer	4'' across
Tray	9½'' dia.

THEE SERVICE
(Flowers And Fancy Trims Series)

PERTINENT DATA:

Identical blanks: None in this book
Known pattern pieces: Tea set with matching cloth and napkins
Point of origin: France
Date: 1890
Classification: Difficult to find in the box with the cloth and napkins
Features attributable to the set: Dusty pink flowers with hints of blue; cloth pinkish red checks

MEASUREMENTS:

Tea pot	2½'' tall
Creamer	2'' tall
Sugar	2'' tall
Cup	1¼'' tall
Saucer	2¼'' across
Small plate	2½'' across
Plate	3¼'' across
Napkin	2¾'' x 2¾''
Cloth	20'' long

THIMBLE TEA
(Flowers And Fancy Trims Series)

PERTINENT DATA:

Identical blanks: None

Known pattern pieces: Tea set
Point of origin: France
Date: Circa 1850
Classification: Rare
Features attributable to the set: Flowers on brown, gold and cream

MEASUREMENTS:

Tea pot	1'' tall
Creamer	¾'' tall
Sugar	1'' tall
Cup	½'' tall
Saucer	1¼'' across
Sewing box	¾'' tall
	1'' across

COMMENTS:

The photo of the French miniature tea set and sewing box brings to mind an old American custom called a "thimble tea". Ladies would gather at a friend's home to make a quilt or to sew for the needy. They would each bring a dish for the evening meal when the husbands would join them. During the day the ladies would enjoy a luncheon provided by the hostess with another small but elegant repast during the afternoon.

The tea set and sewing box are shown on a miniature "lazy Susan" made of maple. The sewing box is silk lined and has all the needed accoutrements. The lid of the box has a porcelain miniature painting.

TINY BLUE AND WHITE
(Flowers And Fancy Trims Series)

PERTINENT DATA:

Identical blanks: None
Known pattern pieces: Tea set
Point of origin: Possibly Germany
Date: Circa 1890
Classification: Difficult to assemble
Features attributable to the set: Shades of blue on white; translucent china; gold trim

MEASUREMENTS:

Tea pot	3¾'' tall
Creamer	3'' tall
Sugar	2¾'' tall
Cup	1¼'' tall
Saucer	3'' across

TREE IN A MEADOW
(Flowers And Fancy Trims Series)

PERTINENT DATA:

Identical blanks: None in this publication
Known pattern pieces: Tea set
Point of origin: Japan
Date: 1930
Classification: Rare if complete
Features attributable to the set: Rich dark colors; pastoral scene

MEASUREMENTS:

Tea pot	3¾'' tall
Creamer	2½'' tall
Sugar	3-1/8'' tall
Cup	1½'' tall
Saucer	3¾'' across
Plate	5¼'' across

TWO TONES RED
AND YELLOW ROSES
(Flowers And Fancy Trims Series)

PERTINENT DATA:

Identical blanks: None
Known pattern pieces: Tea set
Point of origin: Germany
Date: Circa 1900
Classification: Obtainable
Features attributable to the set: Roses and gold trim

MEASUREMENTS:

Tea pot	5'' tall
Creamer	3¼'' tall
Sugar	3¼'' tall
Cup	2'' tall
Saucer	4½'' across
Plate	5½'' across

VICTORIAN ROSES
(Flowers And Fancy Trims Series)

PERTINENT DATA:

Identical blanks: None
Known pattern pieces: Tea set
Point of origin: Germany
Date: Circa 1900-1910
Classification: Available
Features attributable to the set: Tea-cozy shape; warm design of rose bunches

MEASUREMENTS:

Tea pot	4'' tall
Creamer	3'' tall
Sugar	3'' tall
Cup	2¼'' tall
Saucer	4¾'' across
Plate	5'' across

VICTORIAN MAJOLICA
FRUIT AND DESSERT
(Flowers And Fancy Trims Series)

PERTINENT DATA:

Identical blanks: None
Known pattern pieces: Fruit and dessert set
Point of origin: England
Date: Circa 1851-1900
Classification: Very rare
Features attributable to the set: All over typical majolica green

MEASUREMENTS:

Compote	3½'' tall
	5¼'' across
	6'' long
6 plates	4'' across
3 scoop-centered	
servers	4½'' long
	4'' across

COMMENTS:

Majolica is earthenware glazed with a tin oxide. In this case, however, this photo shows an example of Victorian majolica produced from 1851-1900 after the English Crystal Palace Exhibition of 1851. This lead glazed example was named ''majolica'' by the manufacturer but should not be confused with the tin glazed earlier example found in the color section of this book.

Moorish-inspired Spanish pottery was imported to Italy from the island of Majorca. Majolica became the name for the Italian, Dutch, and French tin-glazed earthenware of the sixteenth through the eighteenth centuries. Since tin was expensive the English and Americans produced earthenware glazed with lead. These products were vivid in color and unusual in shape.

WILLOW
(Flowers And Fancy Trims Series)

''Cantonese-Style Blue Willow''

MEASUREMENTS:

Tea pot	2¾'' tall
Creamer	1½'' tall
Sugar	1¾'' tall
Saucer	2¼'' tall
Plate	2-5/8'' tall

''Copeland Blue Willow''

MEASUREMENTS:

Tea pot	4''
Creamer	2¼'' tall
Open sugar	1¾'' tall
Cup	2'' tall
Saucer	5'' tall

''Red Willow With Double Pots'' (Ridgway's Tyrolean; W.R. & Co.)

MEASUREMENTS:

Tallest tea pot	5½'' tall	
	5'' wide	
Short tea pot	3'' tall	
	6½'' wide	
Creamer	2½'' tall	
	3¾'' wide	
Sugar	3'' tall	
	5½'' wide	

Creamer   3'' tall
Sugar   4¼'' tall
Cup   2'' tall
Saucer   4½'' across
Plate   5¼'' across and 5¾'' across

"Brown Willow Staffordshire"

MEASUREMENTS:

Tea pot   4¾'' tall
Creamer   3¼'' tall
Sugar   4¼'' tall
Cup   2¼'' tall
Saucer   4½'' across
Plate   5¾'' across
Waste bowl   2¼'' tall

"Rhone Staffordshire" (William Alsager Adderley;
1876-1885)

MEASUREMENTS:

Tea pot   4¾'' tall

JAPANESE BLUE WILLOW
    One of the most picturesque china patterns familiar to all
collectors is the "Willow" pattern. This design is universal and
still popular even though it has served the world for five cen-

165

turies. It has been selected, at least once, to serve as the official White House china, while most little American hostesses chose this pattern for their official play as well.

There is more to Japanese toy willow ware than first meets the eye. Unlike the East, Western tradition insists on matched table equipage--so Japan gave each tea-set-shape at least four different sizes. The dinner sets have been found, to date, in only three sizes, but the variety of pieces makes up the difference. There are berry and soup sets, tureens and gravy boats, divided "blue plate special" plates, vegetable bowls and platters, and open handled cake plates. The medium in which this pattern is found includes china, tin, and now plastic. One tin set is complete with a dome covered cake saver and matching tea tray. There are even coordinated table cloths and napkin sets to complete the niceties of play.

The slightly askew borders of this romantic motif are due to the method of application. The system was aptly named "transfer". The design was first engraved on copper, the grooves were filled with color and the copper was covered with tissue. The wet tissue was then transferred and pressed to the china. (Sadler and Green of Liverpool, England were credited with the invention of transfer-printing in 1756.)

The "Blue Willow" legend has been issued many times. Other traditional love stories, however, are seldom shared on table ware, making this a very unique soap-opera vehicle. (If "Dallas" is ever portrayed in this medium, we are indeed in for a dining adventure!)

AFTERNOON TEA
(People Series)

PERTINENT DATA:

Identical blanks: None
Known pattern pieces: Tea set
Point of origin: England
Date: 1850
Classification: Rare
Features attributable to the set: Ladies having tea
Color: Mulberry shade, green, blue, brown

Measurements not available.

AMERICAN KATE GREENAWAY
(People Series)

PERTINENT DATA:

Identical blanks: None
Known pattern pieces: Tea set
Point of origin: America
Date: Circa 1900
Classification: Difficult to complete
Features attributable to the set: Willowy girls with fruit, under trees and talking

Color: Salmon, green, cream

MEASUREMENTS:

Tea pot	5" tall
Creamer	3" tall
Sugar	4" tall
Cup	2½" tall
Saucer	5¼" across
Plate	6-5/8" across

BAYREUTH CHILDREN
(People Series)

PERTINENT DATA:

Identical blanks: "Sunbonnet Babies"; "Beach Or

Sand Babies''; ''Sledding Babies'';
''Billowy Girl''; ''Boy With Geese
And Donkey''
Known pattern pieces: Tea set
Point of origin: Royal Bayreuth, Bavaria, Germany
Date: 1914
Features attributable to the set: Children; unusual
''top'' positioned tea
pot handle
Color: Burnished gold, beach browns, hunter green,
distinctive ''Bayreuth'' colors

MEASUREMENTS:

Tea pot	5'' tall
Creamer	2¼'' tall
Sugar	3½'' tall
Cup	2¼'' tall
Saucer	4½'' across

COMMENTS:

The glaze on this set made hot spots in the photographs.
Different methods were used with the same results.
During 1914 Marshall Field & Company sold ''Kringle
Society'' (nine piece) tea sets for $17.00 per dozen. A6863 (Sand
Babies) sold for $30.00 per dozen.

BLACK AND WHITE STAFFORDSHIRE
(People Series)

PERTINENT DATA:

Identical blanks: None
Known pattern pieces: Tea set
Point of origin: England
Date: 1880
Classification: Rare
Features attributable to the set: Detailed black pic-
tures with interesting
accents

MEASUREMENTS:

Tea pot	5¾''
Creamer	2½'' tall
Sugar (open)	1½'' tall
Cup	2¼'' tall
Saucer	5'' across

BLOSSOM CHILDREN
(People Series)

167

BOY AND DOG
(People Series)

PERTINENT DATA:

    Identical blanks: "Southern Belles"
    Known pattern pieces: Tea set
    Point of origin: Germany
    Date: Circa 1890
    Classification: Difficult to locate
    Features attributable to the set: Children wearing flowers; one girl with a "flowerbrella"

MEASUREMENTS:

Tea pot	6" tall
Creamer	3½" tall
Sugar	3¾" tall
Cup	2" tall
Saucer	4½" across
Plate	5¼" across

168

PERTINENT DATA:

Identical blanks: "Titles Rhymes" (cup difference)
Known pattern pieces: Tea set
Point of origin: Germany
Date: 1880
Classification: Difficult to locate
Features attributable to the set: Scroll work on saucers; beading on saucers; girl feeding a flock of birds; boy feeding ducks; dog with a book in its mouth

Color: Pastels

MEASUREMENTS:

Tea pot	5" tall
Creamer	3½" tall
Sugar	3" tall
Cup	2-3/8" tall and 2¾" tall
Saucer	4¼" across
Plate	5" across

BOY AND SWANS
(People Series)

PERTINENT DATA:

Identical blanks: None
Known pattern pieces: Tea set
Point of origin: Germany
Date: Circa 1890
Classification: Difficult to locate
Features attributable to the set: Beaded trim; line incised rays on bases; gold line trim; crooked decals

Color: Pastel decals on white

MEASUREMENTS:

Tea pot	6-3/8" tall
Creamer	2½" tall
Sugar	4" tall
Cup	2-3/8" tall
Saucer	4-5/8" across

BOY ON A BENCH AND FRIENDS
(People Series)

BUSTER BROWN
(People Series)

PERTINENT DATA:

Identical blanks: "Turkeys And Children"; "Lemon
And Green Luster"
Known pattern pieces: Tea set
Point of origin: Germany
Date: Late 1800's
Classification: Difficult to locate
Features attributable to the set: Sway finials;
children talking and
playing
Color: Richly colored decals on white

MEASUREMENTS:

Tea pot	5-7/8'' tall
Creamer	2½'' tall
Sugar	3-5/8'' tall
Cup	2'' tall
Saucer	4¼'' across
Plate	4¾'' across

PERTINENT DATA:

Identical blanks: "Lamb Pulling A Flower Cart"
Known pattern pieces: Tea set
Point of origin: Germany
Date: 1902-1910
Classification: Difficult to assemble
Features attributable to the set: Foliated scroll
handles; sugar bowl
in this text belongs
with another blank
Color: Typical Buster Brown shades

MEASUREMENTS:

Tea pot	6'' tall
Creamer	3'' tall
Sugar	3-5/8'' tall; 2-7/8'' tall different blank
Cup	2¾'' tall; 2½'' tall different blank
Plate	6¼'' across

BUSY DAY
(People Series)

PERTINENT DATA:

Identical blanks: "Clowns" (split handle variation)
Known pattern pieces: Tea set
Point of origin: Germany
Date: 1890
Classification: Difficult to find with dark decals
Features attributable to the set: Sandman on tea pot; daily activities shown on other pieces

Color: Pastel decals on white

MEASUREMENTS:

Tea pot	5½'' tall
Creamer	3¼'' tall
Sugar	3½'' tall
Cup	2'' tall
Saucer	4¼'' across
Plate	6'' across

BUSY GIRL
(People Series)

PERTINENT DATA:

Identical blanks: None; decals are the same as those found on "Industrious Maid"
Known pattern pieces: Tea set
Point of origin: Germany
Date: Circa 1900
Classification: Difficult to locate with short tea pot style
Features attributable to the set: Busy girl; green luster

Color: Green luster; pink dress

MEASUREMENTS:

Tea pot	4-3/8'' tall
Creamer	3'' tall
Sugar	3¼'' tall
Cup	2'' tall
Saucer	4¼'' across
Plate	5'' across

CHILDREN AND TOYS
(People Series)

PERTINENT DATA:

Identical blanks: None
Known pattern pieces: Tea set
Point of origin: Germany
Date: 1900
Classification: Difficult to complete
Features attributable to the set: Children; toys;
                                     animals
Color: Bright decals on white blanks

MEASUREMENTS:

Tea pot	5'' tall
Creamer	3'' tall
Sugar	3½'' tall
Cup	2'' tall
Saucer	4¼'' across
Plate	5¼'' across

CHILDREN AND WAR GAMES
(People Series)

PERTINENT DATA:

Identical blanks: "Children Sailing A Boat" (cups vary in size and shape when compared to "Children And War Games")
Known pattern pieces: Tea set
Point of origin: Germany (gray mark)
Date: 1890
Classification: Difficult to locate intact
Features attributable to the set: Foliated scroll handles

Color: Bright decals on white

MEASUREMENTS:

Tea pot	5-7/8" tall
Creamer	3" tall
Sugar	3-7/8" tall and one 4-1/8" tall
Cup	2" tall and one 2¼" tall
Saucer	4" across and one 4¼" across
Plate	none available for measurement

COMMENTS:

Some of the pictures on the "Children Sailing A Boat" are repeated on other tea sets in this publication.

CHILDREN AT THE TABLE
(People Series)

PERTINENT DATA:

    Identical blanks: ''Girl At The Piano''; ''Sandman''
    Known pattern pieces: Tea set
    Point of origin: Germany
    Date: Circa 1900
    Classification: Blank repeats are easily found, but with different decals, matching is difficult
    Features attributable to the set: All have children
    Color: ''Sandman'' set has very light decals on white; ''Children At The Table'' has rich, dark decals

MEASUREMENTS:

Tea pot	5¼'' tall
Creamer	2½'' tall
Sugar	3¼'' tall
Cup	2'' tall
Saucer	4¼'' across
Plate	5¼'' across

CHILDREN ON SLED
(People Series)

PERTINENT DATA:

    Identical blanks: ''Kissing''; ''Two Girls With Doll''; ''Fairy Tale Variety''
    Known pattern pieces: Tea set
    Point of origin: Germany
    Date: 1900's

Classification: Available
Features attributable to the set: Children playing, sledding, and creating friendships

Color: Luster and pastels

MEASUREMENTS:

Tea pot	6¼'' tall
Creamer	4'' tall
Sugar	4'' tall
Cup	2¼'' tall
Saucer	4½'' across
Plate	5¼'' across

CHILDREN PULLING SLED
(People Series)

PERTINENT DATA:

Identical blanks: None
Known pattern pieces: Tea set
Point of origin: Japan (Nippon)
Date: 1890-1915
Classification: Available
Features attributable to the set: Hand painted children

Color: Pastels

MEASUREMENTS:

Tea pot	3½'' tall
Creamer	2'' tall
Sugar	2¾'' tall
Cup	2'' tall
Saucer	3¾'' across
Plate	4¼'' across

CIRCUS AND CLOWN
(People Series)

PERTINENT DATA:

Identical blanks: None

Known pattern pieces: Tea set
Point of origin: Germany
Date: 1900-1910
Classification: Difficult to complete
Features attributable to the set: Vivid decals on white blank

MEASUREMENTS:

Tea pot	Unavailable for measurement
Creamer	3½'' tall
Sugar	3½'' tall
Cup	2'' tall
Saucer	4'' across (motif repeated on saucers)
Plate	5½'' across

DUTCH BOY AND GIRL
(People Series)

175

DUTCH CHILDREN ON WHITE
(People Series)

PERTINENT DATA:

Identical blanks: None
Known pattern pieces: Tea set
Point of origin: Holland
Date: Circa 1900
Classification: Difficult to locate
Features attributable to the set: Dutch children playing
Color: Sky blue, grass green, vivid red

MEASUREMENTS:

Tea pot	3½'' tall
	5¾'' wide
Creamer	3'' tall
	3½'' wide
Sugar	2¾'' tall
	4½'' wide
Cup	1¼'' tall
Plate	3¾'' across

FLOWER BOAT CHILDREN
(People Series)

PERTINENT DATA:

Identical blanks: "Girls With Bears"; "Yellow Roses With Purple Luster"; "Pink And White Leaved Caladium"
Known pattern pieces: Tea set
Point of origin: Germany
Date: Circa 1890
Classification: Difficult to locate
Features attributable to the set: Two boys and a girl; geese
Color: Vivid greens; splotches of luster; "Girl With Bears" has yellow and green luster

MEASUREMENTS:

Tea pot	6'' tall
Creamer	3½'' tall
Sugar	4'' tall
Cup	2-1/8'' tall
Saucer	4½'' across
Plate	5'' across

PERTINENT DATA:

Identical blanks: None
Known pattern pieces: Tea set
Point of origin: Germany
Date: 1890
Classification: Difficult to complete
Features attributable to the set: Boy poling the craft which is laden with flowers and girls
Color: Lovely shades of colors on a white blank

MEASUREMENTS:

Tea pot	5½'' tall
Creamer	3'' tall
Sugar	3¼'' tall
Cup	2'' tall
Saucer	4'' across
Plate	5¼'' across

GERMAN KITTENS AND CHARIOT
(Animal Series)

PERTINENT DATA:

Identical blanks: "Grandmother's Roses"
Known pattern pieces: Tea set
Point of origin: Germany
Date: 1900
Classification: Difficult to complete
Features attributable to the set: Kittens in a chariot pulled by cats

MEASUREMENTS:

Tea pot	6'' tall
Creamer	3½'' tall
Sugar	3½'' tall
Cup	2¼'' tall
Saucer	4¼'' across
Plate	5'' across

COMMENTS:

The decals on the set "German Kittens And Chariot" are also found on a dinner set which was made in America.

GIRL WITH A WHIP
(People Series)

PERTINENT DATA:

Identical blanks: "White Open Roses"
Known pattern pieces: Tea set
Point of origin: Germany
Date: Circa 1890
Classification: Difficult to assemble
Features attributable to the set: Bud type finials; children at play

Color: Pastels on white blank

MEASUREMENTS:

Tea pot	5½" tall
Creamer	3¼" tall
Sugar	3-3/8" tall
Cup	2" tall
Saucer	4" across
Plate	5¼" across

GOAT CART
(People Series)

PERTINENT DATA:

Identical blanks: None
Known pattern pieces: Tea set
Point of origin: Germany (red mark)
Date: Circa 1900

Classification: Available
Features attributable to the set: Goat; cart, children
Color: Bright decals; gold trim on a plain white blank

MEASUREMENTS:

Tea pot	5-1/8" tall
Creamer	2¾" tall
Sugar	2-5/8" tall
Cup	2" tall
Saucer	4½" across

HAVILAND
(People Series)

PERTINENT DATA:

Identical blanks: None
Known pattern pieces: Tea set
Point of origin: France
Date: 1881
Classification: Very rare
Features attributable to the set: Same group of children doing a variety of things
Color: All over powder blue with dark blue figures

MEASUREMENTS:

Tea pot	4½" tall
	7" wide
Creamer	3¼" tall
	4" wide
Sugar	4" tall
	5½" wide
Cup	2¼" tall
Saucer	4¾" across
Plate	4-7/8" across

COMMENTS:

This set has the green mark on the bases of the pieces, H & Co., 1881.

HAVING A RIDE
(People Series)

Cup	2″ tall
Saucer	4½″ across
Plate	4″ across

COMMENTS:

The children on the following sets are repeated on different blanks: "Having A Ride", "Two Girls With A Doll", "Children On A Sled" and "Kissing".

HUMPHREY'S CLOCK
(People Series)

PERTINENT DATA:

Identical blanks: None
Known pattern pieces: Tea and dinner sets
Point of origin: England (W.R.S. & Co. William Ridgway Co.; Church Works on Cobden Works; Staffordshire Potteries)
Date: 1841-1846
Classification: Very rare
Features attributable to the set: Outdoor scenes

MEASUREMENTS:

Tea pot	4½″ tall
Creamer	1¾″ tall
Sugar (open)	1½″
Cup	1¾″ tall

PERTINENT DATA:

Identical blanks: No identical blanks, just identical decals
Known pattern pieces: Tea set
Point of origin: Germany
Date: 1900's
Classification: Matching the blank rather than matching the decals is the problem with this series
Color: Clear colors on white blank with gold trim

MEASUREMENTS:

Tea pot	5¼″ tall
Creamer	2¾″ tall
Sugar	3″ tall

179

Saucer	4¼'' across
Small platters	5'' long
Large platter	7'' long
Small plates	4'' across
Large plates	4½'' across

Measurements not available for 2 sizes of tureens, gravy boat, covered server, and soup bowls.

KATE GREENAWAY STYLE
(People Series)

PERTINENT DATA:

Identical blanks: No
Known pattern pieces: Dinner set
Point of origin: Possibly American
Date: Circa 1900
Classification: Difficult to complete
Features attributable to the set: Hand painted Kate Greenaway style children; covered compote not shown in photo

MEASUREMENTS:

Plate	7½'' across
Fruit bowl	5'' across
Cup	2-5/8'' tall
Saucer	5¼'' across

COMMENTS:

This rather large child's dinner set features a girl sitting on a branch, a boy and girl with a kite, a girl pushing a child in a chair, a child with a hoop, a boy running, and a girl sitting on a fence.

KITE FLYERS
(People Series)

PERTINENT DATA:

Identical blanks: There is a white set with a blue band available using these blanks, but it is not shown in this publication
Known pattern pieces: Large number of pieces to a dinner set
Point of origin: England (transfer printing attributed to Sadler and Green, Liverpool)
Date: Circa 1800
Classification: Very rare
Features attributable to the set: Boy flying a kite with an adult male watching; boy rolling hoop

Color: Blue on white

MEASUREMENTS:

Platter	4'' long
Tureen	2½'' tall
	3'' long
Platter	4½'' long
Plate	2¾'' long
Plate	2½'' across
Plate	3½'' across
Open dish	2¾'' across
	1'' tall
Soup	3½'' across
Covered square	
dish	2¼'' tall
	3'' across
Gravy	1¼'' tall
	3'' long

COMMENTS:

Joyce Johnston loaned forty-nine pieces of this set for the book's photographs.

LITTLE MAE
(People Series)

PERTINENT DATA:

Identical blanks: Allerton blanks: ''Mae'' (girl in apron); ''Girl with Dog''; ''Punch and Judy''; ''Stag''; ''Water Hen''; ''Goat''; ''Persian'' (with fans, flowers and fish); ''Cresent'' (floral band); ''Gaudy Welsh'' (Wagon Wheel, Tulip, Oyster); ''Stick Spatter''; ''All Over Spatter''
Known pattern pieces: Tea set

Point of origin: England (Charles Allerton & Sons, Park Works, Longton, England)
Date: 1887-1890
Classification: Available
Features attributable to the set: Little Mae on the doorstep with a kitten in her lap in rose, blue, or brown

MEASUREMENTS:

Tea pot	5¼'' tall
Creamer	3¼'' tall
Sugar	4½'' tall
Cup	2'' tall
Saucer	4½'' across
Plate	5½'' across
Waste bowl	2½'' tall
	4'' across

LITTLE SCHOOL TEACHER
(People Series)

PERTINENT DATA:

Identical blanks: None
Known pattern pieces: Tea set
Point of origin: Germany (Altwasser Germany marked in green with flying horse and C.I.)
Date: 1910
Classification: Not easy to assemble
Features attributable to the set: Clear picture and vivid colors

MEASUREMENTS:

Tea pot	5-5/8'' tall
Creamer	2½'' tall
Open sugar	1¼'' tall
	3¼'' across
Cup	2½'' tall
Saucer	5'' across
Plate	unavailable for measurement

LITTLE WOMEN
(People Series)

181

PERTINENT DATA:

Identical blanks: None
Known pattern pieces: Tea set
Point of origin: Germany
Date: Late 1800's
Classification: Difficult to locate
Features attributable to the set: Unusual knobbed feet on the three main pieces; beaded trim; women passing plates and having tea

MEASUREMENTS:

Tea pot	5'' tall
Creamer	3'' tall
Sugar	3½'' tall
Cup	2-1/8'' tall
Saucer	4-5/8'' across
Plate	unavailable for photo

LUSTERED MERRY CHRISTMAS
(People Series)

PERTINENT DATA:

Identical blanks: None
Known pattern pieces: Tea set
Point of origin: Germany (Castle Tower, Lutchenberg)
Date: 1890
Classification: Rare
Features attributable to the set: "Merry Christmas" written in gold; children and Father Christmas
Color: Pink or green luster with gold accent

MEASUREMENTS:

Tea pot	4¾'' tall
Creamer	3'' tall
Sugar	3½'' tall
Cup	2'' tall
Saucer	4½'' across
Plate	6'' across

MERRY CHRISTMAS ANGEL
(People Series)

182

PERTINENT DATA:

Identical blanks: Original blank shown with "Merry Christmas Angel" in this text
Known pattern pieces: Tea set
Point of origin: Germany
Date: 1900
Classification: Rare
Features attributable to the set: Winter scene with angel, star and birds

Color: Winter blue, white, gold

MEASUREMENTS:

Tea pot	5-5/8'' tall
Creamer	2¼'' tall
Sugar	3½'' tall
Cup	2¼'' tall
Saucer	4¼'' across
Plate	6'' across

OLD FASHIONED GIRL AND DOG
(People Series)

PERTINENT DATA:

Identical blanks: "Gold Trimmed Pink Luster"
Known pattern pieces: Tea set, mugs
Point of origin: Germany
Date: 1890
Classification: Available
Features attributable to the set: Girls and dogs

MEASUREMENTS:

Tea pot	5¾'' tall
Creamer	3¼'' tall
Sugar	3¾'' tall
Cup	2'' tall
Saucer	4½'' across
Plate	5¾'' across

PRINCESS DRIVING A BIRD
(People Series)

PERTINENT DATA:

Identical blanks: "Ring Around The Rosy"
Known pattern pieces: Tea set
Point of origin: Germany (Franz Prause 'porcelain factory', N S Nieder-Salzorunn; Niedersulzbrunn Silesia Germany; presently Szczawienko, Poland)
Date: Circa 1900
Classification: Rare
Features attributable to the set: Girl driving bird; elf carrying large flower; crone with pointed hat; crow with ring in its beak
Color: Vivid pictures and gold trim on well made blank

MEASUREMENTS:

Tea pot	6'' tall
Creamer	3¼'' tall
Sugar	3-7/8'' tall
Cup	2¼'' tall
Saucer	4½'' across
Plate	5'' across

ROBINSON CRUSOE
(People Series)

PERTINENT DATA:

Identical blanks: None
Known pattern pieces: Tea set
Point of origin: Germany
Date: 1880's
Classification: Difficult to assemble in good condition
Features attributable to the set: Thin china, but not well made; each of the pieces has a picture telling the Robinson Crusoe story
Color: Splotchy dabs of gold, crooked decals having splashes of good color

MEASUREMENTS:

Tea pot	4-3/8'' tall
Creamer	2¾'' tall
Sugar	2¼'' tall
Cup	2'' tall
Saucer	3'' across
Plate	3-1/8'' across

ROSE O'NEILL KEWPIES
(People Series)

PERTINENT DATA:

Identical blanks: There are other Kewpie sets, this one has them in military helmets
Known pattern pieces: Tea set
Point of origin: Germany
Date: 1915
Classification: Very rare
Features attributable to the set: Kewpies with topknot wisps of hair
Color: Pastels with different colors of luster trim

MEASUREMENTS:

Tea pot	5¼'' tall
Creamer	2½'' tall
Sugar	unavailable for measurement
Cup	2'' tall
Saucer	4½'' across

ROYAL BAYREUTH NURSERY JINGLES
(People Series)

PERTINENT DATA:

Identical blanks: None
Known pattern pieces: Tea set
Point of origin: Germany (Kringle Society toys #A6860)
Date: 1914
Classification: Rare
Features attributable to the set: Mother Goose rhymes in colors and gold

Color: Brilliant

MEASUREMENTS:

Tea pot	4¼'' tall
Creamer	2¾'' tall
Sugar	3½'' tall
Cup	2¼'' tall
Saucer	4'' across

COMMENTS:

In 1914 a dozen sets sold for $17.00.

SANTA WITH PACK
(People Series)

PERTINENT DATA:

Identical blanks: None
Known pattern pieces: Tea set
Point of origin: Japan
Date: Unknown
Classification: Difficult to locate in completion
Features attributable to the set: Santa with pack walking past a brick building

Color: Typical Christmas colors which were not well
  "fired"

MEASUREMENTS:

Tea pot	3¾" tall
Sugar	3¼" tall
Plate	5" across

COMMENTS:

The other members of this set were not available for photos
or measuring.

SEASIDE
(People Series)

PERTINENT DATA:

Identical blanks: None
Known pattern pieces: Dinner set
Point of origin: England
Date: Unknown
Classification: Rare
Features attributable to the set: Transfers showing
  sailboats, anchors, a
  lighthouse, boats,
  and a lady on the
  beach

Color: Teal green on white

MEASUREMENTS:

6 soups	4¾" across
	1" deep
1 serving bowl	5½" across
	1" deep
6 plates	4¾" across
1 serving platter	5½" across
1 platter	6¼" long
2 oval relishes	3¾" long
	2¼" wide
6 butter pats	3½" across
1 footed compote	4¾" across
	2¼" high
1 footed compote	5¾" across
	2½" high
1 soup tureen	5½" across end to end
1 soup tureen	4-7/8" end to end

SKATING CHILDREN
(People Series)

PERTINENT DATA:

Identical blanks: Similar to "Flower Boat Children",
  but not exact
Known pattern pieces: Tea set
Point of origin: Germany
Date: 1890
Classification: Difficult to locate
Features attributable to the set: Children skating,
  walking a doll and
  playing circus
Color: Caramel luster trim, burnished browns

MEASUREMENTS:

Tea pot	5-5/8" tall
Creamer	3" tall
Sugar	3¼" tall
Cup	2¼" tall
Saucer	4¼" across
Plate	5½" across

SLED AND KITE
(People Series)

PERTINENT DATA:

Identical blanks: None
Known pattern pieces: Tea set
Point of origin: Germany
Date: Unknown
Classification: Difficult to locate
Features attributable to the set: Children on sled; kite with a face on it; elephant; Father Christmas; watering can with a flower
Color: Vivid colors, but poorly "fired"

MEASUREMENTS:

Tea pot	2½'' tall
Creamer	1-3/8'' tall
Open sugar	1'' tall
Cup	1¼'' tall
Saucer	2-1/8'' across

THREE GIRLS AND A DOG
(People Series)

PERTINENT DATA:

Identical blanks: None
Known pattern pieces: Tea set
Point of origin: Germany
Date: Unknown
Classification: Difficult to assemble
Features attributable to the set: Three girls and some dogs; girls at play
Color: Very light pictures

MEASUREMENTS:

Tea pot	5½'' tall
Creamer	2¼'' tall
Sugar (open)	1'' tall

Other pieces unavailable for photos

TO GRANDMOTHER'S HOUSE
(People Series)

Set consists of six plates, six cups and saucers, waste bowl, tea pot, sugar and cream pitcher.

TWO GIRLS WITH DOLL
(People Series)

PERTINENT DATA:

Identical blanks: None
Known pattern pieces: Tea set
Point of origin: Germany
Date: 1900
Classification: Difficult to find
Features attributable to the set: Horse pulling sled with one person walking and one riding; person in snowshoes

Color: Winter pastels

MEASUREMENTS:

Tea pot	6-1/8'' tall
Creamer	4'' tall
Sugar	3¾'' tall
Cup	2¼'' tall
Saucer	4¼'' across
Plate	5¼'' across

TOYS AND CHILDREN
(People Series)

PERTINENT DATA:

Identical blanks: None
Known pattern pieces: Tea set
Point of origin: Unknown
Date: Unknown
Classification: Difficult to locate
Features attributable to the set: Pictures of toys, animals, rocking horse, wagon, trumpet and badminton set

PERTINENT DATA:

Identical blanks: No identical blanks, just identical pictures
Known pattern pieces: Tea set
Point of origin: Germany
Date: Early 1900's
Classification: Available
Features attributable to the set: Beautiful children at play; luster decorative handles

188

MEASUREMENTS:

Tea pot	6¼'' tall
Creamer	4'' tall
Sugar	4'' tall
Cup	2¼'' tall
Saucer	4½'' across
Plate	5¼'' across

COMMENTS:

Same children as found on "Sledding"; "Kissing"; and "Having A Ride".

TWO TONED GREEN
DUTCH CHILDREN
(People Series)

PERTINENT DATA:

Identical blanks: None
Known pattern pieces: Tea set; matching jug
Point of origin: Holland
Date: Circa 1890
Classification: Rare
Features attributable to the set: Unusual greens; elegant handles

MEASUREMENTS:

Tea pot	6'' tall
	4-1/8'' wide
Creamer	4'' tall
	3'' wide
Sugar	3'' tall
Cup	1¾'' tall
Saucer	4'' across
Jug	3½'' tall

Rhymes, Jingles And Tales

Literature of the nursery is universal. Every country shares the joy of rhymes and lullabies, allowing a glimpse of the electric images left by another time. Sense and nonsense exist together in sweet reasonableness in the songs, jingles, and rhymes which are repeated in one giddy scene after another on the china toy sets. Much drama is packed on these brief pieces: Miss Muffet's horrific experience with an annoying arachnid; Old Mother Hubbard's eternally empty cupboard; and Little Bo-Peep's cud-chewing strays.

Since the rhymes of Mother Goose are no longer thought of as the special province of children, collectors revel in their lineage, find release and recreation in their memory.

Pictures have always been the major ally in remembering, advertising, packaging and marketing; they assail us in every walk of life. The subjects of the china ware adapt themselves to culture after culture, yet contain a hard core of individuality even when the "blanks" are cloned. (Blanks are the ware products taken from the moulds.)

Jingles, rhymes and tales were not only the entertainment, but the philosophy, the gossip of the time, and the living tradition of masses of unlettered people. These stories were preserved, altered, and adapted by the devices of storytellers, decorators, and manufacturers, outliving succeeding generations of man through these simple mediums.

Of all the creatures on this earth, only man has asked questions--endlessly pursuing the unknown; gathering up ends of the riddles left behind. The margins between the interests of children and the adult collector become indistinct and merge where fantasy is concerned. Fantasy satisfaction cannot be explained nor can the subject of collecting. Collecting is indeed a full blown passion for many thousands of people in this century. Some people are born to it, and as magpies, furnish their nests with tremendous trifles.

The rhymes and jingles of the past usually carried more than surface meaning. This form of literature was a vehicle for gossip, a verbal newspaper. For instance: *Little Jack Horner* is featured on several china sets. The first version of this nursery rhyme was printed around 1720 in a ballad by Henry Carey titled "Namby Pamby". It seems when Henry VIII was taking over all the church property he could get his fingers on, the abbot is said to have sent his steward to the king with a Christmas gift which was intended to appease the greedy man. On the trip, the man Thomas Horner is alleged to have slipped one deed from the pie--that to Mells Manor (a plum indeed). There his lucky descendants live to this day. The Abbot was tried (with Thomas sitting on the jury) and found guilty in having kept gold sacramental cups from the king. He was hanged, beheaded, and quartered--dead at last!

Little Miss Muffet was believed to be Mary Queen of Scots and the "big spider" was John Knox. John Knox was supposed to have denounced Miss Muffet from the pulpit of St. Giles, calling for her renunciation. Another view of the same rhyme was that Miss Muffet was a patient "muffet or moffett" because her father Dr. Thomas Muffet, was an entomologist who admired spiders.

Old King Cole, in rhyme form, first appeared in print around 1708. The brave King Cole of this jingle was a popular ruler in Britain in the third century.

The House That Jack Built is a chant which is an example of the "accumulative" story. A stretch of imagination is needed, however, to connect the subject matter (kid, cat, dog, staff, fire, water, ox, butcher, angel of death) with the marriage of a tattered man and a forlorn milkmaid. This inconsistency, however, has never bothered children . . . only scholars and cranks.

ALICE IN WONDERLAND
(Rhymes, Jingles And Tales Series)

Identical blanks: None
Known pattern pieces: Tea set
Point of origin: Germany (1260/0 on sugar base)
Date: 1900
Classification: Difficult to find
Features attributable to the set: Clear vivid decals with writing, i.e. "The Duchess teased poor Alice with all her ususal Malice"

Color: Mustard trim on cream background

MEASUREMENTS:

Tea pot	3¾'' tall
Creamer	3'' tall
Sugar (open)	1¾'' tall (no picture)
Cup	1¾'' tall
Saucer	4'' across (no picture)

CAT AND THE FIDDLE
(Rhymes, Jingles And Tales Series)

PERTINENT DATA:

Identical blanks: None
Known pattern pieces: Tea set
Point of origin: English
Date: Unknown
Classification: Difficult to assemble
Features attributable to the set: Clean lines; pictures on every member of the unit; writing

Color: Vivid, true to life colors

MEASUREMENTS:

Tea pot	4¾'' tall
Creamer	4'' tall
Sugar	4¾'' tall
Cup	2½'' tall
Saucer	5½'' across
Plate	6'' across

CAT AND FIDDLE
AND OTHER TALES
(Rhymes, Jingles And Tales Series)

PERTINENT DATA:

Identical blanks: None
Known pattern pieces: Tea set
Point of origin: England
Date: 1890-1900
Classification: Difficult to assemble
Features attributable to the set: Nursery rhyme characters and writing

MEASUREMENTS:

Tea pot	4¾'' tall
Creamer	4'' tall
Sugar	unavailable
Waste	3¾'' tall
Cup	2½'' tall
Saucer	5½'' across
Plate	6'' across

CINDERELLA (Staffordshire)
(Rhymes, Jingles And Tales)

PERTINENT DATA:

Identical blanks: None
Known pattern pieces: Tea set
Point of origin: England (Rd. 128955)
Date: Circa 1884
Classification: Rare
Features attributable to the set: Cinderella is pictured on her way to the ball, with the story written with the pictures
Color: Brown and gold on cream or rose on white

MEASUREMENTS:

Tea pot	4¼'' tall
Creamer	2¾'' tall
Sugar (open)	2½'' tall
Waste	4¼'' tall
Cup	2'' tall
Saucer	4½'' across
Plate	4¼'' across

FAIRY TALES
(Rhymes, Jingles And Tales Series)

PERTINENT DATA:

Identical blanks: None
Known pattern pieces: Tea set
Point of origin: Germany
Date: Turn of the century
Classification: Difficult to obtain
Features attributable to the set: Red Riding Hood; Cinderella; Sleeping Beauty; Snow White characters

MEASUREMENTS:

Tea pot	6'' tall
Creamer	3½'' tall
Sugar	3-7/8'' tall
Cup	2¼'' tall
Saucer	3¼'' across
Plate	5'' across

FOUR ON A BLANK
(Rhymes, Jingles And Tales Series)

PERTINENT DATA:

Identical blanks: "Old King Cole"; "Old Mother Hubbard"; "Gold Wedding Band"; "Nursery Jingles"
Known pattern pieces: Tea sets
Point of origin: England
Date: 1870-1890
Classification: Available
Features attributable to the set: Old King Cole series also shows House that Jack Built, Miss Muffet, and Jack Horner

Another set shows Georgie Porgie, Mary Had A Little Lamb, and To Market

One set has only the gold ring

One set, in blue and white, is all about Mother Hubbard

MEASUREMENTS:

Tea pot	4¼'' tall
Creamer	4'' tall
Sugar	4¼'' tall
Cup	2½'' tall
Saucer	5'' across
Plate	5¼'' across
Waste bowl	2½'' tall

GOLLIWAGS (Creatures)
(Rhymes, Jingles And Tales Series)

PERTINENT DATA:

Identical blanks: "Happifats"
Known pattern pieces: Tea set
Point of origin: Germany (Rudolstadt)
Date: Circa 1914
classification: Available
Features attributable to the set: Wild looking stick figures

Color: Excellent, vivid colors

MEASUREMENTS:

Tea pot	5¾'' tall
Creamer	3'' tall
Sugar	2½'' tall
Cup	2'' tall
Saucer	4½'' across
Plate	5½'' across

COMMENTS:

"Happifats" tea sets have either blue trim with strawberries or orange trim and raspberries.

HEY DIDDLE DIDDLE
(Rhymes, Jingles And Tales Series)

PERTINENT DATA:

Identical blanks: None

Known pattern pieces: Tea set
Point of origin: England (Whittaker and Co., Hallfield Pottery)
Date: 1888
Classification: Difficult to obtain
Features attributable to the set: All over detailed pictures and writing
Color: Orange and brown on cream; brown on cream

MEASUREMENTS:

Tea pot	4¼'' tall
Creamer	3-1/3'' tall
Sugar	3¾'' tall
Cup	2'' tall
Saucer	4½'' across
Plate	5'' across
Waste bowl	4'' across
	3'' tall

HOUSE THAT JACK BUILT
(Rhymes, Jingles And Tales Series)

PERTINENT DATA:

Identical blanks: No identical blanks but same decals are used on two different sets
Known pattern pieces: Tea set
Point of origin: Germany
Date: Circa 1900
Classification: Available
Features attributable to the set: Pictures of the tale
Color: Vivid and varied colors

193

MEASUREMENTS:

Tea pot	5¾'' tall and 5-5/8'' tall
Creamer	3¼'' tall
Sugar	3¼'' tall
Cup	2'' tall
Saucer	4'' across
Plate	5¼'' across

JAPAN'S DISNEY CHARACTERS
(Rhymes, Jingles And Tales Series)

LITTLE MISS MUFFET
(Rhymes, Jingles And Tales Series)

PERTINENT DATA:

    Identical blanks: "Snow White"
    Known pattern pieces: Tea set
    Point of origin: Japan
    Date: Made in occupied Japan (c W.D.P.)
    Classification: Obtainable
    Features attributable to the set: Disney characters; typical "Blue Willow" blank

MEASUREMENTS:

Tea pot	3¼'' tall
Creamer	2'' tall
Sugar	2½'' tall
Cup	1¼'' tall
Saucer	3½'' across

PERTINENT DATA:

    Identical blanks: None
    Known pattern pieces: Tea set
    Point of origin: England
    Date: 1940
    Classification: Available
    Features attributable to the set: Great detail in the decals; pinch-penny finial
    Color: Vivid reds, blues and greens

MEASUREMENTS:

Tea pot	4-1/8'' tall
Creamer	2¾'' tall
Sugar	2'' tall
Cup	2'' tall
Saucer	4'' across
Plate	4½'' across

NORITAKE NURSERY RHYMES
(Rhymes, Jingles And Tales Series)

PERTINENT DATA:

Identical blanks: "Meito" (white with gold trim); "Red Roses"
Known pattern pieces: Tea set
Point of origin: Japan
Date: Circa 1900
Classification: Obtainable
Features attributable to the set: Well made with excellent decals and writing

Color: Vivid decals

MEASUREMENTS:

Tea pot	3½'' tall
Creamer	2'' tall
Sugar	2¾'' tall
Cup	1½'' tall
Saucer	4½'' across, also 4''
Plate	5'' across

PALMER COX BROWNIES
(Rhymes, Jingles And Tales Series)

PERTINENT DATA:

Identical blanks: None
Known pattern pieces: Tea set; dinner set in the color section of this publication
Point of origin: Germany
Date: Circa 1900
Classification: Tea set difficult to locate; dinner set very rare
Features attributable to the set: Tea set is a poor quality; dinner set is excellent quality

MEASUREMENTS: (tea set)

Tea pot	4-1/8'' tall Brownie playing a horn
Creamer	2½'' tall
Sugar	2¾'' tall
Cup	1½'' tall
Saucer	2¾'' across
Plate	3-1/8'' across

MEASUREMENTS: (dinner set) see color plate section

Large platter	9-5/8'' long
Small platter	7-1/8'' long
Fruit dishes	5-3/8'' across
Butter pats	3-3/8'' across
(2) tureens	9'' handle to handle
Round dish	5-1/8'' across
Oblong dish	7-1/8'' long
Plate	7-1/8'' across
Cup	2'' high
Saucer	5'' wide

COMMENTS:

Palmer Cox wrote that Brownies, like fairies and goblins, are imaginary little sprites who are supposed to delight in carefree pranks and helpful deeds. Brownies work and sport while tired households sleep. (These little rascals never allowed themselves to be seen by mortal eyes. . .this author has never seen any work they've done around the house either!)

When people find a carver hacked,
A saucer chipped, or a platter cracked,
They should be somewhat slow to claim
That children are the ones to blame;
For Brownies may have used the ware
And failed to show the proper care.

Another Brownie Book
by Palmer Cox

PUNCH AND JUDY
(Rhymes, Jingles And Tales Series)

PERTINENT DATA:

Identical blanks: "Little Mae"; "Girl With Apron"; "Girl With Dog"; "Stag"; "Water Hen"; "Goat"; "Persian"; "Cresent"
Known pattern pieces: Tea set
Point of origin: England
Date: 1890
Classification: Difficult to locate on this particular blank
Features attributable to the set: Bulbous shape; Punch and Judy characters
Color: Rose, blue, brown

MEASUREMENTS:

Tea pot	5¼" tall
Creamer	3" tall
Sugar	4¾" tall
Cup	2" tall
Saucer	4½" across
Plate	5½" across

PERTINENT DATA:

Identical blanks: None
Known pattern pieces: Tea set
Point of origin: Germany
Date: 1900
Classification: Difficult to locate
Features attributable to the set: Light colored decals

MEASUREMENTS:

Tea pot	6½" tall
Creamer	3½" tall
Sugar	2" tall
Cup	2½" tall
Saucer	5" across
Plate	5¾" across

COMMENTS:

The English puppet play, "Punch and Judy", originated in the sixteenth-century. It has delighted and frightened children over the years. Punch is mean and boastful and his wife is unfaithful and obstreperous.

Punch and Judy,
Fought for a pie,
Punch gave Judy
A sad blow to the eye.

Says Punch to Judy,
Will you have more?
Says Judy to Punch
My eye is sore.

PUSS IN BOOTS ON SHORE
(Rhymes, Jingles And Tales Series)

RED RIDING HOOD
(Rhymes, Jingles And Tales Series)

SEE-SAW MARGERY DAW
(Rhymes, Jingles And Tales Series)

PERTINENT DATA:

Identical blanks: None
Known pattern pieces: Tea and dinner set
Point of origin: Knowles, Taylor and Knowles (marked K.T.&K semi-vitreous porcelain)
Date: 1900's
Classification: Difficult to assemble
Features attributable to the set: White with green rims; nursery rhymes and pictures on each piece

MEASUREMENTS:

Cup	1-7/8'' tall
Saucer	3¼'' across
Fruit bowl	4½'' across
Plate	6¼'' wide
Serving bowl	6'' long
Platter	7½'' long
Plate	6'' across

THE WOLF AND RED RIDING HOOD
(Rhymes, Jingles And Tales Series)

PERTINENT DATA:

Identical blanks: None
Known pattern pieces: Tea set
Point of origin: Germany
Date: Circa 1900
Classification: Difficult to locate

PERTINENT DATA:

Identical blanks: "Pink Luster Floral"; "Southern Belles"
Known pattern pieces: Tea set
Point of origin: Germany
Date: 1900
Classification: Available
Features attributable to the set: Red Riding Hood story

MEASUREMENTS:

Tea pot	5½'' tall
Creamer	3½'' tall
Sugar	3-5/8'' tall
Cup	2'' tall
Saucer	4½'' across
Plate	5¼'' across

Features attributable to the set: Fantastic decals; details clear

Color: Vivid and pure

MEASUREMENTS:

Tea pot	4" tall
Creamer	2¼" tall
Sugar (open)	1½" tall
Cup	1¼" tall
Saucer	3½" across
Plate	5" across

CHINA SINGLES, PAIRS AND POSSIBILITIES

"Fairyth" - This tea pot is marked "Fairyth Form N" on the base. 3¾" tall.

"Away To California" - The plate represents a series of small souvenir plates commemorating special events in

"Davenport" - This Davenport plate is a part of a child's set. Davenport (a family name) operated in Longport (a place), Burslem (a suburb of Staffordshire) from 1794-1887. The apple green in this plate was a color used often by this famous company. 3" across.

"Soft Paste Tureen" - This little tureen has a pot which is 1¾" tall and it is 2¾" across its attached plate.

"Bayreuth" - This "Snowbaby" scene is in typical rust and black Bayreuth colors.

"Monastery Hill" - This popular, but difficult to assemble, set is found in blue and rose. Hackwood, Hanley 1827-1855. 3" across.

"Garden Sports" - This set by Thomas, John and Joseph Mayer (Longport) is found in the mulberry shade, brown and blue. Plates, 4" and 3½"; platter, 6"; vegetable, 4¼" x 3¼".

199

"Copeland" - This oval Blue Willow platter represents a dinner set in miniature. The blue is a powder blue and measures 5" long and 3¼" wide. Wedgwood made a similar set in toy form in black and white.

"Taking A Ride" and "The Young Sailors" - These plates represent another series of popular old souvenir plates. 3½" across.

Enamelware Bat-Printed - This is an Enoch & Wood product. 3¼" across.

"Staffordshire Candlestick" - The little girl in this candlestick has a male companion. 2" tall.

Chambersticks - Two different china chambersticks are shown; one has a petal-style socket and is 3" across and

1½'' tall. The other is light blue with hand painted forget-me-nots. It is 3½'' across and 1½'' tall.

"Fishers" - This earthenware dinner set, represented by one plate, can be found in blue, rose or green. It is an Edge Malkin Company product, Newport and Middleport, Burslem, Satffordshire (1873). 2¾'' across.

Enamelware - This abbey-style design is a black print on white enamelware with a rust border. 2¾'' across.

Morley And Asheworth - This plate is blue and white with a flo blue style. 3-1/8'' across.

"Pet Goat" - This sugar bowl from the Oswald collection is the same blank as was used by the Edge Malkin and Co., Newport and Middleport Potteries, Burslem (1870-1902) for their willow miniatures.

Christmas Plates - These plates are from complete sets: children making a snowman, 6'' across; Merry Christmas (playing ball), 7-1/8'', pulling a sled, 6¾'' across

''Babes In The Woods'' - This mug and plate have the appropriate pictures and words. Plate 6'', cup 2¾''.

''Girl And Dogs A B C'' - Alphabet plates with scalloped edges, children and animals are very collectible. 6'' across.

"At The Seaside" - This blue and white china plate has many value enhancing features; Roman Numerals, the alphabet, and children. 7½" across.

"Christmas Holly" - This set is child-sized and functional. Pitcher, 8½" spout to base; bowl, 10" across and 3¾" tall.

"Oliver Twist Asks For More" - This pitcher is Sandland ware, Lancaster and Sandland Ltd. (Hanley England) 4" tall.

Chamberware - This richly colored chamber set has the following measurements: wash bowl, 2½" tall; pitcher, 5½" tall lip to base; soap dish with pouring spout, 1¾" tall and 3¼" across; pomade jar, 2¾" tall; toothbrush, 4" long, 1¾" tall; powder dish, 2¼" tall.

"Red Wing" - The words "Red Wing" are incised on the bottom of the miniature creamer which is 2½" tall and 4" wide. The sugar is 2" high and 3½" wide. Red Wing pottery was made from 1920 to 1967 in Red Wing, Minnesota.

Twin Wash Set - This bath set has decoration applied over the glaze. Magenta orchids, green leaves with gold spattered edges complete the picture. Wash bowl, 5¾" across; pitcher, 4" high; slop jar with reed handles, 2¾"

203

tall; two baby baths, 5¾'' long; two potties, a soap dish and a sponge dish.

Decaled Porcelain Toy Spice Set - This set has fourteen pieces with children and writing. Sugar, barley, coffee, tea, rice measure 3-7/8'' tall; cloves, mustard, ginger, pepper, all spice, nutmeg measure 2¼'' tall; salt with wooden cover measures 3'' tall; pair of oils measures 3-5/8'' tall.

Child's Kitchen Ware - All of these pieces are decorated with over glaze red, blue and gold fuchsias and leafy sprays: china rolling pin, 5¾'' long; two sizes of pitchers; two eared crock and ewer and a handled bottle.

Pennsylvania Redware - A sample of Redware is as follows: child's spitoon, 2½'' across; pair of sponge moulds, 3¼'' across; pair of scalloped edged moulds, 3¾'' wide; applebutter pot, 2¼'' tall and 3'' across. (This set was from an estate auction in Trexlertown, Pa.)

Potter's Sample Set - This is a saltglaze stoneware set with Albany slip interiors in brown: jug, 3-3/8'' tall; crock, 3¼'' across; bowl, 4¼'' across; spitoon, 3'' across. (This set is from an auction in Seemsville, Pennsylvania.)

Child's Pottery - These pieces are all unglazed outside and brown-glazed inside: large, straight-sided bowl, 3¾'' across; small, straight-sided bowl, 3'' across; small, round-sided bowl with wire bail and wooden grip, 2¾'' across.

204

Royal Doulton China (cups, plates, tumblers and mugs from Schmoker collection) - Royal Doulton descriptions and measurements are as follows: "Little Bo-Peep And Pretty Maid" plates, 6¼" diameter; "Hey Diddle Diddle" and "Old Woman In Shoe" tumblers, 3¼" x 4" (matching mush bowl available); mugs: "There Was A Little Man", 2-5/8" x 2¾"; "Jack And Jill", 2½" x 2½"; "Peter Piper", 2¾" x 3"; "Little Boy Blue", 2½" x 2½".

Kate Greenaway

The best loved nursery rhyme art was provided by a plump London artist-authoress named Kate Greenaway. She was childless except for the sober-faced girls and proper boys of her art work. She employed great care and taste in the dressing of her paper family. She became a successful designer, of sorts, much patterned after in America and England. The trends she set are popular today.

Susan C. Stewart of California was kind enough to loan the Kate Greenaway pewter dinner set shown in this book. The set was bought from the Kate Greenaway estate and each piece bears a "K.G." The note with the set reads: "Miniature pewter ware bought at the sale of part of the furniture of Miss Greenaway's house at 39 Frognal (writing unclear here), Hampstead, N.W., 16th December, 1901."

GREENAWAY PEWTER TEA SET
all pieces marked "K.G."

Tea pot	2'' tall
Creamer	1'' tall
Open sugar	¾'' tall
Cup	½'' tall
Mug	¾'' tall
Saucer	1½'' across
Plate	1½'' across
Plate	2'' across
Platter	3¼'' long
(2) covered dishes	2'' long
Gravy	1½'' long
(2) footed dishes	1'' long
Round bowl	1¼'' diam.
	½'' tall

General Accessories

White Mountain Junior Ice Cream Freezer - More than one company made these true-to-life ice cream freezers for children. This one is White Mountain Junior and is 6¼'' tall and 5'' across. It was made by the White Mountain Freezer Company in Nashua, New Hampshire in the early 1900's.

Pot Metal Lamp - This is actually a functional toy lamp with a pot metal base. It is 5½'' tall.

Cannister Set - This is a toy cannister set of tin, wood and aluminum. All of the pieces are painted medium green and decorated with a spray of flowers in red, yellow, white and darker green.

Spool Cabinet - This is a new spool cabinent made by a Mr. Franzer in Cleveland, Ohio. It is a direct copy of the Clark's spool cabinets and is in cherry wood measuring 3½″ x 2-3/8″.

Metal Tea Sets - Starting at the left of the photo there is a miniature sterling silver tea service on a miniature plateau mirror; a sterling silver toy napkin ring; a sterling cake server; a three tiered sweetmeat server and a complete pot metal (type) tea set with tray and sugar tongs. These items are on a cherry tea caddy with beaded hand work in a standard size.

Catalogue Reprint - This photo shows many toy items for children from the 1930 Sears Roebuck and Co. catalogue.

ACCESSORIES RING - This picture includes: center ring--meat grinder, iron trivet, skirt pincher (for keeping skirts out of the mud and out of the way when dancing), two toy napkin rings, double salt dip, German stein; outside ring--onion pattern table ware, bone handle table ware, spoons, turners and strainers, napkin ring, knife rest, name card holders in Dutch design.

ACCESSORIES RING - outside ring--pewter sugar and tea pot (with ebony handle), tin of toy cookie cutters (England 1881), tin lunch bucket with alphabet, sterling toast rack, two hand painted trays, a toy hanging lantern, Red Riding Hood cookie cutters (original box has recipe for sugar cookies), another tin of toy cookie cutters.

SECTION III: FURNITURE

Furniture In Miniature

The mellow wood and accurate detail found in antiques in miniature merits the attention of a variety of today's collectors. They have found a medley of periods can enhance a home giving it a composition of interest and warmth. The patina of the old glowing wood offers the collector a reflection of the diminutive world of a child once housed in a family of "means".

Understandably, the miniature pieces of furniture took as much time to create as the adult items. Quality workmanship was demanded in the miniature objects as well as the large because the tiny objects were often adult "toys", collected with love and displayed with pride. These items were also created for the pampered child who knew quality at an early age.

Since it is impossible to amass standard-sized furniture in a variety of styles and different kinds of wood, the colletor has gleefully assembled small pieces, placing them in the home in special arrangements.

Exact copies of standard-sized pieces were popular many years ago. The miniatures were meant to be placed on top of adult counterparts. For this reason, some pieces of miniature furniture look out of place when viewed from any angle other than from above. Other furniture in miniature was made in child-sized pieces for play as well as functional use.

The misconception that these wooden delights were made as salesman's samples or were made by apprentices to serve as masterpieces is an understandable error. However, the fact is that this was rarely the case. The small furniture was intended as toys, as serviceable household additions or as trinkets for adults.

Even though the museum quality miniatures are captivating, the concentration here has been on the selection of items which may be found by dealers and collectors of today. Accumulations are mustered for daily enjoyment. It is indeed frustrating to encounter tempting delights trapped forever between pages or eternally housed in museums. It is a form of release to have pleasure tickle the eye wherever it might land as we hurl through the house in a daily frenzy of expectations. Through collections, a pungent procession of memories smoothes the edges of duty packed days keeping the collector in tune (through use) with the present while roaming in a recollection of a quieter more mellow era.

FRENCH CYLINDER DESK

DESCRIPTION:

This is a high quality, beautifully executed French cylinder fall-front desk. It is decorated by ropes of floral and bow inlay on the front and back of this delicate toy piece. It stands on French legs of the greatest delicacy. Miniature versions of desks of this quality are incredibly rare.

MEASUREMENTS:

15½'' tall
12¼'' across

208

SIDE CYLINDER BOOKSHELF DESK

DESCRIPTION:

This unusual side cylinder desk has the added feature of a swing-out bookcase and a swing-out ivory-knobbed drawer. The piece is English, dating in the 1700's. The desk has both disc and ring turned legs.

MEASUREMENTS:

    8'' tall
    12½'' wide
    12'' deep

BAKING TABLE

DESCRIPTION:

This table has red buttermilk paint, white porcelain knobs, two curved bottom bin drawers for flour and sugar, two utensil drawers and a pull out bake board. It is pictured with a child's bowl, pie dish and beater jar by Weller. There are kitchen utensils dated Oct. 9, 1923, made by A & J.

MEASUREMENTS:

table	15½'' high
	19½'' wide
	10¼'' deep

LAP DESK

DESCRIPTION:

Miniature lap desks are very rare. This one is English and packs away as a suitcase would. The front falls down displaying writing accoutrements. It is complete with bottles, lids and a key.

MEASUREMENTS:

    6¼'' tall
    8-1/8'' wide
    4'' deep

DAVENPORT DESK

DESCRIPTION:

Nothing is missing from this small rare example of a toy

Davenport desk. The top lifts to expose the necessary drawers and slots to make this an exact replica of the adult desks. All of the knobs pictured pull out to display a work surface, a drawer, or a support system.

MEASUREMENTS:

7¼'' tall
4¾'' wide
12½'' deep

GOVERNOR WINTHROP DESK

DESCRIPTION:

This child's toy desk is a Governor Winthrop. It has bracket feet and was made around 1810. The desk's interior contains two tiny drawers. The drawers and the keyhole are of ivory.

MEASUREMENTS:

12'' tall
10'' wide
1½'' deep

MINIATURE INK BOX

DESCRIPTION:

The lid to this tiny English ink box has a slanted surface for note taking. The wood is beautifully grained. The original bottle is shown in the center slot.

MEASUREMENTS:

4½'' long

ENVIRONMENTAL SETTINGS

These environmental settings from the Dora Rosenberger collection have many outstanding "finds" nestled in the groupings.

BEDROOM DESCRIPTION:

Note the miniature hanging lamp, figure #248 found in *Miniature Lamps* by Ruth E. Smith and her late husband, Frank. Directly under the lamp is a tiny tilt top table with a Musterschutz stein and another miniature lamp (#17). Beside the brass bed is a toy dresser with a tilt mirror. On the dresser is a silver chamberstick and a pitcher and bowl which is white with blue flecking.

COUCH AND CUPBOARD DESCRIPTION:

In this environmental setting the blue velvet fainting couch steals the scene while at the same time the eye strays to the unusual sleigh miniature lamp on the child-sized cupboard. There is an unusual chamber set on top of the cupboard which sports an over-sized pitcher.

KITCHEN CUPBOARD

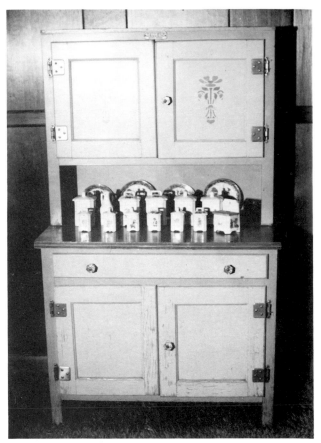

DESCRIPTION:

Typically American Depression era toy cupboards are not readily found. There was a lack of money and spare time during those difficult years. Adults did not worry about providing their children with toys. The counter top sports another example of the times, the "blue plate special" plates in the Blue Willow pattern. In front of the plates is a china cannister set from a more affluent period.

MEASUREMENTS:

45'' tall
15½''counter height

ROLL TOP DESK

DESCRIPTION:

This heavy oak and chestnut roll top desk is an unusual

size. It copies in detail the adult counterpart.

MEASUREMENTS:

15'' high
18'' wide
9'' deep

TURTLE TOP TABLE

DESCRIPTION:

The toy mahogany turtle top table has especially interesting bow-carved legs. The table's skirt is embellished with designs which match the legs of this unusual Victorian beauty.

MEASUREMENTS:

5'' high
5¼'' x 8'' top

OCTAGON WALNUT TABLE

DESCRIPTION:

This is an octagon walnut table with a walnut burl top supported by an ornately carved base.

211

TIGER MAPLE WASHSTAND

DESCRIPTION:

This is unusually fine wood for a toy. The tiger maple miniature washstand has six matching wooden knobs which further illustrates the care taken in the making.

MEASUREMENTS:

    6'' tall
    4'' deep

MURPHY BED

DESCRIPTION:

The chestnut Murphy bed is reminiscent of the Depression era when space was at a premium. This quaint miniature has

a dual purpose of serving as a wardrobe as well as a fall down bed. The bed is flipped back into the rear of the wardrobe for day time (space saving) convenience.

MEASUREMENTS:

    10½'' wide
    15'' high
    6'' deep

DRY SINK

DESCRIPTION:

This early day sink has the original buttermilk paint. It is made of pine and has two doors. The coffee grinder in this picture is a Little Tot. The iron tea kettle in the well has a slide lid. There is also a copper kettle beside this rare American example of a toy dry sink. All items in this photo are from the Welker collection.

MEASUREMENTS:

dry sink	8'' wide
	7½'' high
	3¾'' deep

DRESSER

DESCRIPTION:

A serpentine top drawer enhances the style of this toy oak dresser with the tilt mirror. Brass pulls and bracket legs complete the picture of this miniature example from the Schmoker collection.

MEASUREMENTS:

15'' wide
8'' deep
26'' tall

CURLY CHERRY AND WALNUT EMPIRE CHEST

DESCRIPTION:

A rectangular top with a straight edge and a bit of "over hang" covers the Empire style chest made of curly cherry and walnut. The top drawer, which is made of cherry, extends out and over the smooth wooden knobbed lower drawers. The sides have recessed flat panels. The front feet have the unusual feature of being scrolled.

MEASUREMENTS:

11'' wide
12½'' high
7½'' deep

AMERICAN DRY SINK

DESCRIPTION:

This early American dry sink does not have its original hardware.

MEASUREMENTS:

14'' tall
14'' wide
9½'' deep

HOOSIER CABINET

DESCRIPTION:

This cabinet is painted a typical "Depression" green and has a decal on the center top rail which reads "Schoenhut's Kitchen Cabinets made in U.S.A." The left side has a flour sifter. Sitting on the pullout bread board is a miniature dough tray.

MEASUREMENTS:

17¼'' high
11¼'' wide
7¾'' deep at the
   base
8'' to the work
   surface from
   the floor

DUTCH MARQUETRY SECRETARY

DESCRIPTION:

This is a miniature Dutch Marquetry secretary, circa 1840. It has a shaped front, bun feet and a stepped interior. A pair of standard size candlesticks show the size perspective.

MEASUREMENTS:

33'' tall
17'' wide
13'' deep

OAK ICE BOX

DESCRIPTION:

This little beauty is complete to the last detail, according to the needs of the little hostess. There are three doors on this oak ice box. Behind the top left door is the ice compartment. A drain pipe goes through the bottom (left) section to a pan which rests on the floor. The front apron flips forward to empty the drain water. The food rested on metal shelves on the right. The hardware is nickel plated brass, complete to the tiny rollers in the latches.

MEASUREMENTS:

16½'' tall
5¾'' deep
11¾'' wide

DESK AND SEWING BOX COMBINATION

DESCRIPTION:

This is a beautiful combination of a desk and sewing box and is complete with a secret till. It is made of English walnut

and lined with dusty rose satin. It came equipped with a child's thimble of gold. The front of the desk falls down for writing convenience and rises to meet, and is secured by, the lid.

MEASUREMENTS:

15'' tall
12'' wide
9'' deep

MAHOGANY DINING ROOM SUITE

DESCRIPTION:

Inside the top drawer of this set's buffet is the following label: ''genuine mahogany grows only in West Indies, tropical American and west Coast Africa. This label issued under penalty contract number 587 mahogany association copyright U.S.A.'' A. Green collection.

MEASUREMENTS:

Table top	16'' x 11''
	9'' high
Chairs	11½'' high at the back
	1½'' wide
	6'' floor to seat (slip covered in blue damask)
Buffet	19½'' wide
	8'' deep
	12'' high
Hutch	20½'' high
	15'' wide
	8'' deep at base
	10½'' from floor to work surface

EMPIRE HORSEHAIR SOFA

DESCRIPTION:

This sofa was made in New London, Connecticut around

1840. It has the original black horsehair upholstery. The frame is figured mahogany and has wooden rollers.

MEASUREMENTS:

19½'' high
39½'' wide
12'' deep

MAXEL FURNITURE

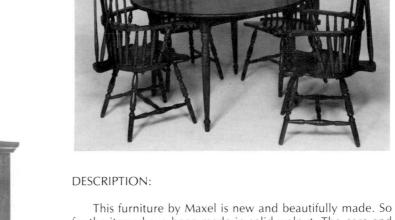

DESCRIPTION:

This furniture by Maxel is new and beautifully made. So far the items have been made in solid walnut. The care and workmanship can be seen and enjoyed in these excellent photographs.

MEASUREMENTS:

Hutch	52'' tall
	45'' long
	12½'' deep
Round table	19¼'' tall
	30'' diameter
Windsor chairs	28'' tall (chair back)
	11½'' seat height
	12'' seat width
Tea cart	17½'' tall

GLASS BIBLIOGRAPHY

Bond, Marcelle. *The Beauty of Albany Glass.* Berne, Ind., Publisher's Printing House, 1972.
_____. *Cambridge Glass Company Catalogue Reprints.* Books 1 and 2.

Florence, Gene. *Akro Agate.* Paducah, Ky., Collector Books. 1975.

Florence, Gene. *Collector's Encyclopedia of Depression Glass.* Paducah, Ky., Collector Books, 1981.

Heacock, William. *Encyclopedia of Victorian Colored Pattern Glass.* Jonesville, Mich., William Heacock. 1974.

Heacock, William. *Opalescent Glass from A to Z.* Marietta, Ohio, Antique Publications. 1975.

Heacock, William. *1,000 Toothpick Holders.* Marietta, Ohio, Antique Publications. Sponsored by the National Toothpick Holder Collectors' Society. 1977.

Heacock, William and Fred Bickenheuser. *U. S. Glass From A to Z.* Marietta, Ohio, Antique Publications. 1978.

Kamm, Minnie Watson. *Pitcher Books.* Numbers 1 to 8. Grosse Pointe, Mich., Kamm Publications, 1950 to 1954.

Lattimore, Colin R. *English 19th-Century Press-Moulded Glass.* London, Barrie & Jenkins Ltd. 1979.

Lechler, Doris and Virginia O'Neill. *Children's Glass Dishes.* Nashville, Tenn., Thomas Nelson. 1976.

Lee, Ruth Webb. *Early American Pressed Glass.* Wellesley Hills, Mass., Lee Publications. 1958.

Manley, Cyril. *Decorative Victorian Glass.* Great Britain. 1981.

Measell, James. *Greentown Glass.* Grand Rapids Public Museum with the Grand Rapids Museum Association. 1979.

Metz, Alice Hulett. *Early American Pattern Glass.* Columbus, Ohio, Spencer Walker Press. 1958.

Miller, Robert W. *Mary Gregory and Her Glass.* Iowa, Wallace-Homestead Co. 1972.

Morris, Barbara. *Victorian Table Glass and Ornaments.* London, Barrie & Jenkins Ltd. 1978.

Revi, Albert Christian. *American Pressed Glass and Figure Bottles.* Nashville, Tenn., Thomas Nelson, Inc. 1964.

Stout, Sandra. *The Complete Book of McKee Glass.* Kansas City, Mo., The Trojan Press. 1972.

Unitt, Doris and Peter. *American and Canadian Goblets.* Peterborough, Ontario, Clock House. 1970.
_____. *Vitro-Porcelain Etc.* Book VIII. *Pattern Book of Fancy Goods.* Book IX. Catalogue Reprints. Sowerbys Ellison Glass Works, Limited, Gateshead-on-Tyne, England. 1882.

Welker, Mary, Lyle, and Lynn. *Cambridge, Ohio Glass in Color.* Books 1 and 2.

CHINA BIBLIOGRAPHY

Chaffers, William. *Marks and Monograms on European and Oriental Pottery and Porcelain.* London. 1932.

Eberlein, Harold and Roger Ramsdell. *The Practical Book of Chinaware.* London. 1925.

Godden, Geoffrey A. *Caughley and Worcester Porcelains 1775-1800.* New York and Washington. 1969.

Godden, Geoffrey A. *An Illustrated Encyclopedia of British Pottery and Porcelain.* New York, Crown Publishers, Inc. 1966.

Godden, Geoffrey A. *British Porcelain.* New York, Clarkson and Motter, Inc. 1974.

Godden, Geoffrey A. *British Pottery.* London, Barrie & Jenkins. 1974.

Godden, Geoffrey A. *Jewitt's Ceramic Art of Great Britain.* Revised by Geoffrey A. Godden. New York, Arco Publishing Company, Inc. 1972.

Godden, Geoffrey A. *British Pottery and Porcelain 1780-1850.* Cranbury, New Jersey, A. A. Barnes and Company, Inc. 1963.

Honey, W. B. *British Pottery.* London, Faber and Faber. Revised by Franklin Barrett. 1977.

Hughes, Bernard and Therle. *The Collector's Encyclopedia of English Ceramics.* London, Abbey Library. 1968.

Lockett, T. A. *Davenport Pottery and Porcelain 1794-1887.* Rutland, Vermont & Tokyo, Japan, Tuttle, Inc. 1972.

Mountford, Arnold R. *Staffordshire Salt-Glaze Stoneware.* New York & Washington, Praeger Publisher. 1974.

Rontgen, Robert E. *Marks on German, Bohemian and Austrian Porcelain 1710 to the Present.* Pa., Schiffer Publisher. 1981.

Schlegelmilch, Clifford J. *R. S. Prussia.* Michigan, Clifford J. Schlegelmilch. 1973.

FURNITURE BIBLIOGRAPHY

Schiffer, Herbert F. and Peter B. *Miniature Antique Furniture.* America, Herbert F. and Peter B. Schiffer. 1972.

Coleman, Evelyn J. *1914 Marshall Field & Company Kringle Society Dolls.* Hobby House Press. Maryland. 1980.

Schroeder, Joseph J. (edited) *The Wonderful World of Toys, Games, and Dolls 1860-1930.* DBI Books, Inc. Illinois.